...ly Recommended

New Edition

OSWAAL BOOKS®
LEARNING MADE SIMPLE

AF731500

NCERT TEXTBOOK SOLUTIONS

CLASS 12

BIOLOGY

Strictly based on the Latest NCERT Textbook

Powered by oswaal.ai LEARNING MADE SMARTER

Smart guidance that helps you learn, practise and improve.

Your Path to Academic Excellence:

1 **...00% ...dated** ...the Latest ...T Textbook

2 **Comprehensive Coverage** with all NCERT concepts

3 **Visual Learning Tools** with Concept Videos

4 **Extensive Revision Tools** with Crisp Revision Notes, Mind Maps & Mnemonics

5 **Complete Question Coverage** with all NCERT textbook questions

OSWAAL BOOKS®

LEARNING MADE SIMPLE

This Edition: 2026

ISBN: 9789359584867

Disclaimer

This publication has been prepared by qualified subject matter experts with rigorous editorial review. Despite our best efforts, errors may exist. Readers are encouraged to report any by scanning the QR code on the Table of Contents page so corrections can reach all users.

This book is a study aid. Examination results depend on multiple factors including individual preparation and the specific examination conducted. No particular outcome is guaranteed.

Links in this book provide access to supplementary content. Accessibility depends on internet connectivity and device compatibility. Third-party content linked herein was verified at the time of printing; however, the Publisher does not guarantee that such content will remain accurate, available, or appropriate over time.

Views expressed by individual contributors are their own and do not represent the Publisher's position. The Publisher does not endorse personal opinions or political statements contained herein.

All maps, boundaries, and diagrams are artistic representations for educational reference only and are not geographically or politically authoritative.

For details on personal data processing, see our Privacy Policy at www.oswaalbooks.com/privacy. This publication is governed by the laws of India. Disputes shall be subject to the exclusive jurisdiction of courts in Agra, Uttar Pradesh.

Published by: Oswaal Books and Learning Private Limited, Oswaal House, 1/11, Sahitya Kunj, M.G. Road, Agra-282002 (U.P.), India

contact@oswaalbooks.com

+91-562-2857671

Printed at: Upkar Print House Pvt. Ltd., Agra

Contents

Stay Informed: NCERT Updates & Recent Improvements

NCERT Updates

Scan to get the latest syllabus updates & changes

Recent Improvements

Scan to stay updated with important changes in the book!

Learning is fun when you're always up to date! Keep scanning!

PREFACE

"Education is the passport to the future, for tomorrow belongs to those who prepare for it today." – Malcolm X

In the pursuit of academic excellence, the journey often begins with curiosity. As students embark on the path to success in the exams, the Oswaal NCERT Textbook Solutions Book for the academic year 2026-27 stands as an invaluable companion, illuminating the way forward.

Success in any exam goes beyond memorization; it involves developing a deep understanding of every concept. The NCERT textbooks provide the essential foundation. Introducing the Oswaal NCERT Textbook Solutions Book, a vital tool to unlock the full potential of every student.

Let's uncover what this book covers for you:

1) **Updated for 2026-27** – The books are 100% updated for the academic year 2026-27, adhering strictly to the latest NCERT guidelines.

2) **Comprehensive Coverage -** We cover all concepts and topics outlined in the most recent NCERT textbooks.

3) **Visual Learning Aids -** Explore theoretical concepts and concept videos that offer a brief description of the topic and help visualize complex concepts.

4) **Effective Revision Tools -** Benefit from crisp Revision Notes, Mind Maps, and Mnemonics designed to facilitate efficient and effective review.

5) **Complete Question Coverage -** All questions from the NCERT textbooks are covered in our solutions, providing a thorough grasp of the subject matter.

What sets this book apart is the expertise behind its creation. The solutions within are the result of the meticulous efforts of expert faculty, individuals with a profound understanding of the curriculum, and the dedication to maintaining the highest quality standards.

May this book be your guide, encouraging you to not just study but to explore and understand.

Wishing you a fulfilling and successful academic journey.

Team,

Oswaal Books

Order Form

ONE FOR ALL OLYMPIADS (Multicolour)
Classes 1 to 8
Mathematics, English, Reasoning, General Knowledge, Science & Cyber

ONE FOR ALL OLYMPIADS Workbooks
Classes 1 to 8
Mathematics, English, Science

ONE FOR ALL WORKBOOKS (Multicolour)
Classes 1 to 5
Mathematics, English, General Knowledge, EVS, Hindi

NCERT WORKBOOKS (B&W)
Classes 1 to 5
English, Hindi, Mathematics & EVS

NCERT & CBSE One For All Workbooks
Classes 6 to 8
Mathematics, English, Science, Social Science, Hindi & Sanskrit

CBSE Work Books
Classes 9 & 10
English Lang. & Literature, Science, Social Science & Mathematics

CBSE & NCERT Laboratory Manual
Classes 6 to 12
Mathematics, Science, Physics, Chemistry & Biology

CBSE QUESTION BANKS (CHAPTER-WISE & TOPIC-WISE SOLVED PAPERS)
Classes 9 & 10
Hindi-A, Hindi-B, English Lang. & Lit. (With NCERT Workbook), Science, Mathematics, Social Science, Computer Applications, Sanskrit & English Communicative (based on CBSE Textbooks), Information Technology (Class-10th only), Artificial intelligence (Class-10th only)

Classes 11 & 12
Hindi Core (For Class-12 Only), English Core, Mathematics, Chemistry, Applied Mathematics (For Class-12 Only), Biology, Physics, Accountancy, Economics, Business Studies, Geography, History, Political Science, Computer Science, Entrepreneurship (For Class-12 Only), Informatics Practices, Physical Education, Sociology (For Class 12th Only), Psychology (For Class 12th Only)

CBSE Textbook Plus
Classes 10 & 12
English Lang. & Lit., Mathematics, Science, Social Science, English Core, Biology, Physics, Chemistry

CBSE Xcellence 95+
Classes 10 & 12
Sanskrit (शेमुषी), Sanskrit Communicative (मणिका), Physics, Chemistry, English Core

NCERT EXEMPLAR PROBLEMS-SOLUTIONS (Hindi & English Medium)
Classes 9 to 12
Science, Mathematics, Physics, Chemistry, Biology, Mathematics, गणित, विज्ञान, भौतिक विज्ञान, रसायन विज्ञान, जीव विज्ञान

NCERT Textbook Solutions
Classes 6 to 8
Mathematics, English, Hindi, Science, Social Science & Sanskrit

Classes 9 to 12
Science, Mathematics, Physics, Chemistry, Biology

CBSE 10 PREVIOUS YEARS' SOLVED PAPERS
Class 10
Combined: English Lang. & Lit, Science, Social Science, Mathematics Stan.

Class 12
Science (PCM)-(Chemistry, Physics, Mathematics & English Core), **Science (PCB)**-(Chemistry, Physics, English Core & Biology) **Commerce**-(Economics, Accountancy, Business Studies, English Core), **Humanities**-(Geography, History, Political Science & English Core)

CBSE Previous Years' Solved Papers Stand alone Series
Class 10
Hindi-A, Hindi-B, Mathematics Basic, Sanskrit, Computer Applications

Class 12
Applied Mathematics, Mathematics

CBSE RMT FLASH CARDS
Class 10
Mathematics, English Lang. & Lit., Social Science & Science

CBSE ONE FOR ALL
Classes 6 to 8
English, Hindi, Mathematics, Science, Social Science & Sanskrit

Class 10
English Lang. & Lit., Social Science, Science, Hindi-A, Hindi-B, Mathematics (Stand.) & Mathematics Basic

Class 12
English Core, Physics, Chemistry, Mathematics, Biology, Accountancy, Business Studies & Economics

FINAL HUSTLE FOR CBSE
Class 10
Science, Mathematics Standard & Social Science

Class 12
Science (Physics, Chemistry, Mathematics, Biology & English Core), **Commerce** (Accountancy, Business Studies, Economics, Mathematics & English Core), **Humanities** (History, Geography, Political Science & English Core)

CBSE SAMPLE QUESTION PAPERS
Class 9
Science, Mathematics

Class 10
Hindi-A, Hindi-B, English Lang. & Lit., Computer Applications, English Communicative, Mathematics Standard, Mathematics Basic, Science, Social Science, Sanskrit, Samajik Vigyan, Information- Technology, Artificial intelligence, Sanskrit Communicative

Class 12
Hindi Core, Hindi Elective, English Core, Mathematics, Applied Mathematics, Physics, Chemistry, Biology, Accountancy, Economics, Business Studies, Geography, History, Political Science, Computer Science, Informatics Practices, Physical Education, Entrepreneurship, Psychology & Sociology

CBSE 20 Combined Sample Question Papers
Classes 9 to 12
Class- 9 & 10: **Combined Book**
Class- 11 & 12: Science, Commerce & Humanities

CBSE Competency Focused Questions Chapter-wise
Classes 10 & 12
Class 10 :- (Combined Book) Science, Social Science & Mathematics Standard
Class 12 :- Science PCM, Science PCB & Commerce

How To Talk To AI

Crafting the Perfect Prompt

oswaal.ai
LEARNING MADE SMARTER

Think of AI as your super-smart study buddy — **the better you ask, the better it answers.** A **prompt** is simply the question or instruction you give to AI. Master this skill, and you'll unlock a powerful tool for learning.

The Basic Prompt Structure

[Role] + [Task] + [Context] + [Format]

Element	What It Means	Example
Role	Tell it who to be	*"Act as a Subject "........" teacher."*
Task	What you want it to do	*"...explain the concept of..."*
Context	Give background details	*"For Class ...., Chapter ...."*
Format	How you want the answer	*"...using bullet points and a diagram."*

Weak Prompt vs. Strong Prompt

☒ **Weak Prompt**
Tell me about this topic "..........".

☑ **Strong Prompt**
"Act as a subject "........" teacher. Explain the topic "........" clearly for school students. Use simple language, include key points, and give one example."

Pro Tips for Better Prompts

Be Specific
Say exactly what you need, not vague requests

Set the Level
Mention your class & board

Ask Examples
Add "with real-life examples" to remember better

Request Format
Ask for tables, flowcharts, or mnemonics

Iterate
Ask follow-ups to simplify or expand

Other Useful AI Tools for Students

ChatGPT
Explains concepts, solves questions, makes notes & projects
chatgpt.com

Google Gemini
Great for diagrams, visuals & numerical explanations
gemini.google.com

Perplexity AI
Research tool with verified info & sources
perplexity.ai

Photomath
Solves Maths problems with step-by-step solutions
photomath.com

Notion AI
Creates notes, organizes syllabus & project structure
notion.so

Quizlet AI
Makes flashcards & quizzes from any chapter
quizlet.com

Canva AI
Makes posters, charts, covers & PPTs easily
canva.com

Otter.ai
Records lectures & converts to written notes
otter.ai

Remember: AI doesn't read minds — it reads prompts. The clearer you are, the more it helps!

Exclusive School Books Suppliers

	KARNATAKA
BENGALURU	Pride Book World, 9448685507, Tanwer Books and Garments, 9916049273, Jipsy, 9620325985
MYSORE	Ragavendra Book Agency, 9591911489
	TELANGANA
HYDERABAD	Shri Sharada store Books & Stationers, 9700768789, Sri Balaji Book Depot, 9676996199, Vishal Book Distributors, 9246333166, Pranavi Publishers, 919948853126, Shri Sharada store Books & Stationers, 9700768789
	TAMIL NADU
CHENNAI	M.K. Stores, 9840030099, Sivaa Book Centre, 9952933315, Kamal Book House, 9841077369
ERODE	Selvam Book Centre, 919843199697
MADURAI	Selvi Book Shoppe, 9345037977, Madurai Book Shop, 9751937519
COIMBATORE CUDDALORE	Indian Book Centre, 9443093053
	MAHARASHTRA
PUNE	Madhusheela Books & Stationers, 7875899892, Pravin Sales, 8888038889
NANDED	Vijay Book Centre, 9822994436
JALNA	Anil Paper Mart, 919422722522
CHHATRAPATI SAMBHAJINAGAR	AARTI BOOK CENTRE, 919422203836
NAGPUR	Sandeep Book Depot, 9371078789
VASAI	Dinvin Books Excellence PVT. LTD. , 9867561128
MUMBAI	New Student Agencies LLP, 8355965098, Ravechi Book Stationery, 9769002371
	ANDHRA PRADESH
VISAKHAPATNAM	VKML Books, 8125168946
NANDYAL	Sathyam Book Store & Fancy, 9052439300
NELLORE	S V S Book Centre, 9347100774
VIJAYAWADA	VKML Books, 9966639957
	HARYANA
ROHTAK	Babu Ram Pradeep Kumar, 9813214692
VIZIANAGARAM	Himamsu Book Distributor, 9493434777
	MADHYA PRADESH
INDORE	Mahesh Book Depot, 9893855543
SHAHDOL	Anjali Book Centre, 917067572992
	JHARKHAND
DEOGHAR	Navyug Sahitya Mandir, 919031917035
BOKARO STEEL CITY	Bokaro Student Friends Pvt. Ltd, 919234628152
	MEGHALAYA
SHILLONG	New Book Centre, 9774088719
	WEST BENGAL
KOLKATA	Oriental Pub. Dist. Pvt. Ltd., 919903879153, United Book House, 9831344622
COOCH BEHAR	S.B. Book Distributors, 9002670771
	UTTAR PRADESH
PRAYAGRAJ	Saraswati book depot, 7706855403
KANPUR	Raj Book, 9235616506
MATHURA	Sapra Traders, 9410076716, Agrawal Book House, 7906527213
GHAZIABAD	Vani Enterprises, 919891276834
	DELHI
DELHI	Mittal Books, 919810133323, Prakash Brothers, 919811179840, R.D. Chawla & Sons, 9810045752, Ameen Global Services, 919716028892, Need Prakashan Pvt Ltd, 9968383261
	GUJARAT
VADODARA	Career Skills Education and Research Foundation, 8469149288
BHARUCH	J.D. Agency, 9099944480
	KERALA
ERNAKULAM	Novel House School Supplies, 8792342807
	ASSAM
GUWAHATI	Central Book Agency, 9954707165
SILCHER	New Book Stall, 919435712617
JORHAT	Bajrang stationery, 9706978968
	RAJASTHAN
ANUPGARH	City Pride Departmental Store, 919414095677
BARMER	Dev Indra Enterprises, 7073282106
	MANIPUR
IMPHAL	Global Agencies, 917641814494
	PUNJAB
TARN TARAN	Sital Di Hatti, 919988206890
KHAMMAM	Sri Nivasa Book Stall, 919948247838
	CHHATTISGARH
RAIPUR	Central Book House, 9406016308

Our Distributors

	ANDHRA PRADESH
VISAKHAPA-THAM	Sri Rajeshwari Book Link, 9848036014,
VIJAYAWADA	Sree Vidya Book Depot, 9491830839
	ANDAMAN & NICOBAR ISLAND
PORTBLAIR	Krishna Book Centre, 9474205570, Andaman Book Centre, 9434264521
	ARUNACHAL PRADESH
NAHARLAGUN	New Pothi Ghar, 8731832947
	ASSAM
SILCHAR	Book Emporium, 9675972993, 6000763186,
	New Book Stall, 9435712617
GUWAHATI	Kayaan Enterprises, (0361) 2630443,
	BIHAR
PATNA	Nova Publisher & Distributors, (0612) 2666404, Gyan Ganga Limited, 9304826651,
	Rishu Pustak Bhandar, 8294576789, Sri Durga Pustak Mandir, 9334477386,
	Vikas Book Depot, 919504780402,
	Bokaro Student Friends Pvt. Ltd, 7277931285
BIHAR SHARIF	Good Books , 8210685462
MUZAFFARPUR	Pustak Bhandar, 7870834225
	CHATTISGARH
AMBIKAPUR	M.P Department Stores, 9425254264
BOKARO	Bokaro Student Friends Pvt. Ltd, Bokaro, 7277931285
DURG	Bhagwati Bhawani Book Depot, 0788-2327620, 9827473100
RAIPUR	Gupta Pustak Mandir, 7974220323, Anil Publication, 7999078802
BILASPUR	Pustak Bhawan, 9300667909, Agrawal Book Depot, 9711088843
	DELHI
DELHI	Mittal Books, (011) 23288887, 9899037390, A One Books, New Delhi, 8800497047,
	Batheja Super Store, 9871833924, 9811182352, Zombozone, 9871274082,
	LDS Marketing, 9811182352/9999353491, R.D. Chawla & Sons, 9810045752,
	Janta Book Depot, 9313046321
	Bokaro Student Friends Pvt. Ltd, 7004074900
	GUJARAT
AHMEDABAD	Patel Book Agencies, 9898184248, 9824386112, 9825900335,
	Shalibhadra Stationers, 9904477855, Hardik Book Agency, 9904659821
VAPI	Goutam Book Sellers, 9081790813
VADODARA	Shree ji Book Depot, 9824649375, Nilesh Book Centre, 9924458748
	Umakant Book Sellers & Stationer, 6359396370
	Sagar Book Suppliers, 9879402375
AHMEDNAGAR	Hira Stationers, 9970150300
	HARYANA
ROHTAK	Swami Kitab Ghar, 9355611088, Babu Ram Pradeep Kumar, 9813214692
	Dhruv Book Depot, 8901352187
GURGAON	Book Care Centre Venture, 9654564783
REWARI	Repro Books Ltd, 8657315914, Annu book depot, 9053246268
	JHARKHAND
BOKARO	Bokaro Student Friends Pvt. Ltd. (0654) 2233094, 7360021503,
	Bharati Bhawan Agencies, 06542-265302, 9431740797
HAZARIBAGH	Khandelwal Book Depot, 9708607489
DEOGHAR	Navyug Sahitya Mandir, 9031917035
RANCHI	Pustak Mandir, 9431115138, Agarwal Book Depot, 9334869210, Jayshree Book House, 8434430311
	Bokaro Student Friends Pvt. Ltd, 7360021508
DHANBAD	Bokaro Student Friends Pvt. Ltd, 6202834756
	KARNATAKA
HUBLI	Renuka Book Distributor, (0836) 2244124,
	Vidyamandir Book Distributors, 9980773976
BENGALURU	Krishna book house, 9739847334,
	Sapna Book House Pvt. Ltd., 9980513242,
	Sree Sai Ram Book Traders, 9738881088
	MADHYA PRADESH
INDORE	Pustak Bhawan, 8982150100, Bhaiya Store, 9425318103
	S.P. & Publication, 7000025933
UJJAIN	Shreenath Book Depot, 9827544045
GWALIOR	Agarwal Book Depot, 9425116210
JABALPUR	Vinay Pustak Sadan, 8962362667,
	Anand Books and Stationers, 9425323508
	Akash Book Distributor, 8989111444, Bharat Book House, 9826541542
KATNI	Shri Mahavir Agency, 9425363412
	MAHARASHTRA
AMRAVATI	Delta Pen House, 9890350073

15/05/26

Our Distributors

PUNE	Vikas Book House, 9921331187, Pravin Sales, 9890683475, New Saraswati Granth Bhandar, 9422323859 Sai Book Collection, 9623224343 Yash Agencies, 9850956542
MUMBAI	New Student Agencies, 7045065799, Shivam Books & Stationery, 8619805332
KOLHAPUR	Jai Book Co. 9404671543
NAGPUR	Laxmi Pustakalay and Stationers, (0712) 2727354, Vijay Book Depot, 9860122094 Renuka Book Distributor, 9765406133, Novelty Book Depot, 9657690220, Shree Mahalaxmi Pustakalaya, 7507099360
DHULE	Navjeevan Book Stall, 7020525561
YAVATMAL	Shri Ganesh Pustkalaya, 9423131275
NASHIK	Vishal Book Centre, Nashik - 8208249434
VASAI	Prime Book Centre, Vasai, 9890293662
LATUR	Tara Book Stall, 9657709101
	ODISHA
CUTTACK	A. K. Mishra Agencies, 9437025991, 9437081319
BHUBANESHWAR	M/s Pragnya, 8847888616, 9437943777, Padmalaya, 9437026922,
KEONJHAR	Students Corner, 7008435418
KORAPUT	Ambica Book Centre, 7008585008
	PUNJAB
AMBALA	Bharat Book Depot, 7988455354
PATIALA	Goel Sons, 9463619978, Adarsh Enterprises, 9814347613
JALANDHAR	Cheap Book Store, 9872223458, 9878258592, City Book Shop, 9417440753, Subhash Book Depot, 9876453625, B.P. Publishers and Distributors, 7009571805 Gaurav Book world, 9478821183
LUDHIANA	Amit Book Depot, 9815807871, Bhatia Book Centre, 9815277131, Gupta Brothers, 9888200206
CHANDIGARH	Mohindra Book Depot, 9814920226
BATHINDA	Goyal Sons , 9464478362, Bhagwati Book Depot, 9463120564
BARNALA	Nav Chetan Book Depot, 9417906880
	RAJASTHAN
AJMER	Laxmi General Store, Ajmer, 0145- 2428942 9460652197
KOTA	Raj Traders, 9309232829, A J Book Seller, 9571365020
BHILWARA	Nakoda Book Depot, (01482) 243653, 9214983594,
JAIPUR	Saraswati Book House, (0141) 2610823, 9829811155, Goyal Book Distt., 9460983939, 9414782130,
JODHPUR	Kitab Mahal, 9460957875
BHIWADI	Alankar Book Depot, 9414707462
	TRIPURA
AGARTALA	Books Corner, 8794894165, 8984657146
	TAMIL NADU
IBATORE	Majestic Book House, 9791966665
CHENNAI	M.R. Book Store (044) 25364596, Kalaimagal Store, (044) 5544072, 9940619404, Vijaya Stores, 9381037417, Bookmark It-Books & Stat. Store, 7305151653, M.K. Stores, 9840030099, Tiger Books Pvt. Ltd., 9710447000,
MADURAI	Selvi Book Shoppe, 9843057435
	KERALA
ERNAKULAM	Academic Book House, (0484) 2376613, H & C Store, 9864196344
KOTTAYAM	Asad Book Centre, (0481) 2566992
CALICUT	Aman Book Stall, (0495) 2721282,

KOZHIKODE	T.B.S. Publishers Distributors, 7559822223
	TELANGANA
HYDERABAD	Sri Balaji Book Depot, (040) 27613300, 9866355473 Vishal Book Distributors, 9246333166, Aditya Navneet Book World, 6281055905 Insta Book Store, 9866589298
	UTTARAKHAND
DEHRADUN	Inder Book Agencies, 9634045280 Brothers Pustak Bhandar, 9897833882
ROORKEE	Universal Book Depot, 9897503504
	UTTAR PRADESH
AGRA	Sparsh Book Agency, 9412257817, Sanjay Publication, 8126699922 Arti book centre, 8630128856, Om Pustak Mandir, (0562) 2464014, 9319117771 Panchsheel Books, 9412257962, 9412257961 Manav Book World, 9760316933
DEORIA	Kanodia Book Depot, 9415277835
MATHURA	Sapra Traders, 9410076716
PRAYAGRAJ	Mehrotra Book Agency, (0532) 2266865, 9415636890
AZAMGARH	Sasta Sahitya Bhandar, 9450029674
ALIGARH	K.B.C.L. Agarwal, 9897124960,
NAJIBABAD	Gupta News Agency, 8868932500
KANPUR	Radha News Agency, 8957247427, Raj Book Dist., 9235616506, H K Book Distributors, 9506033137/9935146730
GORAKHPUR	Vidyarthi Sahitya Bhandar, 6394026706
LUCKNOW	Om Book Depot, 7705871398, Azad Book Depot Pvt. Ltd., 7317000250, Ashirwad Book Depot, 9235501197, Book.com, 7458922755, Universal Books, 9450302161, Sheetla Book Agency, 9235832418, Vidyarthi Kendra Publisher & Distributor Pvt Ltd, 9554967415, Tripathi Book House, 9415425943, Navyug Book Agencies, 8073564410, Pustak Vatika, 7905317119 Book Sadan, 8318643277
MEERUT	Ideal Book Depot, (0121) 4059252, 9837066307
NOIDA	Goyal Books Overseas Pvt.Ltd., 1204655555, 9873387003
PRAYAGRAJ	Kanhaiya Pustak Bhawan, 9415317109
RENUKOOT	Om Stationers, 7007326732
VARANASI	Bokaro Student Friends Pvt. Ltd , 9798050654, Gupta Books, 8707225564
	WEST BENGAL
KOLKATA	Oriental Publishers & Distributor (033) 40628367, Katha 'O' Kahini, (033) 22196313, 22419071, Saha Book House, (033), 22193671, 9333416484, United Book House, 9831344622, Bijay Pustak Bhandar, 8961260603, Shawan Books Distributors, 8336820363
PUDUCHERRY	Sri Lakshmi Book Stall, 7871555145
SILIGURI	Agarwal Book House, 9832038727
NORTH DINAJPUR	Sarkar Book Suppliers, 9830949359
COOCH BEHAR	S.B. Book Distributor, 9002670771
KHARAGPUR	Subhani Book Store, 9046891334
SINGRAULI	Ambedkar Book Depot, 9826115292
KANPUR	Lamba Book Stall, 9839024277
KARNAL	Chopra Book Store, 8950322681
JAMMU	Harnamdass & Bros Agency, 9419180999
	MANIPUR
IMPHAL	P.C. Jain & Company, 9856084649

15/05/26

CHAPTER 1

SEXUAL REPRODUCTION IN FLOWERING PLANTS

Introduction

- Sexual reproduction in flowering plants involves transformation of diploid sporophytic cells into haploid gametophytic cells.
- This occurs through meiosis and subsequent fusion of haploid (n) gametes from opposite sex to form a zygote (2n).
- All flowering plants show sexual reproduction. The diversity of structures of the inflorescences, flowers and floral parts, shows an amazing range of adaptations to ensure formation of the end products of sexual reproduction, the fruits and seeds.

Flower-Fascinating Organ of Angiosperms

➢ **Flowers:** Flowers are the main reproductive organs, found in angiosperms.

- Flowers can be classified into two categories, based on presence of male and female reproductive parts.
  - **(i) Monoecious:** Such flowers bear both male and female reproductive parts.
  - **(ii) Dioecious:** Such flowers either bear male or female reproductive parts.
- Male reproductive structure (androecium or stamen) consists of anther and filament.
- Female reproductive structure (gynoecium or carpel) consists of stigma, style and ovary.

➢ **Parts of a Typical Flower:**

- The flower is the reproductive unit in the angiosperms. It is meant for sexual reproduction.
- A typical flower has four different kinds of whorls arranged successively on the swollen end of the stalk or pedicle, called thalamus or receptacle. These are calyx, corolla, androecium (stemen) and gynoecium (capel).

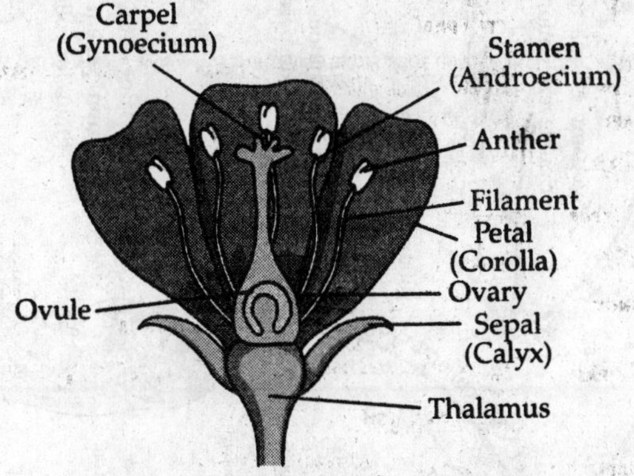

Fig. 1.1 Vertical section of a flower

- **Calyx** is the outermost whorl of the flower, its single unit is called a sepal. Generally, sepals are green, leaf like and protect the flower in the bud stage.
- **Corolla** is composed of petals. Petals are usually brightly coloured to attract insects for pollination.
- **Androecium** is composed of stamens. Each stamen which represents the male reproductive organ consists of a stalk or a filament and an anther.
- **Gynoecium** is the female reproductive part of the flower and is made up of one or more carpels.
- A carpel consists of three parts namely stigma, style and ovary.
- Ovary is the enlarged basal part, on which lies the elongated tube, the style.
- The style connects the ovary to the stigma.
- The stigma is usually at the tip of the style and is the receptive surface for pollen grains.
- The ovary holds the ovules, the female gametophytes. When the ovules are fertilised, the ovule becomes the seed and the ovary becomes the fruit.
- A flower can be bisexual (contains both male and female reproductive parts) or unisexual (only one of the reproductive part is present).

Pre-fertilisation Structures and Events

- A flower is the branch of the stem specially modified for sexual reproduction. Several hormonal and structural changes are initiated leading to differentiation and development of floral primordium.
- Inflorescences are formed which bear floral buds and then flowers. In the flower, the androecium (male reproductive part) and gynoecium (female reproductive part) differentiate and develop.

Scan to know more about this topic

Pre - Fertilisation Events

MNEMONICS

Concept Name: Male Reproductive Structures

Mnemonics: **M**obiles **A**sk **F**or **C**onnectivity

Interpretation: Male, Anther, Filament, Connective

➢ **Stamen, Microsporangium and Pollen Grain:**

- **Stamen (Androecium):** It is the male reproductive unit of angiosperm. It consist of:
  - **(i) Anther:** Terminal and bilobed part of stamens attached with filament.
  - **(ii) Filament:** Long and slender, stalk part of the stamen. Proximal end of the filament is attached to the thalamus or petals of the flower.
- **Connective:** The structure which connects the anther lobes of the stamen together is known as connective.

➢ **Structure of Anther:**

- A typical angiosperm anther has two lobes (bilobed). Each lobe consists of two theca. Fig. 1.2 (a).
- A bilobed anther is called dithecous and separated by longitudinal groove running lengthwise.
- In a cross section, the anther is a (four - sided) tetragonal structure, which consist of four microsporangia located at the corners two in each lobe. Fig. 1.2 (b)

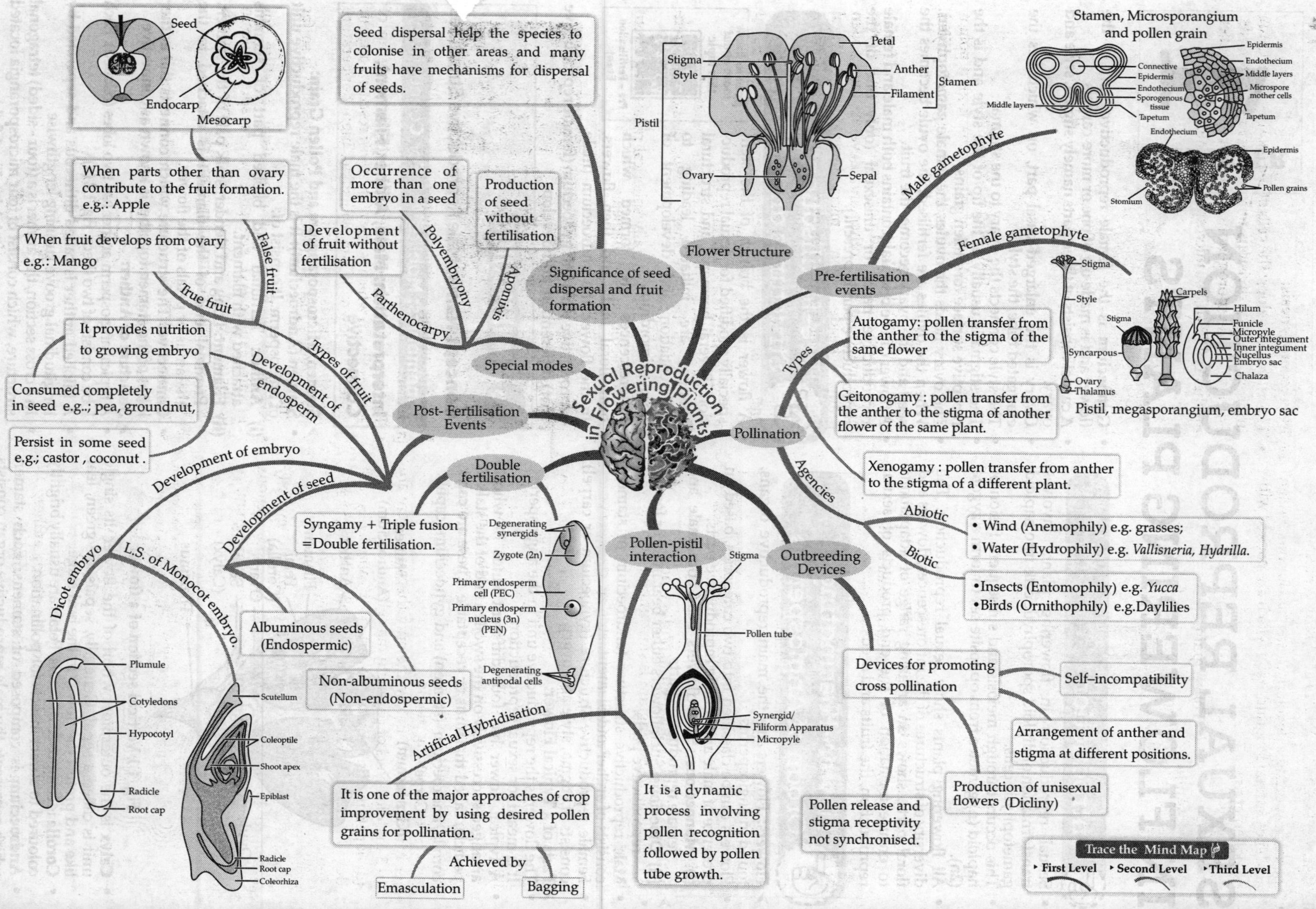
Sexual Reproduction in Flowering Plants
Flower Structure
Petal
Stigma
Style
Anther
Filament
Stamen
Pistil
Ovary
Sepal
Pre-fertilisation events
Male gametophyte
Stamen, Microsporangium and pollen grain
Epidermis
Endothecium
Middle layers
Microspore mother cells
Tapetum
Connective
Epidermis
Endothecium
Sporogenous tissue
Tapetum
Middle layers
Endothecium
Epidermis
Stomium
Pollen grains
Female gametophyte
Stigma
Style
Syncarpous
Ovary
Thalamus
Stigma
Carpels
Hilum
Funicle
Micropyle
Outer integument
Inner integument
Nucellus
Embryo sac
Chalaza
Pistil, megasporangium, embryo sac
Pollination
Types
Autogamy: pollen transfer from the anther to the stigma of the same flower
Geitonogamy : pollen transfer from the anther to the stigma of another flower of the same plant.
Xenogamy : pollen transfer from anther to the stigma of a different plant.
Agencies
Abiotic
• Wind (Anemophily) e.g. grasses;
• Water (Hydrophily) e.g. Vallisneria, Hydrilla.
Biotic
•Insects (Entomophily) e.g. Yucca
•Birds (Ornithophily) e.g.Daylilies
Outbreeding Devices
Devices for promoting cross pollination
Self–incompatibility
Arrangement of anther and stigma at different positions.
Production of unisexual flowers (Dicliny)
Pollen release and stigma receptivity not synchronised.
Pollen-pistil interaction
Stigma
Pollen tube
Synergid/ Filiform Apparatus
Micropyle
It is a dynamic process involving pollen recognition followed by pollen tube growth.
Artificial Hybridisation
It is one of the major approaches of crop improvement by using desired pollen grains for pollination.
Achieved by
Emasculation
Bagging
Double fertilisation
Degenerating synergids
Zygote (2n)
Primary endosperm cell (PEC)
Primary endosperm nucleus (3n) (PEN)
Degenerating antipodal cells
Syngamy + Triple fusion =Double fertilisation.
Post- Fertilisation Events
Development of seed
Albuminous seeds (Endospermic)
Non-albuminous seeds (Non-endospermic)
Development of embryo
Dicot embryo
Plumule
Cotyledons
Hypocotyl
Radicle
Root cap
L.S. of Monocot embryo.
Scutellum
Coleoptile
Shoot apex
Epiblast
Radicle
Root cap
Coleorhiza
Development of endosperm
It provides nutrition to growing embryo
Consumed completely in seed e.g..; pea, groundnut,
Persist in some seed e.g.; castor , coconut .
Types of fruit
True fruit
When fruit develops from ovary e.g.: Mango
False fruit
When parts other than ovary contribute to the fruit formation. e.g.: Apple
Seed
Endocarp
Mesocarp
Special modes
Parthenocarpy
Development of fruit without fertilisation
Polyembryony
Occurrence of more than one embryo in a seed
Apomixis
Production of seed without fertilisation
Significance of seed dispersal and fruit formation
Seed dispersal help the species to colonise in other areas and many fruits have mechanisms for dispersal of seeds.
Trace the Mind Map
First Level
Second Level
Third Level

The microsporangia develop further and become pollen sacs. They extend longitudinally which are packed with the pollen grains.

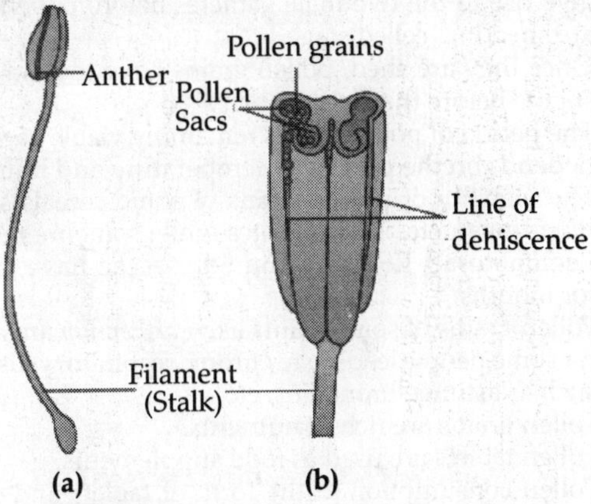

Fig. 1.2 (a) A typical stamen;
(b) Three-dimensional cut section of an anther

MNEMONICS

Concept Name: Structures of microsporangium or pollen sac

Mnemonics: Eating **T**omato

Interpretation: Endothecium, Tapetum

➢ **Structure of microsporangium (Pollen sac):**

- A typical microsporangium is surrounded by four wall layers.

  (a) Epidermis : Protects and helps in dehiscence of anther to release the pollens.

  (b) Endothecium : It is also called fibrous layer. They have specialised cells that develop fibrous thickenings, particularly on the radial and inner walls, except at the junctions of two adjacent pollen sacs. These fibrous thickenings are involved in the mechanism that allows the anther to open and release pollen during pollination, which is crucial for the reproductive process in flowering plants.

  (c) Middle layers : Below the endothecium, there are 1 - 3 middle layers of parenchyma cells.

  (d) Tapetum (innermost layer) : It nourishes the developing pollen grains. The cells of tapetum possess dense cytoplasm and generally have more than one nucleus.

  (e) When the anther is young, a group of compactly arranged homogenous cells called the sporogenous tissue occupies the centre of each microsporangium.

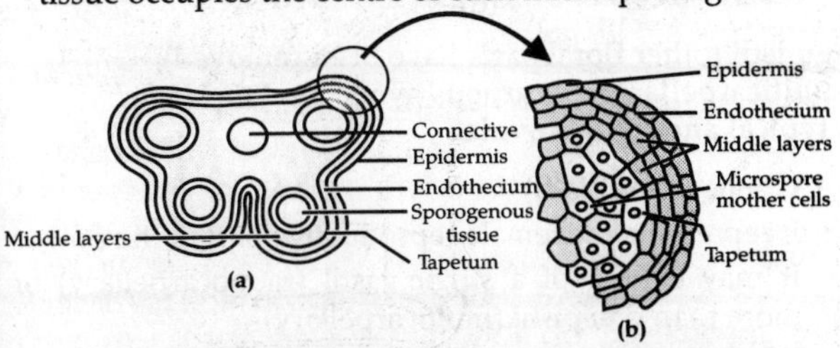

Fig. 1.3 : (a) Transverse section of a young anther;
(b) Enlarged view of one microsporangium showing wall layers

➢ **Microsporogenesis:**

- The anther develops; the cells of the sporogenous tissue undergo meiotic divisions to form microspore tetrads. Each cell of the sporogenous tissue is a potential pollen mother cell (PMC) or microspore mother cell.

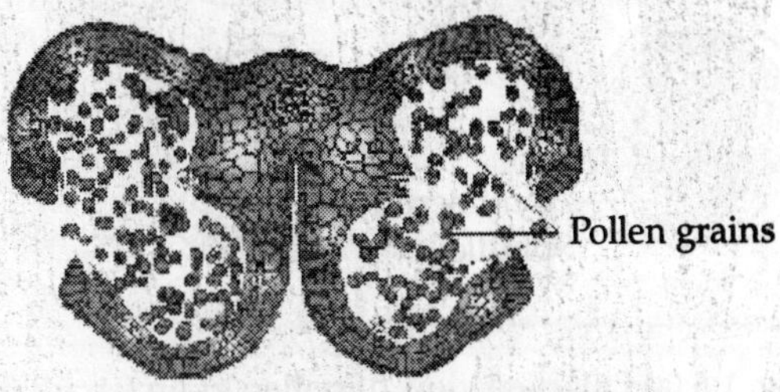

Fig. 1.4 A mature dehisced anther.

- The process of formation of microspore from a pollen mother cell through the process of meiosis is called microsporogenesis.

➢ **Dehiscence of anther:**

- The anthers mature and dehydrate, the microspores dissociate from each other and develop into pollen grains. Inside each microsporangium, several thousands of microspores or pollen grains are formed that are released with the dehiscence of anther.
- In general, dehiscence of anther occurs through the rupture of anther lobe walls which causes release of several thousands of pollen grains at a time.

➢ **Pollen grain (Male Gametophyte)**

- The pollen grains represent the male gametophytes.
- They vary in their size, shape, colour, design, etc., from species to species.
- Pollen grains are generally spherical measuring about 25 - 50 micrometers in diameter.
- Pollen grains are made up two layered walls.

Fig. 1.5 Scanning electron micrographs of pollen grains.

(a) Exine:

- The hard outer layer called the exine is made up of sporopollenin which is one of the most resistant organic material known. It can withstand high temperature and strong acids and alkali.
- No enzymes that degrade the sporopollenin is so far known.
- Pollen grains have prominent distal aperture for germinations called germpore where sporopollenin is absent. Pollen grains are well preserved as fossils because of the presence of sporopollenin.

(b) Intine :

- The inner wall of the pollen grain is called intine. It is thin and chiefly composed of cellulose and pectin.

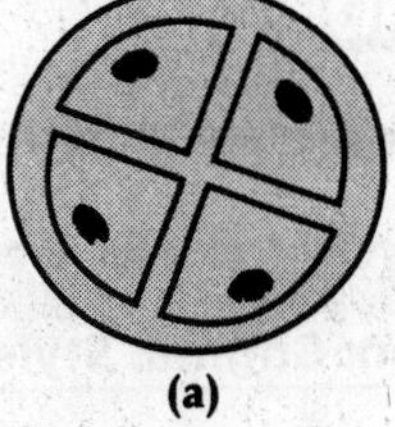

(a)

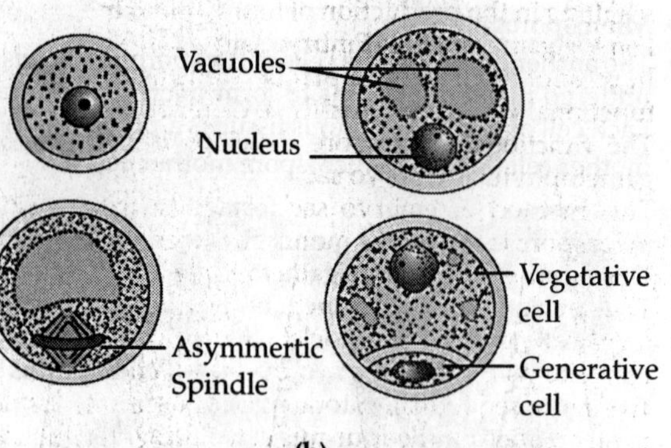

(b)

Fig. 1.6 (a) Enlarged view of pollen grain tetrad; (b) Stages of a microspore maturing into a pollen grain

➤ **Mature Pollen:-**

- At maturity the pollen grain contains two cells, vegetative cell and generative cells.

	Vegetative cells	Generative cells
1.	Large with irregularly shaped nucleus. Nucleus is dormant.	Small and spindle shaped. Nucleus actively participates in division.
2.	Non - reproductive in nature.	Reproductive in nature.
3.	Abundant food reserve	Involves in syngamy
4.	Involved in the formation of the pollen tube to pass the male gametes to the embryo sac.	Involved in the formation of male gametes.

- The pollen grains are generally shed at the 2-celled stage in flowering plants.
- In other plants, the generative cell divides mitotically to give rise to the two male gametes before pollen grains are shed in 3-celled stage.
- Once they are shed, pollen grains have to land on the stigma before they lose viability.
- The period of pollen grains remaining viable varies and depends on the prevailing temperature and humidity.
- The viability of pollen grains of some cereals such as rice, wheat, etc. is 30 minutes while some members of Leguminosae, Rosaceae and Solanaceae have viability for months.
- Pollen grains of some plants like *Parthenium* are allergic for some people leading to chronic respiratory disorders such as asthma, bronchitis, etc.
- Pollen grains are rich in nutrients.
- Pollen tablets are used as food supplements.
- Pollen consumption in the form of tablets and syrups increases the performance of athletes and race horses.
- It is possible to store pollen grains for years in liquid nitrogen (–196°C).
- The pollen can be stored in pollen banks for crop breeding programmes.
- Few methods of pollen storage being used are:
  - **Dry and cold storage:** This method involves keeping pollen grains in a dry environment at sub-freezing temperatures. By reducing metabolic activity, this method can maintain pollen viability for several years.
  - **Organic solvents:** Pollen grains can be stored in organic solvents such as acetone, benzene, ethanol, ether, chloroform, and phenol. These solvents help prevent desiccation (drying out) and maintain the structural integrity of the pollen grains.

➤ **Female Reproductive Structure**

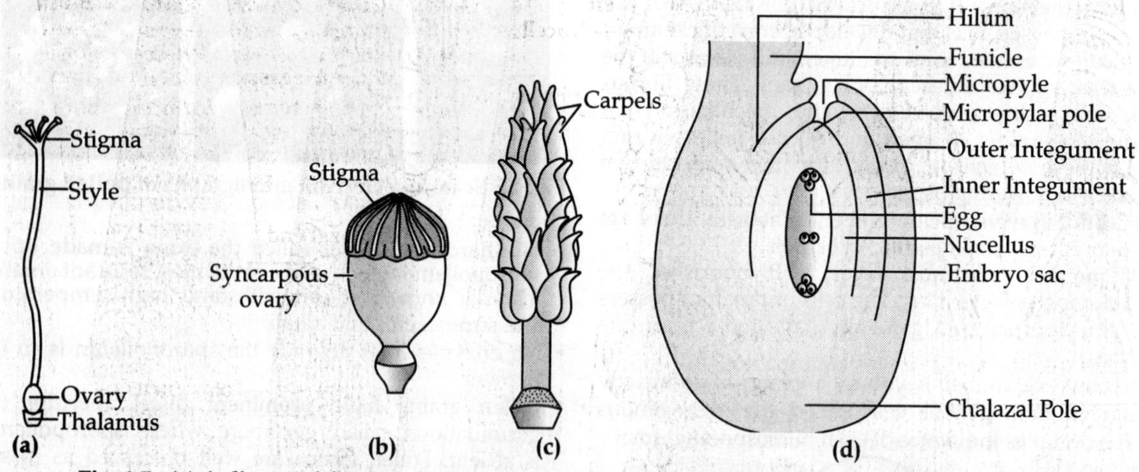

Fig. 1.7 : (a) A dissected flower of *Hibiscus* showing pistil (other floral parts have been removed); (b) Multicarpellary, syncarpous pistil of *Papaver*; (c) A multicarpellary, apocarpous gynoecium of *Michelia*; (d) A diagrammatic view of a typical anatropous ovule.

MNEMONICS

Concept Name: Female Reproductive Structures

Mnemonics: **S**mall **S**oft **O**rnament

Interpretation: Stigma, Style, Ovary

➤ **Gynoecium (Pistil)**

- It represents the female reproductive part of the flower.
- It may consist of a single pistil (monocarpellary) or more than one pistil (multicarpellary).
- When there are more than one, the pistils may be fused together (syncarpous) or may be free (apocarpous).
- Each carpel has three parts, the Stigma, Style and Ovary
  (i) **Stigma**: It is a landing platform for pollen grains.

(ii) Style: It is an elongated slender part beneath the stigma.

(iii) Ovary: It is the basal swollen part of the carpel.

Inside the ovary is the ovarian cavity called locule, where the placenta is located.

Placenta contains the ovules or megasporangia.

The number of ovules in an ovary may be one as seen in wheat, paddy, mango, etc., or many as seen in papaya, watermelon, orchids, etc.

➢ **Structure of Megasporangium (Ovule):**

It is a small structure attached to the placenta by a stalk called funicle.

The junction where the body of ovule and funicle fuse is called hilum.

- Each ovule has one or two and sometimes three protective coverings called integuments.
- Integuments encircle the ovule except at the tip where a small opening called micropyle is organised.
- Opposite to the micropylar end is the chalaza, which is the basal part of the ovule.
- Within the integuments, there is a mass of cells called nucellus, which contains reserve food materials.
- Inside the nucellus there is embryo sac, which is also called as the female gametophyte.
- An ovule has a single embryo sac usually formed from a single haploid megaspore.

➢ **Megasporogenesis:**

- The formation of haploid megaspores from the diploid megaspore mother cell (MMC) as a result of meiosis is called **megasporogenesis**.
- A single megaspore mother cell is differentiated in the micropylar region of the nucellus.
- The megaspore mother cell is a large cell containing dense cytoplasm and a prominent nucleus.
- The megaspore mother cell undergoes meiotic division resulting in the production of four haploid megaspores.

➢ **Female gametophyte (Embryo sac)**

- In most of the flowering plants, only one megaspore is functional while the other three degenerate.
- The functional megaspore develops into the female gametophyte or embryo sac.
- This method of embryo sac formation from a single megaspore is termed as monosporic development.

➢ **Development of Female gametophyte**

- The nucleus of the functional megaspore divides mitotically to form two nuclei which move towards the opposite poles, forming two-nucleated embryo sac.
- Two more sequential mitotic nuclear divisions result in the formation of the four-nucleated and later the eight nucleated stages of the embryo sac.
- These divisions are strictly free nuclear, i.e. nuclear divisions are not followed immediately by cell wall formation.
- After eight-nucleate stage, the organisation of the typical female gametophyte or embryo sac takes place.
- Generally six of the eight nuclei are surrounded by cell walls and organised into cells.
- The remaining two nuclei called the polar nuclei are found below the egg apparatus in the large central cell.

➢ **Distribution of the cells within the embryo sac**

- The three cells consisting of two synergids and one egg cell which are grouped together at the micropylar end constitute the egg apparatus.
- The synergids have special cellular thickenings at the micropylar tip called filiform apparatus.
- The filiform apparatus helps to guide the pollen tubes into the synergid.
- Three cells at the chalazal end organise as the antipodals.
- Thus, a typical mature angiosperm embryo sac at maturity is eight-nucleate and seven-celled.

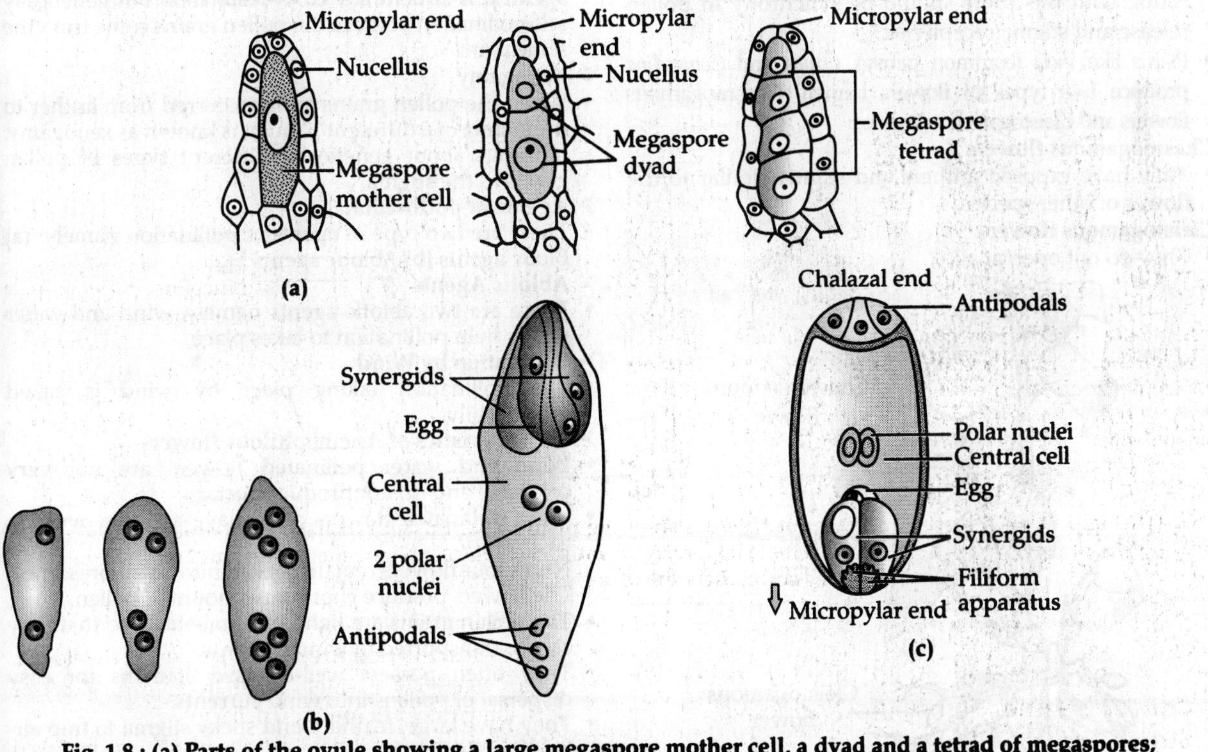

Fig. 1.8 : (a) Parts of the ovule showing a large megaspore mother cell, a dyad and a tetrad of megaspores; (b) 2,4 and 8-nucleate stages of embryo sac and a mature embryo sac; (c) A diagrammatic representation of the mature embryo sac

➤ **Pollination**

- Pollination is the act of transferring pollen grains from the male anther of a flower to the female stigma.
- Flowers rely on vectors to move pollen. These vectors include wind, water, birds and other animals that visi flowers. We call animals or insects that transfer poller from plant to plant as **"Pollinators"**

➤ **Kinds of pollination:**

Scan to know more about this topic

Pollination

Pollination
- Self Pollination
  - Autogamy (Same flower)
  - Geitonogamy (Different flower of the same plant)
- Cross Pollination (Xenogamy)
  - Abiotic Agencies
    - 1. Anemophily (Wind)
    - 2. Hydrophily (Water)
  - Biotic Agencies
    - 1. Entomophily (Insects)
    - 2. Chiropterophily (Bats)
    - 3. Malacophily (Snails and slugs)
    - 4. Ornithophily (Birds)

The Pollination is of three types based on the source of pollens namely,

(a) Autogamy

(b) Geitonogamy

(c) Xenogamy

➤ **Autogamy**

- When the pollen grains are transferred from the anther to the stigma of the same flower, it is known as autogamy.
- In flowers with exposed anthers and stigma, a complete autogamy is rare and hence the anthers and stigma should lie close to each other to enable self-pollination. Along with this there should be synchrony in pollen release and stigma receptivity.
- Plants like *Viola* (common pansy), *Oxalis* and *Commelina* produce two types of flowers namely Chasmogamous flowers and Cleistogamous flowers.

Chasmogamous flowers

- They have exposed anthers and stigma similar to the flower of other species.

Cleistogamous flowers

- They do not open at all.

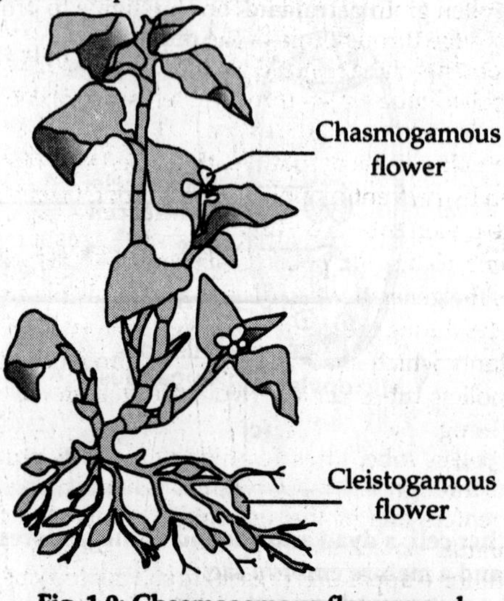

Fig. 1.9: Chasmogamous flowers and Cleistogamous flowers.

- Anthers and stigma lie close to each other.
- They are autogamous as there is no chance of cross-pollination.
- When anthers dehisce in the flower buds, pollen grains come in contact with the stigma for pollination.
- Cleistogamous flowers produce assured seed-set even in the absence of pollinators.

➤ **Geitonogamy**

- When the pollen grains are transferred from the anther to the stigma of another flower of the same plant, it is known as geitonogamy.
- It involves pollination with the help of a pollinating agent. It is structurally cross-pollination but genetically self-pollination because the pollen grains come from the same plant.

➤ **Xenogamy**

- When the pollen grains are transferred from anther to the stigma of a different plant, it is known as xenogamy. It brings about genetically different types of pollen grains to the stigma.

➤ **Agents of pollination:**

- There are two type of agents of pollination namely: **(a)** Biotic agents **(b)** Abiotic agents

➤ **Abiotic Agents**

- There are two abiotic agents namely, wind and water which help pollination to takes place.

➤ **Pollination by Wind**

- The pollination taking place by wind is called anemophily.

➤ **Characteristics of Anemophilous flowers**

- Wind and water pollinated flowers are not very colourful and do not produce nectar.
- Wind pollinated flowers often have a single ovule in each ovary.
- Numerous flowers remain packed into an inflorescence.
- The flowers produce enormous amount of pollen.
- The pollen grains are light and non-sticky so that they can be transported in wind currents.
- They often possess well-exposed stamens for easy dispersal of pollens into wind currents.
- They have large, feathery and sticky stigma to trap air-borne pollen grains.
- Examples – In corn cob, the tassels are the stigma and style which wave in the wind to trap pollen grains. Wind pollination is commonly seen in grasses.

MNEMONICS

Concept Name: Pollination

Mnemonics: **W**orld **a**ssociation for **V**isually **H**andicapped

Interpretation: Water Pollinated: *Vallisneria, Hydrilla*

➤ **Pollination by Water**
- The pollination taking place by water is called hydrophily.
- It is limited to about 30 genera, mostly monocotyledons.
- In *Vallisneria*, the female flowers reach the surface of water by the long stalk and the male flowers or pollen grains are released on to the surface of water. These male flowers or pollen grains are carried by water currents and reach the female flowers.
- In sea grasses, the female flowers remain submerged in water and the long, ribbon-like pollen grains are carried inside the water and reach the stigma.
- The pollen grains of most of the water-pollinated species have a mucilaginous covering to protect from wetting.
- Not all aquatic plants use hydrophily. For example, in aquatic plants like water hyacinth, water lily, etc., the flowers emerge above the level of water for entomophily or anemophily i.e., for pollination to takes place by insects or wind.
- Some examples of water pollinated plants are *Vallisneria* and *Hydrilla* (fresh water) and several marine sea-grasses such as *Zostera*.

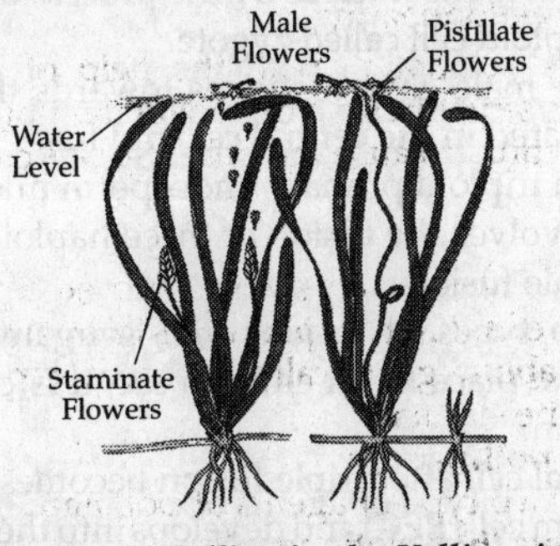

Fig. 1.10 (a) Pollination by *Vallisneria*;

➤ **Biotic Agents**
- Some flowering plants use animals as pollinating agents like bees, butterflies, flies, beetles, wasps, ants, moths, birds (sunbirds and humming birds) bats, some primates (lemurs), arboreal (tree-dwelling) rodents, reptiles (gecko lizard and garden lizard) etc.
- When the pollination takes place by insects, it is known as entomophily.
- Often flowers of animal pollinated plants are specifically adapted for a particular species of animal.
- When the animal comes in contact with the anthers, the body gets a coating of pollen grains and when it comes in contact with the stigma, it results in pollination.
- Some plants provide safe places as floral reward to lay eggs as seen in *Amorphophallus*, the tallest flower.
- There is a very close obligatory symbiotic relationship between the species of moth (*Pronuba*) and the plant *Yucca*.
- They cannot complete their life cycles without each other. The moth deposits its eggs in the locule of the ovary and the flower gets pollinated by the moth. The larvae of the moth come out of the eggs as the seeds start developing.
- There are many insects which consume pollen or nectar without bringing about pollination. They are called pollen/nectar robbers.

➤ **Characteristics of Entomophilous Flowers**
- Flowers are large, colourful, fragrant and rich in nectar. When the flowers are small, they form inflorescence to make them visible.
- The flowers pollinated by flies and beetles secrete foul odours to attract these animals.
- The pollen grains are generally sticky.

➤ **Out-breeding Devices**
- In order to avoid self-pollination, cross-pollination is encouraged in plants as follows :

(a) Avoiding Synchronisation
- In some species, pollen release and stigma receptivity are not synchronised.
- Either the pollen is released before the stigma becomes receptive or stigma becomes receptive before the release of pollen i.e., the anther and stigma mature at different times. This is called dichogamy. It prevents autogamy.

(b) Arrangement of anther and stigma at different position
- In some species, the arrangement of anther and stigma at different position prevents autogamy.

(c) Self-incompatibility
- It is a genetic mechanism which prevents pollen of one flower to germinate on the stigma of the same flower of the same plant due to the presence of similar sterile genes in pollen and stigma.

(d) Production of Unisexual Flowers (Dicliny)
- Monoecious plants such as castor and maize, where the male and the female flowers are present on the same plant prevents autogamy but not geitonogamy. On the other hand, dioecious plants like papaya, where the male and female flowers are present on different plants prevent both autogamy and geitonogamy.

➤ **Pollen-pistil Interaction**
- It is a dynamic process involving pollen recognition followed by promotion or inhibition of the pollen.
- This interaction takes place through the chemical components produced by them.
- If the pollen is compatible, then the pistil accepts it and promotes post- pollination events.
- The pollen grain germinates on the stigma to produce a pollen tube through one of the germpores.
- The contents of the pollen grain move into the pollen tube.
- The pollen tube grows through the tissues of the stigma and style and reaches the ovary.
- If the pollen is incompatible, then the pistil rejects the pollen by preventing pollen germination on the stigma or the pollen tube growth in the style.
- In some plants, the pollen grains are shed at two-celled stage, the generative cell divides and forms the two male gametes during the growth of pollen tube on the stigma.
- In plants which shed pollen in the three-celled stage, the pollen tubes carries two male gametes from the beginning.
- The pollen tube, after reaching the ovary, enters the ovule through the micropyle/chalaza/integuments and then enters one of the synergids through the filiform apparatus.
- The filiform apparatus present at the micropylar part of the synergids guides the entry of pollen tube.

- A plant breeder can manipulate pollen-pistil interaction, even in incompatible pollinations, to get desired hybrids.

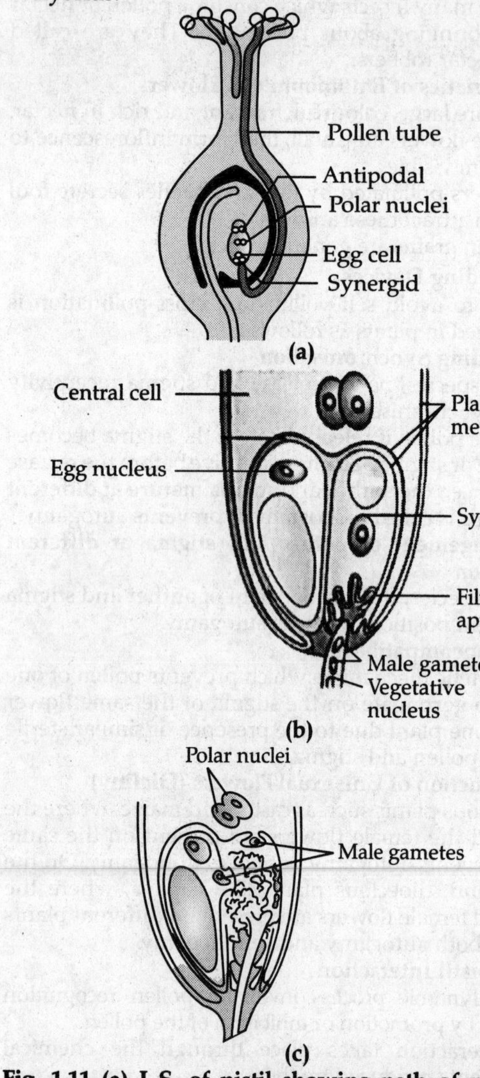

Fig. 1.11 (a) L.S. of pistil showing path of pollen tube growth; (b) enlarged view of an egg apparatus showing entry of pollen tube into a synergid; (c) Discharge of male gametes into a synergid and the movements of the sperms, one into the egg and the other into the central cell.

➤ **Artificial Hybridisation**

- It is one of the major approaches of crop improvement programme by using desired pollen grains for pollination.
- This is achieved by emasculation and bagging techniques.
- Emasculation is the removal of anthers by using forceps from the bisexual flower bud of female parent before the anther dehiscence.
- The emasculated flowers are then covered with a suitable bag made up of butter paper to prevent contamination of its stigma with unwanted pollen. This is called bagging.
- When the stigma attains receptivity, the mature pollen grains collected from anthers of the male parent are dusted on the stigma. Then the flowers are rebagged and allowed to develop the fruits.
- If the female parent produces unisexual flowers, there is no need for emasculation.
- The female flower buds are bagged before the flowers open.
- When the stigma becomes receptive, pollination is carried out using the desired pollen and the flower rebagged.

Double Fertilisation

- The pollen tube after entering one of the synergids releases its contents including the two male gametes into the cytoplasm of the synergid.
- One of the male gametes moves towards the egg cell and fuses with its nucleus by the process of syngamy to form a diploid cell called zygote.
- The other male gamete moves towards the two polar nuclei located in the central cell and fuses with them to produce a triploid primary endosperm nucleus (PEN).
- As this involves the fusion of three haploid nuclei, it is called triple fusion.
- Since two types of fusions viz., syngamy and triple fusion take place in an embryo sac, it is called double fertilisation.
- The central cell after triple fusion becomes the primary endosperm cell (PEC) and develops into the endosperm. while the zygote develops into an embryo. It is an event unique in flowering plants.

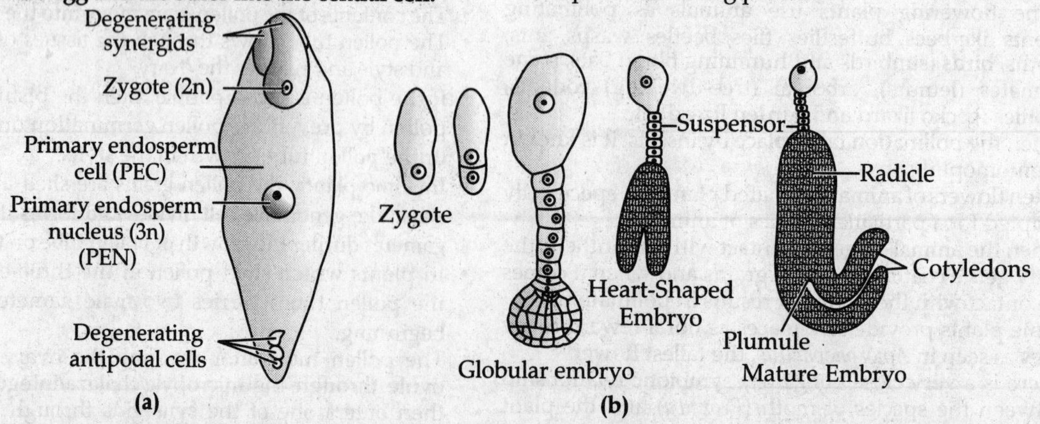

Fig. 1.12 (a) Fertilised embryo sac showing zygote and Primary Endosperm nucleus (PEN); (b) Stages of embryo development in a dicot (shown in reduced size as compared to (a)

Post - Fertilisation : Structures and Events:

➤ All those events, which occur in a flower after fertilisation are collectively known as post - fertilisation events.

Scan to know more about this topic

Post Fertilisation Events

Post - Fertilisation

- Development of endosperm
- Development of embryo
- Maturation of ovules into seeds
- Maturation of ovary into fruits

➤ **Endosperm Development**

- The primary endosperm cell divides repeatedly by mitosis to form a triploid endosperm tissue.
- Endosperm cells are filled with reserve food materials which are used for the nutrition of the developing embryo.
- During the endosperm development, the primary endosperm nucleus undergoes successive mitotic nuclear divisions to give rise to free nuclei. This stage is called free-nuclear endosperm.
- Then the endosperm becomes cellular due to the cell wall formation.
- For example, the tender coconut water is a free-nuclear endosperm which is made up of thousands of nuclei and the surrounding white kernel is the cellular endosperm.

➤ **Development of Embryo**

- The development process of an embryo from the zygote is known as embryogeny. This is the second post- fertilisation events.
- In most cases, after some endosperm formation, the zygote starts dividing. The zygote gives rise to the pre-embryo and subsequently to the globular, heart-shaped and mature embryo.
- The stages of embryogeny are similar for dicot and monocot plants. They have different structures.

MNEMONICS

Concept Name: L.S. of Monocot Embryo

Mnemonics: Personal Assistant Engineer and Senior Commandant of Railway Police Crops.

Interpretation: Pericarp, Aleurone layer, Endosperm, Scutellum, Coleoptile, Radicle, Plumule, Coleorhiza

➤ **Dicotyledonous Embryo**

- A typical dicotyledonous embryo consists of an embryonal axis and two cotyledons.
- The portion of embryonal axis above the level of attachment of cotyledon is the epicotyl which terminates into plumule or stem tip.
- The cylindrical portion below the level of cotyledons is hypocotyl that terminates at its lower end into radicle or root tip. The root tip is covered with a root cap.

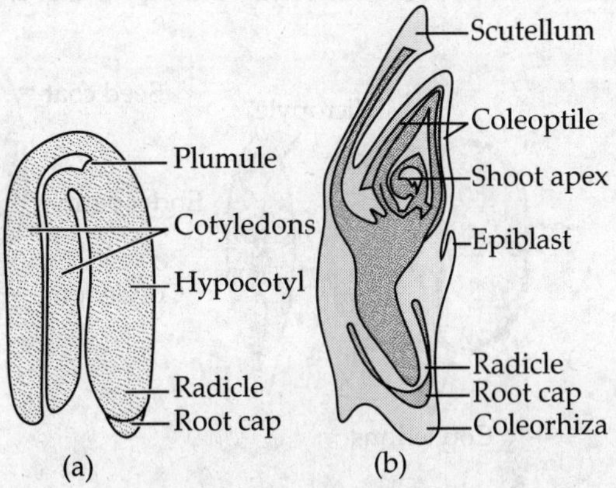

Fig. 1.13 (a) A typical dicot embryo; (b) L.S. of an embryo of grass.

MNEMONICS

Concept Name: Dicot Embryo

Mnemonics: Personal Care Heals Rare Remorse

Interpretation: Plumule, Cotyledon, Hypocotyl, Radicle, Root cap

➤ **Monocotyledonous Embryo:-**

- They possess only one cotyledon.
- In the grass family, the cotyledon is called scutellum which is situated lateral to the embryonal axis.
- At its lower end, the embryonal axis has the radicle and root cap enclosed in an undifferentiated sheath called coleorhizae.
- The portion of embryonal axis above the level of attachment of scutellum is the epicotyl.
- It has a shoot apex and a few leaf primordia enclosed in a hollow foliar structure called coleoptiles e.g., Grass, Banana, Bamboo, Palm etc.

➤ **Seed**

- Seed is the final product of sexual reproduction.
- It is the fertilised ovule formed inside fruits.
- It consists of seed coat(s), cotyledon(s) and an embryonal axis.
- The cotyledons are simple, thick and swollen due to storage of food as seen in most of the dicots.
- Mature seeds may be non-albuminous or albuminous.

➤ **Non-albuminous or Non-endospermic Seeds**

- These seeds have no residual endosperm as it is completely consumed during embryo development.
- Examples - pea, groundnut, beans.

➤ **Albuminous or Endospermic Seeds**

- These seeds retain a part of endosperm as it is not completely used up during embryo development.
- Examples, wheat, maize, barley, castor, coconut, sunflower.
- In some seeds like black pepper, beet, etc., the remnants of nucellus is also persistent. It is called perisperm.
- Integuments of ovules harden as tough protective seed coats.
- It has a small pore (micropyle) through which oxygen and water enter into the seed during germination.
- As the seed matures, its water content gets reduced and the seeds become dry (10-15 % moisture by mass). The general metabolic activity of the embryo slows down.
- The embryo may enter a state of inactivity called dormancy.
- If favourable conditions are available such as adequate moisture, oxygen and suitable temperature, they germinate.

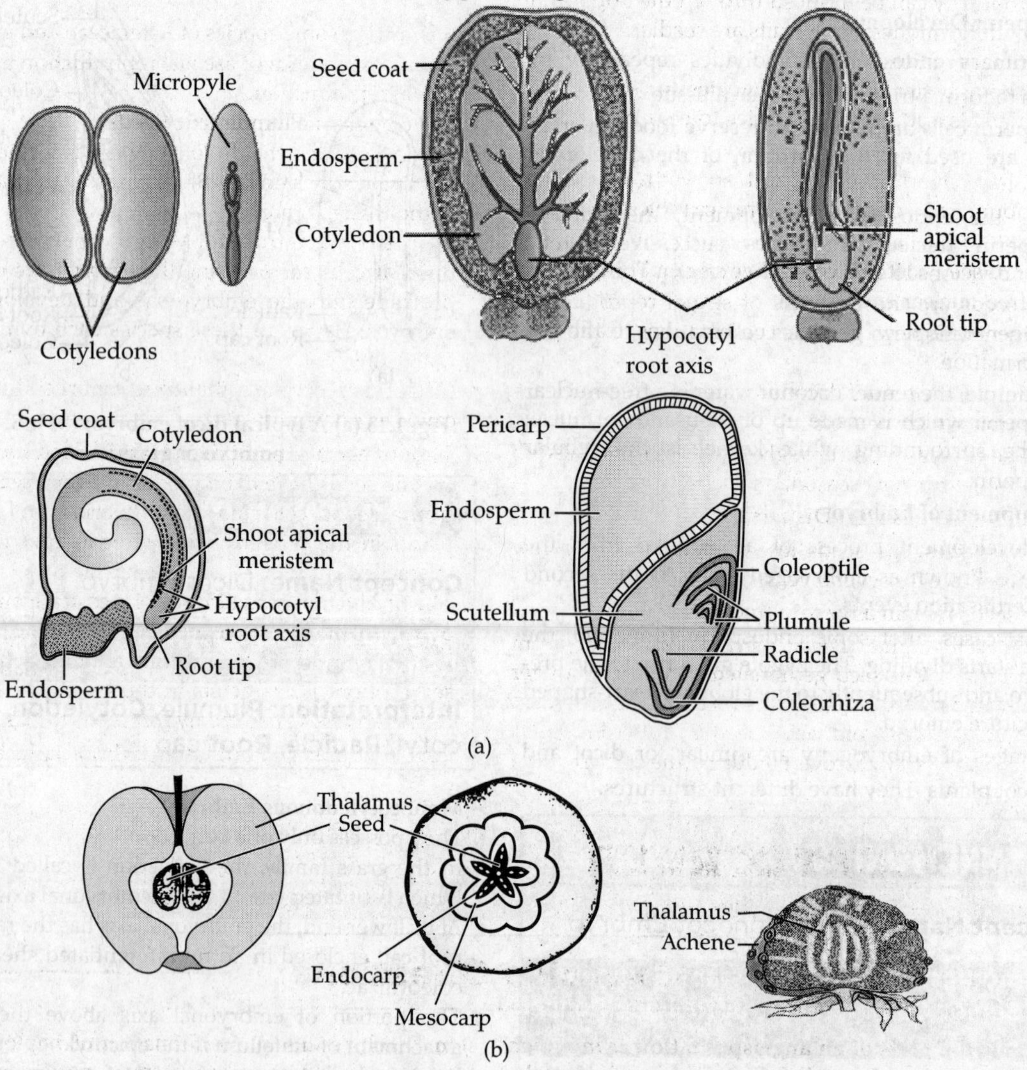

Fig. 1.14 (a) Structure of some seeds ; (b) False fruits of apple and strawberry

➤ **Fruit**

- The ovary develops into a fruit after pollination and fertilisation.
- The transformation of ovules into seeds and ovary into fruit proceeds simultaneously.
- The wall of ovary develops into pericarp.
- The fruits may be fleshy as seen in guava, orange, mango, etc., or may be dry as seen in groundnut, mustard, etc.,
- Many fruits have mechanisms for dispersal of seeds.
- Fruits are of two types namely :

MNEMONICS

Concept Name: Types of of Fruit : True fruit and False fruit

Mnemonics: Too **M**any **F**ake **A**cronyms

Interpretation: True Fruit= **M**ango; **F**alse Fruit= **A**pple

(a) **True fruits:** True fruits are formed when the fruit originates exclusively from the ovary of a flower, while the other floral components deteriorate and detach as the fruit matures. Examples: mango, maize, grape etc.

(b) False fruits: When components of the flower, aside from the ovary, play a role in the formation of the fruit, they are referred to as false fruits. Examples: apple, strawberry, cashew, etc.

➢ **Parthenocarpic fruits.**

- In some species such as banana, the fruits develop without fertilisation, these fruits are called parthenocarpic fruits.
- Parthenocarpy can be induced through the application of growth hormones. Such fruits are seedless.

➢ **Advantages of Seeds**

- Seeds have better adaptive strategies for dispersal to new habitats and help the species to colonise in other areas.
- They have food reserves and so young seedlings are nourished until they are capable of doing photosynthesis.
- The hard seed coat protects the young embryo.
- Since seeds are the products of sexual reproduction, they generate new genetic combinations leading to variations.
- The dehydration and dormancy of mature seeds are crucial for storage of seeds.
- It can be used as food throughout the year and also to raise crop in the next season.

➢ **Viability of Seeds after Dispersal**

- In few species, the seeds lose viability within a few months or live for several years.
- Some seeds remain alive for hundreds of years.
- The oldest is lupine (*Lupinus arcticus*) excavated from Arctic Tundra. The seed germinated and flowered after an estimated record of 10,000 years of dormancy. A recent record of 2000 years old viable seed is of the date palm (*Phoenix dactylifera*), discovered during the archeological excavation at King Herod's palace near the Dead Sea.

➢ **Apomixis and Polyembryony**

- Apomixis (apo = without; mixis = mixing together) means the production of seeds without fertilisation.

Types of Apomixis
- Diplospory
- Apospory
- Adventitious

- It is seen in some species of Asteraceae and grasses.
- Apomixis is a form of asexual reproduction that mimics sexual reproduction.

➢ **Development of Apomictic Seeds**

- In some species, the diploid egg cell is formed without reduction division and develops into the embryo without fertilisation.
- In species like Citrus and Mango varieties, some of the nucellar cells surrounding the embryo sac divide and protrude into the embryo sac and develop into the embryos. Hence, in these species each ovule contains many embryos.
- Occurrence of more than one embryos in a seed is called as polyembryony.

➢ **Importance of Apomixis in Hybrid Seed Industry**

- Hybrid seeds have to be produced every year.
- If the seeds collected from hybrids are sown, the plants in the progeny will segregate and lose hybrid characters.
- The production of hybrid seeds is costly. Hence the cost of hybrid seeds is also expensive for the farmers.
- If the hybrids are made into apomicts, there is no segregation of characters in the hybrid progeny. This helps farmers to use the hybrid seeds to raise new crop year after year without losing hybrid characteristics.

NCERT CORNER

Exercise Questions

Q. 1. Name the parts of an angiosperm flower in which development of male and female gametophyte take place. [NCERT, Ex. Q. 1, Page 24]

Ans. The male gametophyte or the pollen grain develops inside the pollen chamber of the anther, whereas the female gametophyte (also known as the embryo sac) develops inside the nucellus of the ovule from the functional megaspore.

Q. 2. Differentiate between microsporogenesis and megasporogenesis. Which type of cell division occurs during these events? Name the structures formed at the end of these two events. [NCERT, Ex. Q. 2, Page 24]

Ans. Both events (Microsporogenesis and megasporogenesis) involve the process of meiosis or reduction division which results in the formation of haploid gametes from the microspore and megaspore mother cells.

Microsporogenesis results in the formation of haploid microspores from a diploid microspore mother cell. On the other hand, megasporogenesis results in the formation of haploid megaspores from a diploid megaspore mother cell.

Q. 3. Arrange the following terms in the correct developmental sequence: Pollen grain, sporogenous tissue, microspore tetrad, pollen mother cell, male gametes. [NCERT, Ex. Q. 3, Page 24]

Ans. The correct developmental sequence is as follows:

Sporogenous tissue – pollen mother cell – microspore tetrad – Pollen grain – male gametes.

During the development of microsporangium, each cell of the sporogenous tissue acts as a pollen mother cell and gives rise to a microspore tetrad, containing four haploid microspores by the process of meiosis (microsporogenesis). As the anther matures, these microspores dissociate and develop into pollen grains. The pollen grains mature and give rise to male gametes.

Q. 4. With a neat, labelled diagram, describe the parts of a typical angiosperm ovule. [NCERT, Ex. Q. 4, Page 24]

Ans. For Diagram: Refer Topic 1- Revision Notes- Fig 1.7 (d).

An ovule is a female megasporangium where the formation of megaspores takes place.

The various parts of an ovule are:

- **Funiculus:** It is a stalk-like structure which represents the point of attachment of the ovule to the placenta of the ovary.
- **Hilum:** It is the point where the body of the ovule is attached to the funiculus.
- **Integuments:** They are the outer layers surrounding the ovule that provide protection to the developing embryo.
- **Micropyle:** It is a narrow pore formed by the projection of integuments. It marks the point where the pollen tube enters the ovule at the time of fertilisation.
- **Nucellus:** It is a mass of the parenchymatous tissue surrounded by the integuments from the outside. The nucellus provides nutrition to the developing embryo. The embryo sac is located inside the nucellus.
- **Chalazal:** It is the basal swollen part of the nucellus from where the integuments originate.

Q. 5. What is meant by monosporic development of female gametophyte? [NCERT, Ex. Q. 5, Page 24]

Ans. The female gametophyte or the embryo sac develops from a single functional megaspore. This is known as monosporic development of the female gametophyte. In most flowering plants, a single megaspore mother cell present at the micropylar pole of the nucellus region of the ovule undergoes meiosis to produce four haploid megaspores. Later, out of these four megaspores, only one functional megaspore develops into the female gametophyte, while the remaining three degenerate.

Q. 6. With a neat diagram explain the 7-celled, 8-nucleate nature of the female gametophyte. [NCERT, Ex. Q. 6, Page 24]

Ans. The female gametophyte (embryo sac) develops from a single functional megaspore. This megaspore undergoes three successive mitotic divisions to form eight nucleate embryo sac.

The first mitotic division in the megaspore forms two nuclei. One nucleus moves towards the micropylar end while the other nucleus moves towards the chalazal end. Then, these nuclei divide at their respective ends and re-divide to form eight nucleate stages. As a result, there are four nuclei each at both the ends i.e., at the micropylar and the chalazal end in the embryo sac. At the micropylar end, out of the four nuclei only three differentiate into two synergids and one egg cell. Together they are known as the egg apparatus.

Similarly, at the chalazal end, three out of four nuclei differentiates as antipodal cells. The remaining two cells (of the micropylar and the chalazal end) move towards the centre and are known as the polar nuclei, which are situated in a large central cell. Hence, at maturity, the female gametophyte appears as a 7-celled structure, though it is 8 nucleate.

For Diagram : Refer Topic 2/ Revision notes/Fig 1.8-(c), Pg. 6.

Q. 7. What are chasmogamous flowers? Can cross-pollination occur in cleistogamous flowers? Give reasons for your answer. [NCERT, Ex. Q. 7, Page 25]

Ans. Chasmogamous flowers have exposed anthers and stigma similar to the flowers of other species.

Cross-pollination cannot occur in cleistogamous flowers. This is because cleistogamous flowers never open at all. Also, the anther and the stigma lie close to each other in these flowers. Hence, only self-pollination is possible in these flowers.

Q. 8. Mention two strategies evolved to prevent self-pollination in flowers. [NCERT, Ex. Q. 8, Page 25]

Ans. Self-pollination involves the transfer of pollen from the stamen to the pistil of the same flower. Two strategies that have evolved to prevent self-pollination in flowers are as follows:

- In certain plants, the stigma of the flower has the capability to prevent the germination of self- pollen and hence, prevent the growth of the pollen tube. It is a genetic mechanism to prevent self-pollination called self-incompatibility. Incompatibility may be between individuals of the same species or between individuals of different species. Thus, incompatibility prevents breeding.
- In some plants, the gynoecium matures before the androecium or vice- versa. This phenomenon is known as protogyny or protandry respectively. This prevents the pollen from coming in contact with the stigma of the same flower.

Q. 9. What is self-incompatibility? Why does self-pollination not lead to seed formation in self-incompatible species? [NCERT, Ex. Q. 9, Page 25]

Ans. Self-incompatibility is a genetic mechanism in angiosperms that prevents self-pollination. It develops genetic incompatibility between individuals of the same species or between individuals of different species.

The plants which exhibit this phenomenon have the ability to prevent germination of self-pollen and thus, prevent the growth of the pollen tube on the stigma of the flower. This prevents the fusion of the gametes along with the development of the embryo. As a result, no seed formation takes place.

Q. 10. What is bagging technique? How is it useful in a plant breeding programme? [NCERT, Ex. Q. 10, Page 25]

Ans. The bagging technique is an integral part of plant breeding programs. It involves the removal of the anthers from bisexual flowers, leaving the female reproductive part (the pistil) intact through a process called emasculation. After emasculation, these flowers are enclosed or wrapped in bags to protect them from unwanted pollen grains and prevent unintended pollination.

This technique holds significance in plant breeding programme as it ensures that pollen grains of only desirable plants are utilised for fertilisation of the stigma to develop the desired plant variety.

Q. 11. What is triple fusion? Where and how does it take place? Name the nuclei involved in triple fusion.

[NCERT, Ex. Q. 11, Page 25]

Ans. Triple fusion is the fusion of the male gamete with two polar nuclei inside the embryo sac of the angiosperm. This process of fusion takes place inside the embryo sac.

When pollen grains fall on the stigma, they germinate and give rise to the pollen tube that passes through the style and enters into the ovule. After this, the pollen tube enters one of synergids and releases two male gametes there. Out of the two male gametes, one gamete fuses with the nucleus of the egg cell and forms the zygote (syngamy). The other male gamete fuses with the two polar nuclei present in the central cell to form a triploid primary endosperm nucleus. Since this process involves the fusion of three haploid nuclei, it is known as triple fusion. It results in the formation of the endosperm.

One male gamete nucleus and two polar nuclei are involved in this process.

Q. 12. Why do you think the zygote is dormant for sometime in a fertilised ovule?

[NCERT, Ex. Q. 12, Page 25]

Ans. The zygote is formed by the fusion of the male gamete with the nucleus of the egg cell. The zygote remains dormant for some time and waits for the endosperm to form, which develops from the primary endosperm cell resulting from triple fusion. The endosperm provides food for the growing embryo and after the formation of the endosperm, further development of the embryo from the zygote starts.

Q. 13. Differentiate between:

(a) Hypocotyl and epicotyl;

(b) Coleoptile and coleorrhiza;

(c) Integument and testa;

(d) Perisperm and pericarp.

[NCERT, Ex. Q. 13, Page 25]

Ans.

(a)	**Hypocotyl**	**Epicotyl**
	Hypocotyl is the region of embryonal axis between radicle and the point of attachment of cotyledons.	Epicotyl is the region of embryonal axis between plumule and the point of attachment of cotyledon.
(b)	**Coleoptile**	**Coleorrhiza**
	Coleoptile is the foliaceous sheath that covers the plumule in the embryo of cereals. It belongs to shoot system.	Coleorrhiza is a protective sheath of radical or root cap in the embryo of cereals. It belong to root system.
(c)	**Integument**	**Testa**
	It is the protective covering of ovule.	It is the outer covering of a seed.
(d)	**Perisperm**	**Pericarp**
	Perisperm is the remnant of the nucellus in a seed. It is a part of the seed.	Pericarp is the fruit wall which is formed from the ovary wall. It is the part of a fruit.

Q. 14. Why is apple called a false fruit? Which part(s) of the flower forms the fruit?

[NCERT, Ex. Q. 14, Page 25]

Ans. Fruits that are derived from the thalamus and other accessory floral parts are called false fruits. On the contrary, true fruits are those fruits which develop from the ovary, but do not consist of the thalamus or any other floral part. In an apple, the fleshy receptacle forms the main edible part. Hence, it is a false fruit.

Q. 15. What is meant by emasculation? When and why does a plant breeder employ this technique?

[NCERT, Ex. Q. 15, Page 25]

Ans. Emasculation is the process of removing anthers from bisexual flowers without affecting the female reproductive part (pistil), which is used in various plant hybridisation techniques.

Emasculation is performed by plant breeders in bisexual flowers to obtain the desired variety of a plant by crossing a particular plant with the desired pollen grain. To remove the anthers, the flowers are covered with a bag before they open. This ensures that the flower is pollinated by pollen grains obtained from desirable varieties only. Later, the mature, viable, and stored pollen grains are dusted on the bagged stigma by breeders to allow artificial pollination to take place and obtain the desired plant variety.

Q. 16. If one can induce parthenocarpy through the application of growth substances, which fruits would you select to induce parthenocarpy and why?

[NCERT, Ex. Q. 16, Page 25]

Ans. Parthenocarpy is the process of developing fruits without involving the process of fertilisation or seed formation. Therefore, the seedless varieties of economically important fruits such as orange, lemon, water melon, etc. are produced using this technique. This technique involves inducing fruit formation by the application of plant growth hormones such as auxins.

Q. 17. Explain the role of tapetum in the formation of pollen-grain wall. [NCERT, Ex. Q. 17, Page 25]

Ans. Tapetum is the innermost layer of the microsporangium. It provides nourishment to the developing pollen grains. During microsporogenesis, the cells of tapetum produce various enzymes, hormones, amino acids, and other nutritious material required for the development of pollen grains. It also produces the exine layer of the pollen grains, which is composed of the sporopollenin.

Q. 18. What is apomixis and what is its importance?

[NCERT, Ex. Q. 18, Page 25]

Ans. Apomixis is the mechanism of seed production without involving the process of meiosis and syngamy. It plays an important role in hybrid seed production. The method of producing hybrid seeds by cultivation is very expensive for farmers. Also, by sowing hybrid seeds, it is difficult to maintain hybrid characters as characters segregate during meiosis. Apomixis prevents the loss of specific characters in the hybrid. Also, it is a cost-effective method for producing seeds.

□□

HUMAN REPRODUCTION

CHAPTER 2

Introduction

➤ Humans are asexually reproducing and viviparous (giving birth to young ones). The reproductive events in humans include formation of gametes (gametogenesis), i.e., sperms in males and ovum in females, transfer of sperms into the female genital tract (insemination) and fusion of male and female gametes (fertilisation) leading to formation of zygote. It is followed by implantation of blastocyst, its embryonic development and parturition (delivery of the baby).

Male Reproductive System

➤ It consists of:

(a) A pair of testes

(b) Accessory ducts

(c) Accessory glands

(d) External genitalia

Testes

➤ Testes are the primary sex organs that produce sperms and testosterone **hormone**.

➤ They are contained in the scrotum located between upper thighs.

➤ The scrotum helps in maintaining the low temperature of the testes (2 – 2.5°C less than the normal internal body temperature) necessary for spermatogenesis.

➤ Each testis is oval in shape and has about 250 (200 – 300) compartments called testicular lobules.

➤ Each lobule is filled with connective tissue and contains 1-3 coiled seminiferous tubules in which sperm are produced.

➤ Seminiferous tubule is lined internally with spermatogenic cells called spermatogonia or primary male germ cells and sertoli cells or supporting cells.

➤ Spermatogonia undergo meiotic divisions and leads to sperm formation.

➤ Sertoli cells give shape and nourishment to developing spermatogenic cells and therefore also called as **nurse cells.**

➤ The regions outside the seminiferous tubules are the interstitial spaces which contain small blood vessels and interstitial cells or Leydig cells.

➤ The Leydig cells are endocrine in nature and secrete testicular hormones called androgens.

➤ Immunologically competent cells are also present.

Accessory Ducts

➤ The duct system includes **rete testis, vasa efferentia, epididymis** and **vas deferens.**

➤ The seminiferous tubules open into the vasa efferentia through rete testis.

➤ The vasa efferentia open into epididymis.

➤ The epididymis leads to vas deferens that ascends into the abdomen and loops over the urinary bladder.

➤ It receives a duct from seminal vesicle and opens into urethra as the ejaculatory duct.

➤ These ducts store and transport the sperms from the testis to the outside through urethra.

➤ The urethra originates from the urinary bladder and extends through the penis to its external opening called urethral meatus.

Accessory Male Genital Glands

➤ It includes paired seminal vesicles, prostate and paired bulbourethral glands (Cowper's glands).

➤ The secretions of these glands constitute the seminal plasma, which is rich in fructose, calcium and certain enzymes.

➤ Seminal vesicles produce seminal fluid and form 60 - 70% of semen.

➤ The secretion of bulbourethral glands is alkaline and is rich in mucus. It helps in the lubrication of the penis, supplies nutrient to sperms and provides an alkaline medium to counteract the acidity of the uterus.

External Genitalia

➤ The penis is the male external genitalia.

➤ It is made up of special tissue that helps in erection of the penis to facilitate insemination.

➤ The enlarged end of penis called the glans. Penis is covered by a loose fold of skin called foreskin.

The Female Reproductive System

➤ It consists of a pair of ovaries along with a pair of oviducts, uterus, cervix, vagina and the external genitalia located in pelvic region.

MNEMONICS

1. Concept Name: Accessory Male Genital Glands

Mnemonics: Supreme Power is Back

Interpretation: Seminal vesicles, Prostate, Bulbourethral glands

2. Concept Name: Parts of Oviduct (Fallopian tube)

Mnemonics: I Am Intelligent than yoU

Interpretation: Infundibulum, Ampulla, Isthmus, Uterine part

Ovaries

➤ Ovaries are located one on each side of the lower abdomen.

➤ They are the primary female sex organs which produce ova or the female gametes. It secretes a number of steroid ovarian hormones such as estrogen and progesterone.

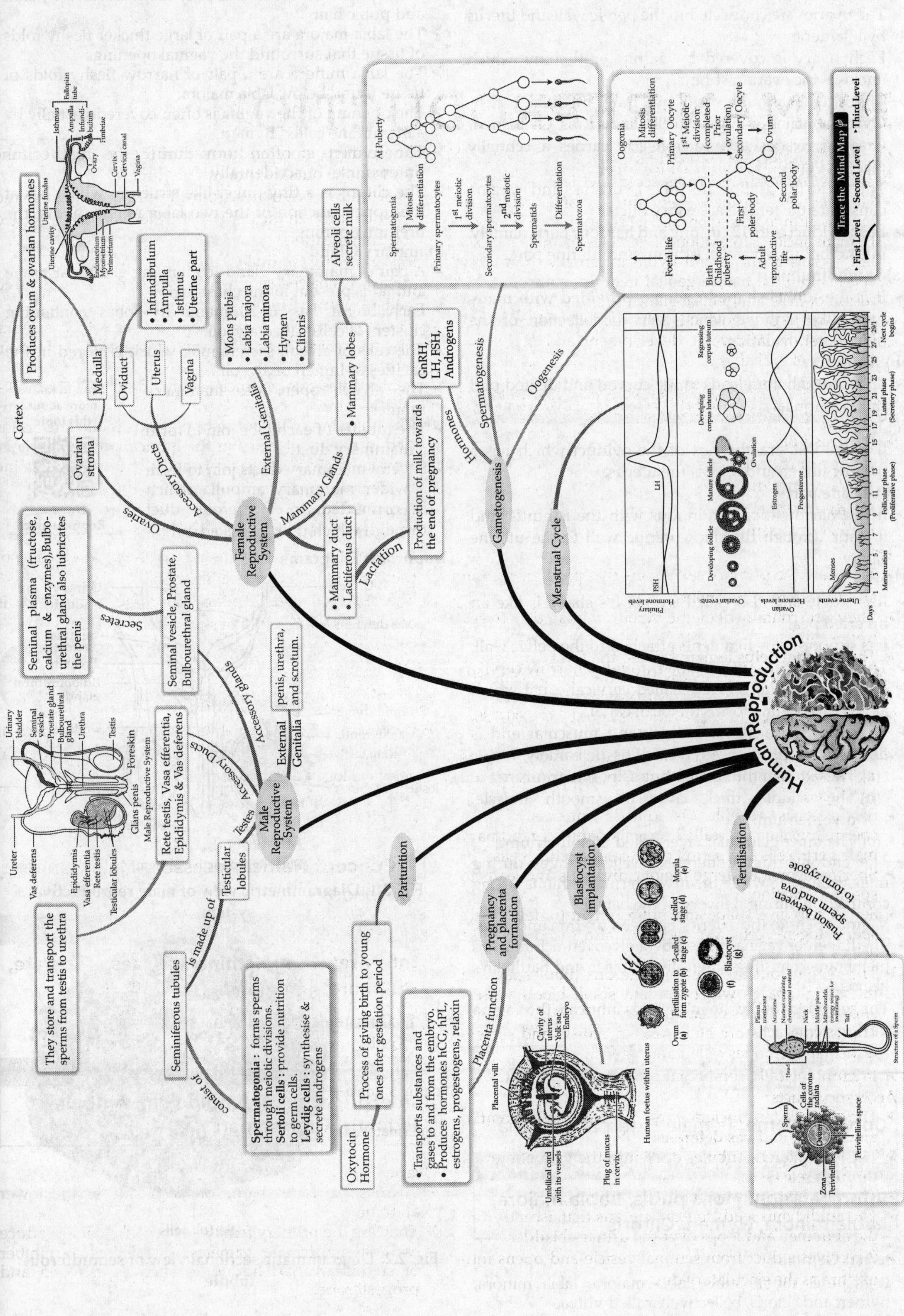
Human Reproduction
Male Reproductive System
Testes
Testicular lobules
is made up of
Seminiferous tubules
consist of
Spermatogonia : forms sperms through meiotic divisions.
Sertoli cells : provide nutrition to germ cells.
Leydig cells : synthesise & secrete androgens
Accessory Ducts
Rete testis, Vasa efferentia, Epididymis & Vas deferens
They store and transport the sperms from testis to urethra
Accessory glands
Seminal vesicle, Prostate, Bulbourethral gland
Secretes
Seminal plasma (fructose, calcium & enzymes),Bulbourethral gland also lubricates the penis
External Genitalia
penis, urethra, and scrotum.
Ureter
Vas deferens
Epididymis
Vasa efferentia
Rete testis
Testicular lobules
Glans penis
Foreskin
Testis
Urethra
Bulbourethral gland
Prostate gland
Seminal vesicle
Urinary bladder
Male Reproductive System
Female Reproductive System
Ovaries
Ovarian stroma
Cortex
Medulla
Produces ovum & ovarian hormones
Accessory Ducts
Oviduct
• Infundibulum
• Ampulla
• Isthmus
• Uterine part
Uterus
Vagina
Uterine fundus
Uterine cavity
Isthmus
Ampulla
Infundibulum
Fallopian tube
Ovary
Fimbriae
Cervix
Cervical canal
Vagina
Endometrium
Myometrium
Perimetrium
External Genitalia
• Mons pubis
• Labia majora
• Labia minora
• Hymen
• Clitoris
Mammary Glands
• Mammary lobes
Alveoli cells secrete milk
Mammary duct
Lactiferous duct
• Mammary duct
• Lactiferous duct
Lactation
Production of milk towards the end of pregnancy
Gametogenesis
Hormones
GnRH, LH, FSH, Androgens
Spermatogenesis
At Puberty
Spermatogonia
Mitosis differentiation
Primary spermatocytes
1st meiotic division
Secondary spermatocytes
2nd meiotic division
Spermatids
Differentiation
Spermatozoa
Oogenesis
Foetal life
Birth Childhood puberty
Adult reproductive life
Oogonia
Mitosis differentiation
Primary Oocyte
1st Meiotic division (completed Prior ovulation)
First polar body
Secondary Oocyte
Ovum
Second polar body
Menstrual Cycle
Pituitary Hormone levels
FSH
LH
Ovarian events
Developing follicle
Mature follicle
Ovulation
Developing corpus luteum
Regressing corpus luteum
Ovarian Hormone levels
Estrogen
Progesterone
Uterine events
Menses
Days
Menstruation
Follicular phase (Proliferative phase)
Luteal phase (Secretory phase)
Next cycle begins
Fertilisation
Fusion between sperm and ova to form zygote
Sperm
Cells of the corona radiata
Ovum
Perivitelline space
Zona Pellucida
Plasma membrane
Acrosome
Nucleus containing chromosomal material
Head
Neck
Middle piece
Mitochondria (energy source for swimming)
Tail
Structure of a Sperm
Blastocyst implantation
Ovum (a)
Fertilisation to form zygote (b)
2-celled stage (c)
4-celled stage (d)
Morula (e)
Blastocyst (g)
(f)
Pregnancy and placenta formation
Placenta function
• Transports substances and gases to and from the embryo.
• Produces hormones hCG, hPL, estrogens, progestogens, relaxin
Placental villi
Umbilical cord with its vessels
Cavity of uterus
Yolk sac
Embryo
Plug of mucus in cervix
Human foetus within uterus
Parturition
Process of giving birth to young ones after gestation period
Oxytocin Hormone
Trace the Mind Map
First Level
Second Level
Third Level

- It is about 2-4 cm in length.
- The ovaries are connected to the pelvic wall and uterus by ligaments.
- Each ovary is covered by a thin epithelium which encloses the ovarian stroma.
- The stroma has outer cortex and inner medulla.
- Ovary contains groups of cells known as Ovarian or Graafian follicles and each follicle carries a centrally placed ovum.
- The oviducts (fallopian tubes), uterus and vagina constitute the female accessory ducts.
- Each oviduct is 10-12 cm long and has four parts namely, infundibulum, ampulla, isthmus and uterine part.

(a) Infundibulum

- It is the funnel-shaped opening provided with many finger-like fimbriae which help in collection of the ovum after ovulation.

(b) Ampulla

- The infundibulum leads to the curved and dilated part called ampulla.

(c) Isthmus

- It is the last straight part of the oviduct which has a narrow lumen and it joins the uterus.

(d) Uterine part

- It is a narrow tube continuous with the isthmus, and it leads through the thick uterine wall to the uterine cavity.

Uterus

- It is single and also called womb. It's shape is like an inverted pear.
- It is supported by ligaments attached to the pelvic wall.
- The uterus opens into vagina through a narrow cervix.
- The cavity of the cervix is called cervical canal which along with vagina forms the birth canal.
- The wall of the uterus is thick and muscular and is differentiated into three layers of tissue namely,
  (a) The external thin membranous perimetrium.
  (b) The middle thick layer of smooth muscle, myometrium.
  (c) The inner glandular layer called endometrium.
- The endometrium undergoes cyclic changes during menstrual cycle while the myometrium exhibits strong contraction during delivery of the baby.
- Vagina opens to the exterior between urethra and anus.
- The lumen of vagina is lined by a glycogen-rich mucous membrane consisting of sensitive papillae and Bartholin's glands.
- The secretions of Bartholin's glands lubricate the vagina during sexual act.

MNEMONICS

Concept Name: Female External genitalia

Mnemonics: Mobiles Light Led Him Crazy

Interpretation: Mons pubis, Labia majora, Labia minora, Hymen, Clitoris

External Genitalia

- It includes mons pubis, labia majora, labia minora, hymen and clitoris, collectively called vulva.
- Mons pubis is a cushion of fatty tissue covered by skin and pubic hair.
- The labia majora are a pair of large thicker fleshy folds of tissue that surround the vaginal opening.
- The labia minora are a pair of narrow fleshy folds of tissue found below labia majora.
- The opening of the vagina is often covered partially by a membrane called hymen.
- The hymen is often torn during the first coitus (intercourse) or accidentally.
- The clitoris is a tiny finger-like structure which lies at the upper junction of the two labia minora above the urethral opening.

Mammary Gland

- A pair of mammary glands containing glandular tissue and fat is present in the chest region.
- Each breast has 15-20 mammary lobes containing clusters of cells called alveoli.
- The cells of alveoli secrete milk which is stored in the cavities or lumen of alveoli.
- The alveoli open into mammary tubules.
- The tubules of each lobe join to form a mammary duct.
- Several mammary ducts join to form a wider mammary ampulla which is connected to lactiferous duct through which milk is sucked out.

Scan to know more about this topic

Human Reproduction

Important Diagrams

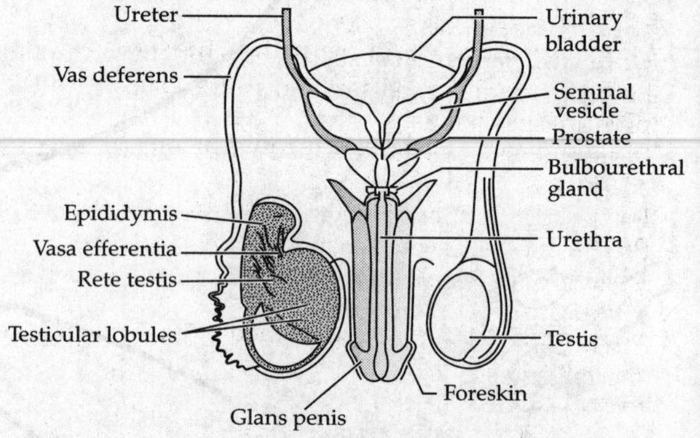

Male Reproductive System

Fig. 2.1: Diagrammetric view of male reproductive system

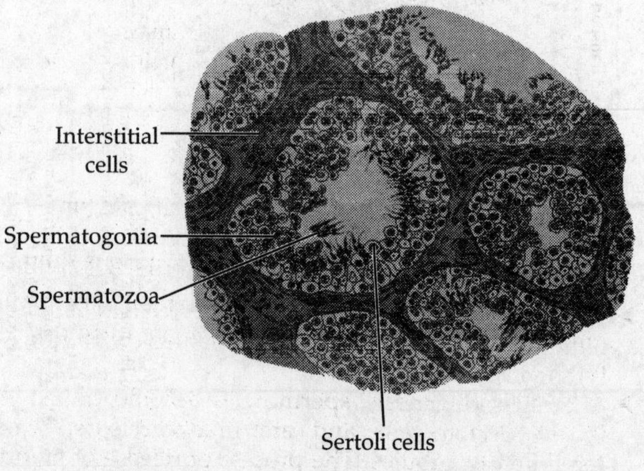

Fig. 2.2: Diagrammatic sectional view of seminiferous tubule

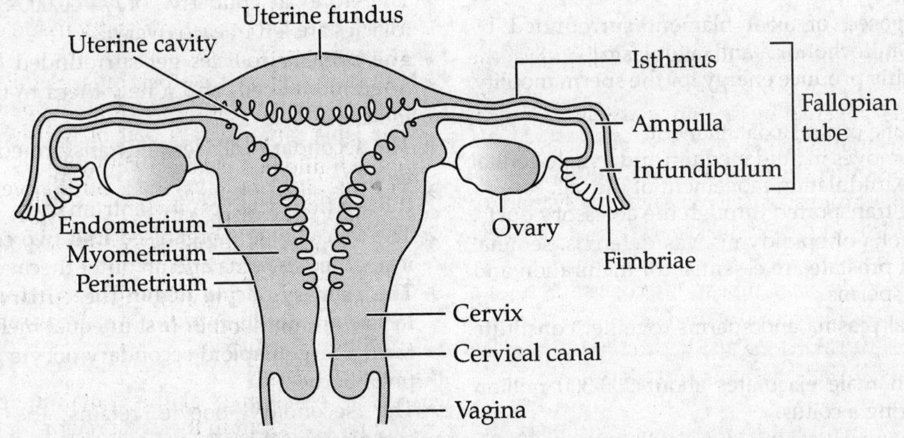

Fig. 2.3: Diagrammatic sectional view of the female reproductive system

Scan to know more about this topic

Female Reproductive system

Gametogenesis

Scan to know more about this topic

Gametogenesis

- It is the process of formation of gametes or sex cells.
- It includes spermatogenesis and oogenesis.

Spermatogenesis

- It is the process of formation of sperms in seminiferous tubules of testes.
- It has two stages namely,
  (a) Formation of spermatids
  (b) Spermiogenesis
- During the formation of spermatids, the spermatogonia i.e., sperm mother cells or immature male germ cells produce spermatids.
- In spermiogenesis, the spermatids are transformed into sperm.
- Each primary spermatocyte undergoes meiosis-I and produces two haploid secondary spermatocytes.
- Each secondary spermatocyte divides by meiosis-II and produces two haploid spermatids.
- Thus, four spermatids are formed from each primary spermatocyte.

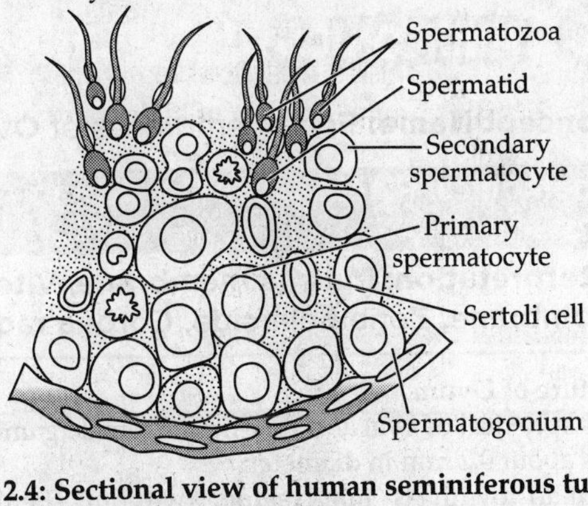

Fig. 2.4: Sectional view of human seminiferous tubule

- The spermatids, under the influence of FSH of anterior pituitary are converted into spermatozoa. The process is called spermiogenesis.
- After spermiogenesis, sperm head become embedded in the Sertoli cells and are finally released from seminiferous tubules. The process of release of mature spermatozoa from the sertoli cells into the lumen of seminiferous tubules is known as spermiation.

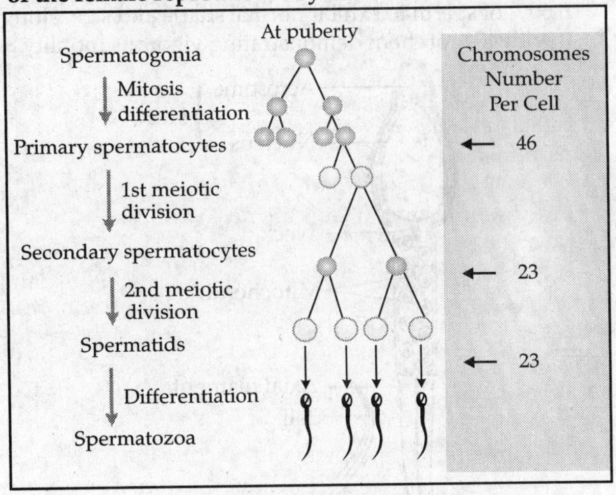

Fig. 2.5: Spermatogenesis

Hormones in Spermatogenesis

- Hypothalamus releases large amount of Gonadotropin releasing hormone (GnRH).
- GnRH stimulates the anterior pituitary gland to secrete two gonadotropins namely Luteinising hormone (LH) and Follicle stimulating hormone (FSH).
- LH acts on the Leydig cells and stimulates synthesis and secretion of androgens which in turn stimulate the spermatogenesis.
- FSH acts on the Sertoli cells and stimulates secretion of some spermogenic factors which help in the process of spermiogenesis.

Structure of Sperm

- It is a microscopic structure.
- A mature sperm measures about 60 μm (0.06 mm) long.
- A plasma membrane envelops the whole body of sperm.
- Sperm consists of four parts namely, head, neck, a middle piece and a tail region.

(a) Head

- It is oval shaped, consisting of nucleus and acrosome.
- Acrosome is formed from Golgi complex which contains lytic enzymes, that help in fertilisation of the ovum.

(b) Neck

- Behind the head is a neck containing proximal and distal centrioles.
- The distal centriole of the neck is connected to axial filament.

(c) Middle Piece

- It is composed of axial filament surrounded by numerous mitochondria and cytoplasm.
- Mitochondria produce energy for the sperm motility.

(d) Tail

- It consists of a central axial filament.
- The sperm moves in fluid medium and female genital tract by the undulating movement of the tail.
- Sperms are transported through the accessory ducts.
- The secretions of epididymis, vas deferens, seminal vesicle and prostate are essential for maturation and motility of sperms.
- The seminal plasma and sperms together constitute the semen.
- The human male ejaculates about 200-300 million sperms during a coitus.
- To achieve normal fertility, it is necessary for at least 60% of sperm to exhibit normal shape and size, along with 40% of them demonstrating vigorous motility.

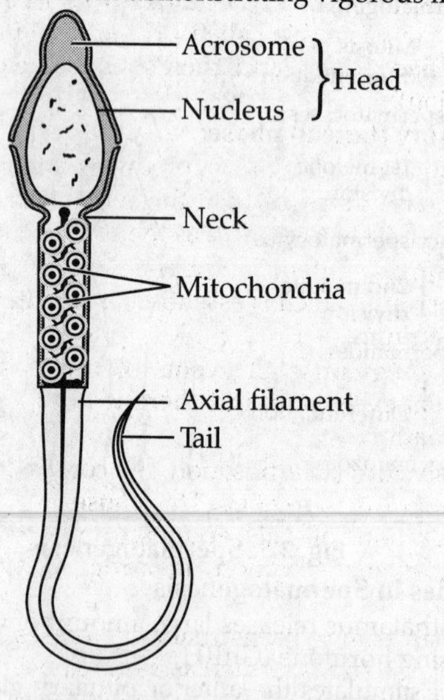

Fig. 2.6: Structure of a Sperm

MNEMONICS

Concept Name: Structure of Sperm

Mnemonics: High Node Magnification Time

Interpretation: Head, Neck, Middle Piece, Tail

Oogenesis

- It is the process of formation and maturation of ovum.
- It takes place in Graafian follicles.
- It is initiated in embryonic stage when millions of egg mother cells (oogonia) are formed within each ovary.
- No oogonia are formed and added after birth.
- Oogonia multiply to form primary oocytes which enter into prophase-I of the meiosis and get temporarily arrested at that stage.
- Each primary oocyte gets surrounded by a layer of granulosa cells to form primary follicle.
- A large number of primary follicles degenerate during the phase from birth to puberty.
- Therefore at puberty only 60,000-80,000 primary follicles are left in each ovary.
- The primary follicles get surrounded by more layers of granulosa cells and a new theca to form secondary follicles.
- The secondary follicles get transformed into a tertiary follicle.
- It has a fluid filled cavity (antrum).
- The theca layer is organised into two components: an inner theca interna and an outer theca externa.
- The primary oocyte within the tertiary follicle grows in size and undergoes first unequal meiotic division to form a large haploid secondary oocyte and a tiny first polar body.
- The secondary oocyte retains the nutrient rich cytoplasm of the primary oocyte.
- It is unknown, whether the first polar body divides further or degenerates.
- The tertiary follicle further changes into the mature follicle (Graafian follicle).
- The secondary oocyte forms a new membrane (zona pellucida).
- The Graafian follicle now ruptures to release the secondary oocyte (ovum) from the ovary. This is called ovulation.

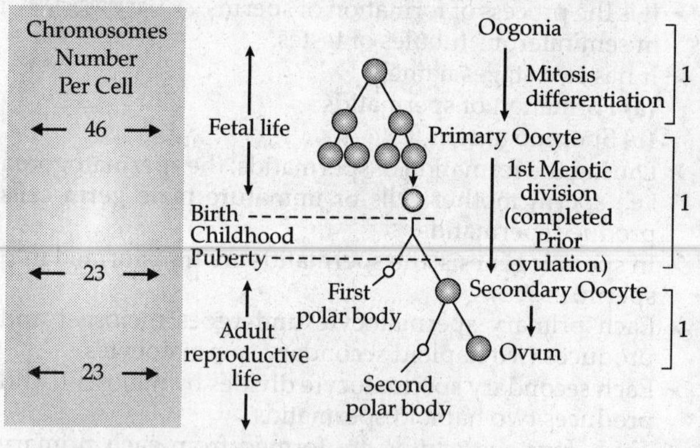

Fig. 2.7: Oogenesis

MNEMONICS

Concept Name: Four membranes of Ovum

Mnemonics: Please Cross Via Zebra Crossing

Interpretation: Plasma membrane, Vitelline membrane, Zona pellucida, Corona radiata

Structure of Ovum

- It is spherical or oval and non-motile female gamete.
- It is about 0.2 mm in diameter.
- Human ovum is non-cleidoic (without shell) and alecithal (without yolk).
- Ovum has four membranes namely,
  - **(a) Plasma membrane (Oolemma):** Innermost layer.
  - **(b) Vitelline membrane:** Attached to plasma membrane.
  - **(c) Zona pellucida:** Transparent non-cellular, thick, glycoprotein rich layer found outer to the vitelline membrane.

(d) Corona radiata: Outer layer formed of follicle cells. These cells are held together by mucopolysaccharide called hyaluronic acid.

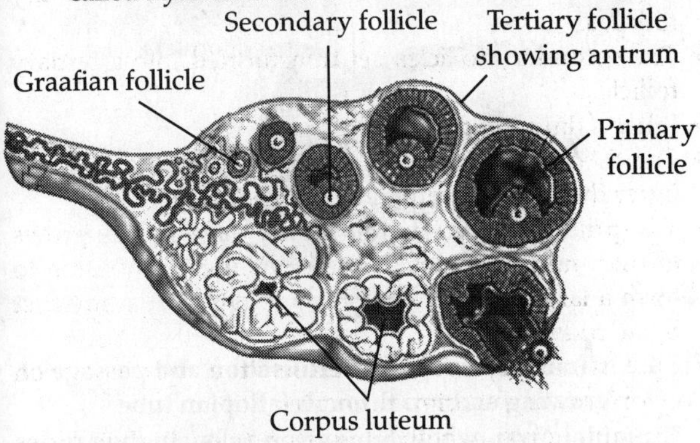

Fig. 2.8: Diagrammatic Section view of ovary

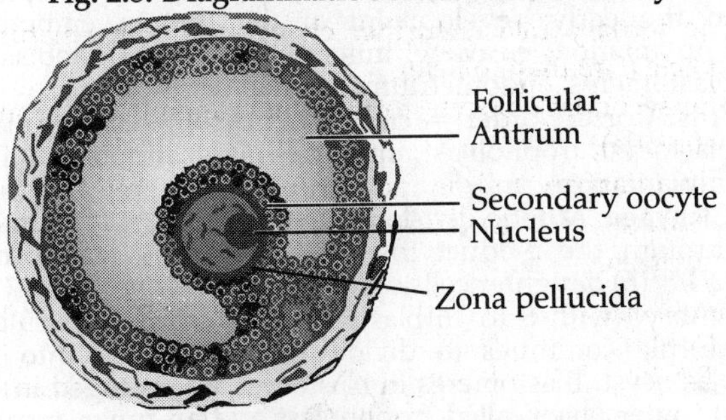

Fig. 2.9: Structure of the Graafian follicle

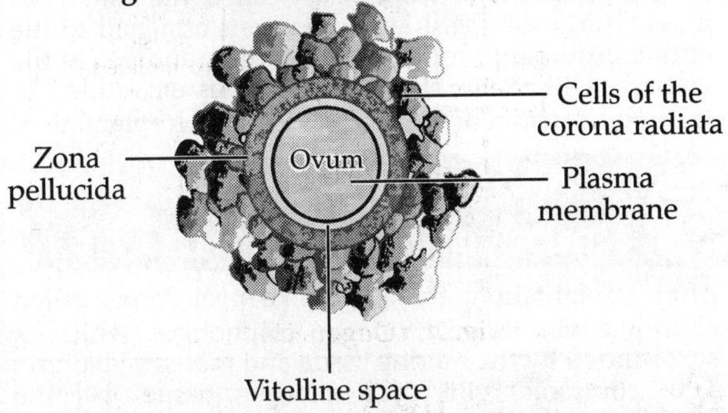

Fig. 2.10: Diagrammatic view of human ovum

Menstrual Cycle

- The reproductive cycle in the human female and related primates is called menstrual cycle.
- The first menstruation begins at puberty (at the age of 10-12 years) and is called menarche.
- In human females, menstruation is repeated at an average interval of about 28/29 days and the cycle of events starting from one menstruation till the next one is called the menstrual cycle.
- One ovum is released during the middle of each menstrual cycle.

Menstrual cycle has the following phases:

(i) Menstural phase:

- The cycle starts with the menstrual phase, when menstrual flow occurs, it lasts for 3-5 days.
- The menstrual flow results due to breakdown of endometrial lining of the uterus and its blood vessels which form the liquid that comes out through vagina.
- Menstruation occurs only if the released ovum is not fertilised.
- Lack of menstruation may be indicative of pregnancy or may also be caused due to some other underlying causes like stress, poor health, etc.

(ii) Follicular (Proliferative) phase:

- The menstrual phase is followed by the follicular phase.
- During follicular phase, the primary follicles in the ovary grow to become a fully mature Graafian follicle and simultaneously the endometrium of uterus regenerates through proliferation. These changes in the ovary and the uterus are induced by changes in the levels of pituitary and ovarian hormones.
- The secretion of gonadotropins (LH and FSH) increases gradually during the follicular phase and stimulates follicular development as well as secretion of estrogens by the growing follicles.

(iii) Ovulatory phase:

- Both LH and FSH attain a peak level in the middle of cycle (about 14th day).
- Rapid secretion of LH leading to its maximum level during the mid-cycle called LH surge induces rupture of Graafian follicle and thereby the release of ovum (ovulation).

(iv) Secretory (Luteal) phase:

- The ovulation (ovulatory phase) is followed by the luteal phase during which the remaining parts of the Graafian follicle transform as the corpus luteum.
- The corpus luteum secretes large amounts of progesterone, which is essential for maintenance of the endometrium.
- During pregnancy, all events of the menstrual cycle stop and there is no menstruation.
- In the absence of fertilisation, the corpus luteum degenerates. This causes disintegration of the endometrium leading to menstruation, marking a new cycle.
- In human beings, menstrual cycle ceases at around 50 years of age and is termed as menopause.
- Cyclic menstruation is an indicator of normal reproductive phase and extends between menarche and menopause.

Scan to know more about this topic

Menstruation

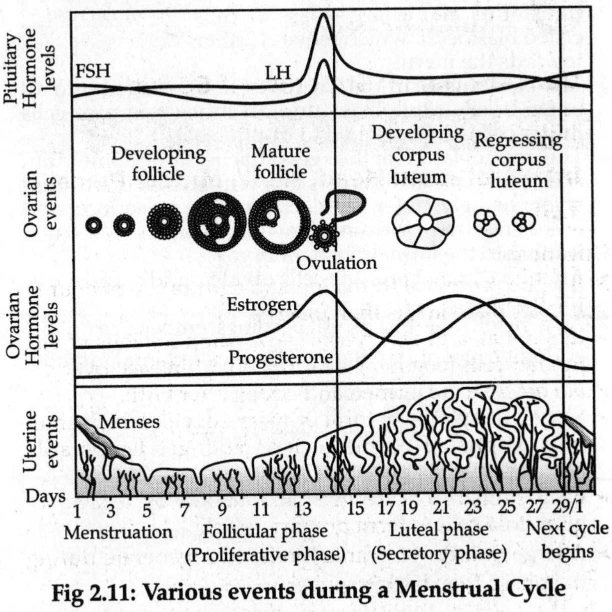

Fig 2.11: Various events during a Menstrual Cycle

Fertilisation and Implantation

Fertilisation

Scan to know more about this topic

Fertilisation

- The process of fusion of male gamete (sperm) with the female gamete (ovum) is called fertilisation.
- During copulation, semen is released through the penis into the vagina (insemination).
- After insemination, the sperms swim through the cervix and enter into the uterus and reach the ampullary-isthmic junction of the oviduct where fertilisation takes place.
- The process of fertilisation takes place as follows:
  - Sperms → vagina → cervical canal → uterus → isthmus → ampullary-isthmic junction → Fertilisation
  - Ovum (from ovary) → fimbriae → infundibulum → ampulla→ ampullary-isthmic junction → Fertilisation
- Fertilisation (sperm + ovum → zygote) occurs only if ovum & sperms are transported simultaneously. So all copulations do not lead to fertilisation and pregnancy.
- As soon as sperm contacts with zona pellucida, it induces changes in the membrane that block entry of additional sperms.
- With the help of enzymes of the acrosome, which dissolve the zona pellucida and plasma membrane of the ovum, the sperm enters into the cytoplasm of the ovum. This induces second meiotic division of the secondary oocyte to form a second polar body and a haploid ovum (ootid).
- The haploid nuclei of the sperm and ovum fuse together to form a diploid zygote.

Implantation

Scan to know more about this topic

Implantation of embryo

- The mitotic division (cleavage) starts as the zygote moves through the isthmus of oviduct towards the uterus and forms 2, 4, 8, 16 daughter cells called blastomeres.
- The embryo with 8-16 blastomeres is called a morula.
- Morula continues to divide and transforms into a large mass of cells called blastocyst, which moves further towards the uterus.
- The blastomeres in the blastocyst are arranged into an outer layer (trophoblast) and an inner group of cells (inner cell mass) attached to trophoblast.
- The trophoblast layer then gets attached to endometrium and the inner cell mass gets differentiated to three germ layers namely: outer ectoderm, middle mesoderm and inner endoderm forming 3-layered structure (gastrula) leading to the formation of embryo.
- After attachment, uterine cells divide rapidly and cover the blastocyst.
- As a result, the blastocyst becomes embedded in the endometrium of the uterus. This is called implantation.

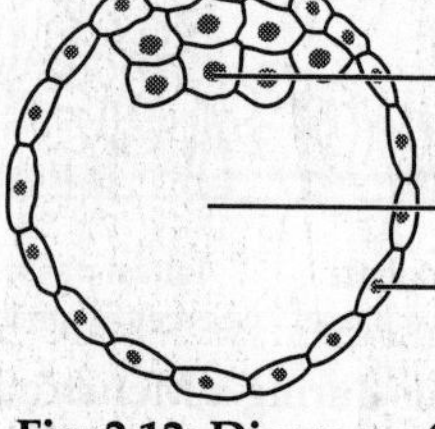

Fig. 2.12: Diagram of a Blastocyst

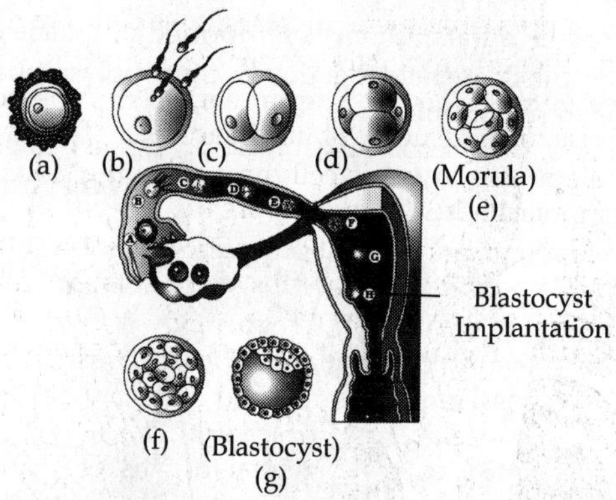

Fig. 2.13: Transport of ovum, fertilisation and passage of growing embryo through fallopian tube

Example: Arrange the terms given below in their order of occurrence describing their structure and function in the early development of the human embryo: Implantation; cleavage; inner cells mass; trophoblast; blastomeres; endometrium; morula; blastocyst.

Ans. Correct order = cleavage, blastomeres, morula, blastocyst, trophoblast, inner cell mass, endometrium, implantation.

Cleavage: Mitotic division starts as the zygote moves through the oviduct towards the uterus and form (2/4/8/16) daughter cells called blastomeres.

Embryo with 8 to 16 blastomeres is called a morula. Morula continues to divide and transforms into a blastocyst. Blastomeres in blastocyst are arranged into an outer layer called trophoblast and an inner group of cells attached to trophoblast called the inner cell mass. The trophoblast layer then gets attached to the endometrium and inner cell mass differentiates as the embryo. Ultimately blastocyst becomes embedded in the endometrium of uterus. This is called Implantation.

Pregnancy and Embryonic Development

- After implantation, the finger-like projections called chorionic villi appear on the trophoblast which is surrounded by the uterine tissue and maternal blood.
- The chorionic villi and uterine tissue become interdigitated with each other and form a structural and functional unit between developing embryo and the maternal body called placenta.
- The placenta is a structural and functional unit between embryo (foetus) and maternal body.
- Placenta is connected to the embryo by an umbilical cord.
- The umbilical cord helps to transport substances to and from the embryo.

Functions of Placenta

- It acts as barrier between the foetus and mother.
- Soluble inorganic and organic materials, nutrients, hormones, antibodies, etc., can pass through the placenta from the mother to foetus.
- It helps in the gas exchange between mother and foetus.
- It helps to eliminate nitrogenous wastes of foetus.
- It acts as an endocrine gland by secreting several hormones like human chorionic gonadotropin (hCG), human placental lactogen (hPL), oestrogens, progesterone and relaxin.

Pregnancy

- During pregnancy, levels of estrogen, progestogen, cortisol, prolactin, thyroxine, etc., are also increased in maternal blood.

- They support the foetal growth, metabolic changes in the mother and maintain pregnancy.
- Three germ layers (ectoderm, endoderm, mesoderm) give rise to all tissues (organs) in adults.
- The stem cells in inner cell mass have the potency to give rise to all the tissues and organs.
- Human pregnancy (gestation period) lasts 9 months (for cats: 2 months, dogs: 2 months, elephants: 21 months).

Changes in Embryo during Pregnancy

- After one month of pregnancy: Heart is formed.
- End of second month: Limbs and digits are developed.
- End of 12 weeks (first trimester): The major organs such as limbs, external genital organs etc., are well developed.
- During 5th month: First movement of foetus and appearance of hair on the head.
- End of 24 weeks (second trimester): Body is covered with fine hair, eyelids separate and eye lashes are formed.
- End of 9 months: Ready for delivery.

Parturition (Labour) and Lactation

- The process of giving birth to young ones after the gestation period of nine months is known as parturition.
- Parturition is induced by neuroendocrine mechanism.
- The signals originating from the foetus and placenta induce mild uterine contractions (foetal ejection reflex). This causes the release of oxytocin from maternal pituitary.
- Oxytocin causes stronger uterine muscle contractions which in turn stimulate further secretion of oxytocin. This process is continued leading to expulsion of the baby out of the uterus through the birth canal.
- After parturition, the umbilical cord is cut off.
- The placenta and remnants of umbilical cord are expelled from the maternal body after parturition. This is called "after birth".

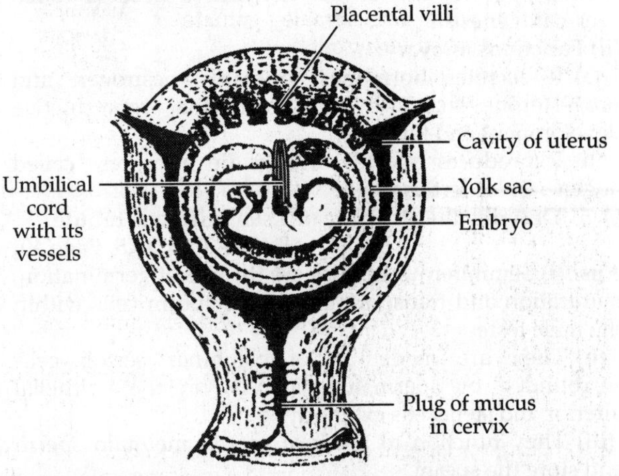

Fig. 2.14: Transport of ovum, fertilisation and passage of growing embryo through fallopian tube

Lactation

- The mammary glands produce milk towards the end of pregnancy by the process called lactation.
- The yellowish milk produced during the initial few days of lactation is called colostrum.
- The colostrum contains several antibodies essential to develop resistance for the new born babies.

NCERT CORNER

Exercise Questions

Q. 1. Fill in the blanks.

(a) Humans reproduce __________. (asexually/ sexually)

(b) Humans are __________. (oviparous, viviparous, ovoviviparous)

(c) Fertilisation is __________ in humans. (external/ internal)

(d) Male and female gametes are __________. (diploid/haploid)

(e) Zygote is __________. (diploid/haploid)

(f) The process of release of ovum from a mature follicle is called __________.

(g) Ovulation is induced by a hormone called __________.

(h) The fusion of male and female gametes is called __________.

(i) Fertilisation takes place in __________.

(j) Zygote divides to form __________ which is implanted in uterus.

(k) The structure which provides vascular connection between foetus and uterus is called __________.

[NCERT Ex. Q.1, Page 39]

Ans. (a) Sexually, **(b)** Viviparous, **(c)** Internal, **(d)** Haploid, **(e)** Diploid, **(f)** Ovulation, **(g)** Luteinising hormone (LH), **(h)** Fertilisation, **(i)** ampullary region of Fallopian tube, **(j)** Blastocyst **(k)** Placenta

Q. 2. Draw a labelled diagram of male reproductive system. [NCERT Ex. Q.1, Page 40]

Ans.

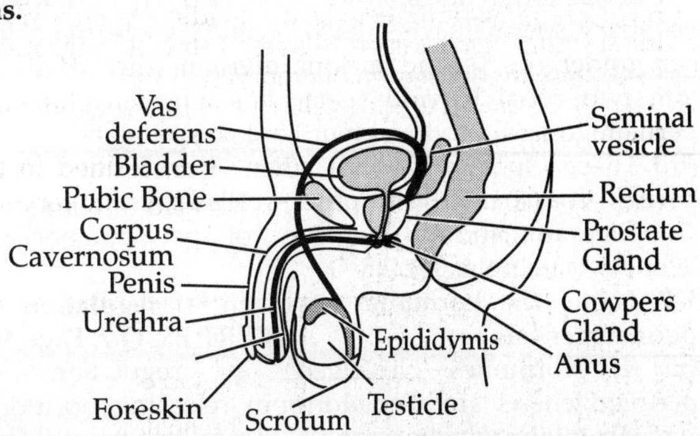

Q. 3. Draw a labelled diagram of female reproductive system. [NCERT Ex. Q.3, Page 40]

Ans. For diagram refer: Revision notes/ Fig 2.3.

Q. 4. Write two major functions each of testis and ovary. **[NCERT Ex. Q.4, Page 40]**

Ans. (i) Functions of testis:

(a) It produces male sex hormone, testosterone.

(b) It produces sperm. Sperms are produced in the seminiferous tubules of the testes in a process called spermatogenesis.

(ii) Functions of ovary:

(a) It secretes hormones, primarily oestrogen and progesterone that are vital to normal reproductive development and fertility.

(b) It produces oocytes or eggs (in a process called oogenesis) for fertilisation.

Q. 5. Describe the structure of a seminiferous tubule. **[NCERT Ex. Q.5, Page 40]**

Ans. (i) Seminiferous tubules are the site of germination, maturation and transportation of the sperm cells within the male testes.

(ii) They are made up of columnar sertoli cells surrounded by spermatogenic cells on the epithelial interior and stem cells exteriorly.

(iii) They function to produce sperm, maintain sperm and store the sperm.

(iv) During the process of meiosis, the sertoli cells that line the seminiferous tubules undergo the process of differentiation to be converted into sperm.

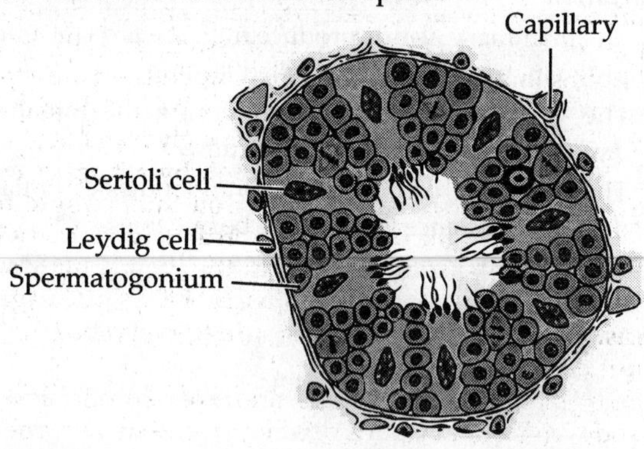

Q. 6. What is spermatogenesis? Briefly describe the process of spermatogenesis. **[NCERT Ex. Q.6, Page 40]**

Ans. (i) Spermatogenesis is the process of the production of sperms from the immature germ cells in males. It takes place in seminiferous tubules.

(ii) During spermatogenesis, a diploid spermatogonium (male germ cell) divides by mitosis and produces primary spermatocyte (diploid). This primary spermatocyte undergoes first meiotic division (meiosis I) which is a reductional division to form two equal haploid secondary spermatocytes. Each secondary spermatocyte then undergoes second meiotic division (meiosis II) to form two equal haploid spermatids. Hence, a diploid spermatogonium produces four haploid spermatids.

(iii) These spermatids are then transformed into spermatozoa (sperm) by the process called spermiogenesis.

(iv) Diagrammatic representation of spermatogenesis : Refer Revision notes/Fig 2.5.

Q. 7. Name the hormones involved in regulation of spermatogenesis. **[NCERT Ex. Q.7, Page 40]**

Ans. (i) Hormones involved in regulation of spermatogenesis are Gonadotropin releasing hormone (GnRH), luteinizing hormone (LH), follicle stimulating hormone (FSH) and inhibin.

(ii) GnRH reaches to the pituitary via the hypophyseal portal vessels and causes release of FSH and LH.

(iii) FSH and testosterone hormone both promotes the production of spermatozoa.

(iv) Inhibin feeds back to the pituitary gland to switch off FSH release.

Q. 8. Define spermiogenesis and spermiation. **[NCERT Ex. Q.8, Page 40]**

Ans. (i) Spermiogenesis is a process in which the spermatids differentiate into mature, motile spermatozoa.

(ii) Spermiation is a process in which sertoli cells release the elongated, non-motile spermatids into the lumen of the seminiferous tubules prior to their passage to the epididymis.

Q. 9. Draw a labelled diagram of sperm. **[NCERT Ex. Q.9, Page 40]**

Ans. For diagram refer to Revision notes/ Fig 2.6.

Q. 10. What are the major components of seminal plasma? **[NCERT Ex. Q.10, Page 40]**

Ans. (i) The major components of the seminal plasma in the male reproductive system are mucus, spermatozoa and various secretions of accessory glands.

(ii) The seminal plasma is rich in fructose, calcium, ascorbic acid and certain enzymes. It provides nourishment and protection to sperms.

Q. 11. What are the major functions of male accessory ducts and glands? **[NCERT Ex. Q.11, Page 40]**

Ans. (i) Male accessory ducts are vasa efferentia, epididymis, vas deferens and rete testis. They play an important role in the transport and temporary storage of sperms.

(ii) Male accessory glands are seminal vesicles, prostate glands and bulbo-urethral glands. These glands secrete fluids that lubricate the reproductive system and sperms.

(iii) Sperms get dispersed in the fluid which makes their transportation into the female body easier. The fluid is rich in fructose, ascorbic acid and certain enzymes. They also provide nutrients and activate the sperm.

Q. 12. What is oogenesis? Give a brief account of oogenesis. **[NCERT Ex. Q.12, Page 40]**

Ans. (i) Oogenesis is the process by which the female gametes, or ovum are produced in the ovaries. It involves meiosis and occurs after puberty until menopause. Human normally produces only one oocyte during each ovarian cycle.

(ii) During oogenesis, a diploid oogonium gets transformed into a diploid primary oocyte. This diploid primary oocyte then undergoes first meiotic division to form two unequal haploid cells. The smaller cell is known as the first polar body, while the larger cell is known as the secondary oocyte.

(iii) This secondary oocyte undergoes second meiotic division and gives rise to a second polar body and an ovum.

(iv) Hence, in the process of oogenesis, a diploid oogonium produces a single haploid ovum while two or three polar bodies are produced.

Q. 13. Draw a labelled diagram of a section through ovary. **[NCERT Ex. Q.13, Page 40]**

Ans. For diagram: Revision notes/ Fig 2.8.

Q. 14. Draw a labelled diagram of a Graafian follicle? **[NCERT Ex. Q.14, Page 40]**

Ans. For diagram: Revision notes/ Fig 2.9, Page 43.

Q. 15. Name the functions of the following.

(a) Corpus luteum **(b) Endometrium**

(c) Acrosome **(d) Sperm tail**

(e) Fimbriae **[NCERT Ex. Q.15, Page 40]**

Ans.

S. No.	Term	Functions
(a)	Corpus luteum	• Secretes progesterone hormone. • Essential for establishing and maintaining pregnancy in females
(b)	Endometrium	• Place where implantation of blastocysts and formation of placenta takes place. • Development of embryo.
(c)	Acrosome	• Helps the sperm get through the egg's protective coat with the help of hydrolytic enzymes released during acrosome reaction • Allow the plasma membranes of the sperm and egg to fuse during fertilisation.
(d)	Sperm tail	• Helps in propelling or swim the sperm cell forward to meet the egg.
(e)	Fimbriae	• Responsible for capturing the egg when it is released from the ovary. • Help egg to move from the ovaries to uterus.

Q. 16. Identify True/False statements. Correct each false statement to make it true.
(a) Androgens are produced by Sertoli cells.
(b) Spermatozoa get nutrition from Sertoli cells.
(c) Leydig cells are found in ovary.
(d) Leydig cells synthesise androgens.
(e) Oogenesis takes place in corpus luteum.
(f) Menstrual cycle ceases during pregnancy.
(g) Presence or absence of hymen is not a reliable indicator of virginity or sexual experience.
[NCERT Ex. Q.16, Page 40]

Ans. (a) False. Androgens are produced by Leydig cells found in seminiferous tubules of the testis.

(b) True. Spermatozoa get nutrition from Sertoli cells. Sertoli cells support and nourish the immature sperm cells by giving them nutrients and blood products.

(c) False. Leydig cells are found in the seminiferous tubules of the testis. Leydig cells, also known as interstitial cells of Leydig, produce testosterone in the presence of luteinising hormone (LH).

(d) True. Leydig cells synthesise androgens. It produces testosterone in the presence of LH.

(e) False. Oogenesis takes place in the ovary and leads to the formation of a single egg cell or ovum.

(f) True. Menstrual cycle ceases during pregnancy because if the woman gets pregnant around the mid-cycle, the fetus's placenta starts secreting human chorionic gonadotropin (hCG). hCG causes the remnant of the ruptured follicle to start growing (and make the yellow body, corpus luteum) and start secreting progesterone. This will sustain the thickness of the uterine wall during the pregnancy and cause the periods to stop during the pregnancy.

(g) True. Presence or absence of the hymen is not a reliable indicator of virginity or sexual experience.

Q. 17. What is menstrual cycle? Which hormones regulate menstrual cycle? [NCERT Ex. Q.17, Page 40]

Ans. (i) Menstrual cycle may be defined as the monthly cycle of changes in the ovaries and the lining of the uterus (endometrium). This will start the preparation of an egg for fertilisation.

(ii) Hormones, which regulate the menstrual cycle, are following:

(a) FSH and LH (secreted by the pituitary gland)
(b) Oestrogen (secreted by the ovaries)
(c) Progesterone (secreted from corpus luteum).

Q. 18. What is parturition? Which hormones are involved in induction of parturition? [NCERT Ex. Q.18, Page 40]

Ans. (i) Parturition is the process of delivery of the foetus at the end of pregnancy.

(ii) The hormones involved in the induction of parturition are oxytocin and relaxin.

(a) Oxytocin leads to the contraction of smooth muscles of myometrium of the uterus, which directs the full term foetus towards the birth canal.

(b) Relaxin causes relaxation of the pelvic ligaments and prepares the uterus for child birth.

Q. 19. In our society the women are blamed for giving birth to daughters. Can you explain why this is not correct ? [NCERT Ex. Q.19, Page 40]

Ans. Women are homogametic, i.e., they produce only one type of egg, each having 22 autosomes and one X chromosome. Male is heterogametic and produces two types of sperms: 50% with X chromosome and 50% with Y chromosome. The sex of the baby depends on the type of sperm fuses with the egg so sex of the baby is determined by the father. Thus, mothers are wrongly blamed.

Q. 20. How many eggs are released by a human ovary in a month? How many eggs do you think would have been released if the mother gave birth to identical twins? Would your answer change if the twins born were fraternal? [NCERT Ex. Q.20, Page 40]

Ans. (i) An ovary releases a single egg every month.

(ii) Identical twins:

(a) As the identical twins are monozygotic and are produced from two parts of same zygote so only one egg was released from the ovary.

(b) Therefore, twins are produced from a single egg by the separation of early blastomeres resulting from the first zygotic cleavage. As a result, the young ones formed will have the same genetic make-up and are thus, called identical twins.

(iii) Fraternal twin:

(a) If the twins born are fraternal, then they would have developed from two separate eggs.

(b) This happens when two eggs (one from each ovary) are released at the same time and gets fertilised by two separate sperms and produce two zygotes. Hence, the young ones developed will have separate genes and are therefore, called non-identical or fraternal twins.

Q. 21. How many eggs do you think were released by the ovary of a female dog which gave birth to 6 puppies? [NCERT Ex. Q.21, Page 41]

Ans. (i) Dogs and rodents are poly-ovulatory species.

(ii) In these species, more than one ovum is released from the ovary at the time of ovulation. Hence, six eggs were released by the ovary of a female dog to produce six puppies.

□□

CHAPTER 3

REPRODUCTIVE HEALTH

➢ The term 'reproductive health' simply refers to healthy reproductive organs with normal functions. According to WHO (World Health Organisation), the word 'reproductive health' means a total well-being in all aspects of reproduction i.e., physical, emotional, behavioural and social.

➢ Reproductive health in a society forms a crucial part of general health.

Reproductive Health - Problems and Strategies

➢ **Problems Associated with Reproductive Health:**

(a) Lack of awareness and sex education in people.
(b) A number of myths and misconceptions about sex related aspects.
(c) Common occurrence of sexually transmitted diseases due to lack of knowledge about hygiene about reproductive organs.
(d) Illegal abortions and female foeticides.
(e) Sex abuse and sex related crime.

➢ **Strategies of Reproductive Health Programmes**

To ensure total reproductive health, programmes called 'family planning' were initiated in 1951.

➢ Improved programmes covering wider reproduction-related areas are currently in operation under the popular name 'Reproductive and Child Health Care (RCH) programmes'.

➢ **The aim of Reproductive and Child Care Programme was to:**

(a) **Create awareness** in both males and females about various reproductive aspects with the help of audio-visual and print media by both governmental and non-governmental agencies.
(b) Provide **sex education** in schools to save the young generation from myths and misconceptions about sex related issues.
(c) **Prevention and control of sexually transmitted diseases** by providing correct information about reproductive organs, adolescence and safe and hygienic sexual practices.
(d) **Educate the fertile couples** and those in marriageable age about birth control devices, pre-natal and post-natal care of mother and child, importance of breast feeding etc.
(e) Provide awareness about **ill-effects of population explosion, sexual abuses, sex discrimination and sex related crimes.**
(f) **Provide medical facilities and support** like infrastructural facilities, professional expertise and material support to decrease maternal and infant mortality rates.
(g) Lessen the **problem of infertility** by promoting the Assisted Reproductive Techniques (ARTs).

➢ **Steps Taken to Maintain a Reproductively Healthy Society**

1. Imposing a statutory ban on amniocentesis (analysis of Amniotic Fluid-Foetal Sex Determination.)
2. Rigorous implementation of immunisation programs.
3. Creation of specialised health centers like infertility clinic for diagnosis and corrective treatment of some infertility disorders.
4. Better awareness about sex related matters and sex-related problems etc.
5. Increase in the number of medically assisted deliveries and better post-natal care.
6. Increase in number of couples with small families.
7. Early detection and cure of STDs.

Population Stabilisation and Birth Control

➢ **Population Explosion:** Tremendous increase in size and growth rate of population is called population explosion.

➢ **Reasons for Population Explosion:**

1. Rapid decline in death rate.
2. More longevity, longer life span.
3. Advanced medical facilities.
4. Prevention of diseases.
5. Developed techniques in agriculture.
6. Better transport facilities.
7. Protection from natural factors.
8. Increase in number of people in reproductive age.

➢ **Consequences of Population Explosion:** Poverty, unemployment, shortage of food, unhygienic conditions, education problems, residential problems, pollution, crime, excessive consumption of natural resources, etc.

➢ **Control measures to check population explosion:**

1. Motivate smaller families by using contraceptive methods.
2. Aware peoples about a slogan Hum Do Hamare Do (we two, our two). Many couples have adopted a 'one child norm'.
3. Statutory rising of marriageable age of the female (18 years) and males (21 years).

➢ **Birth Control Measures:**

- Governments have come out with various programmes that encourage smaller families by means of various contraceptive methods.
- Contraceptive devices are used to prevent unwanted pregnancy and to prevent the spreading of STDs.

➢ **An ideal contraceptive should be**

- User-friendly, easily available, effective and reversible.
- With no or least side-effects.
- Non-interfering with sexual drive, desire & sexual act.

➢ **They are grouped as follows:**

1. **Natural or Traditional Methods:** Natural methods work on the principle of avoiding chances of ovum and sperms meeting.
It includes:
(a) **Coitus interruptus:** This involves withdrawal of penis by male partner before ejaculation so that semen is not deposited in the vagina. It is the oldest method of voluntary fertility control. This method has certain limitations:

Scan to know more about this topic

Natural Contraceptive Methods

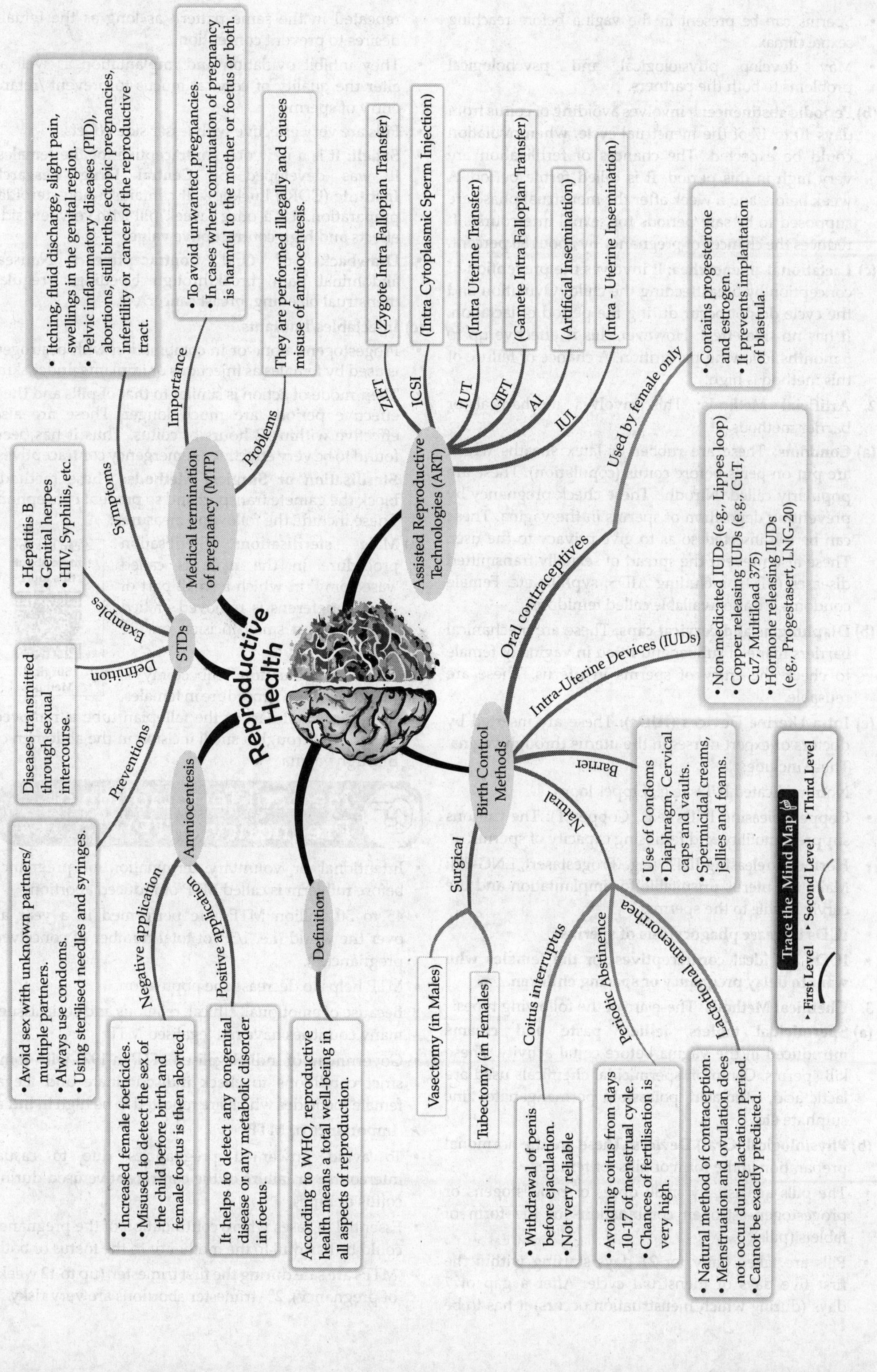
Reproductive Health
STDs
Definition
Diseases transmitted through sexual intercourse.
Examples
• Hepatitis B
• Genital herpes
• HIV, Syphilis, etc.
Symptoms
• Itching, fluid discharge, slight pain, swellings in the genital region.
• Pelvic inflammatory diseases (PID), abortions, still births, ectopic pregnancies, infertility or cancer of the reproductive tract.
Preventions
• Avoid sex with unknown partners/ multiple partners.
• Always use condoms.
• Using sterilised needles and syringes.
Medical termination of pregnancy (MTP)
Importance
• To avoid unwanted pregnancies.
• In cases where continuation of pregnancy is harmful to the mother or foetus or both
Problems
They are performed illegally and causes misuse of amniocentesis.
Assisted Reproductive Technologies (ART)
ZIFT
(Zygote Intra Fallopian Transfer)
ICSI
(Intra Cytoplasmic Sperm Injection)
IUT
(Intra Uterine Transfer)
GIFT
(Gamete Intra Fallopian Transfer)
AI
(Artificial Insemination)
IUI
(Intra Uterine Insemination)
Amniocentesis
Negative application
• Increased female foeticides.
• Misused to detect the sex of the child before birth and female foetus is then aborted.
Positive application
It helps to detect any congenital disease or any metabolic disorder in foetus.
Definition
According to WHO, reproductive health means a total well-being in all aspects of reproduction.
Birth Control Methods
Oral contraceptives
Used by female only
• Contains progestrone and estrogen.
• It prevents implantation of blastula.
Intra-Uterine Devices (IUDs)
• Non-medicated IUDs (e.g., Lippes loop)
• Copper releasing IUDs (e.g. CuT, Cu7, Multiload 375)
• Hormone releasing IUDs (e.g., Progestasert, LNG-20)
Barrier
• Use of Condoms
• Diaphragm, Cervical caps and vaults.
• Spermicidal creams, jellies and foams.
Natural
Coitus interruptus
• Withdrawal of penis before ejaculation.
• Not very reliable
Periodic Abstinence
• Avoiding coitus from days 10-17 of menstrual cycle.
• Chances of fertilisation is very high
Lactational amenorrhea
• Natural method of contraception.
• Menstruation and ovulation does not occur during lactation period
• Cannot be exactly predicted.
Surgical
Vasectomy (in Males)
Tubectomy (in Females)
Trace the Mind Map
• First Level • Second Level • Third Level

- Sperms can be present in the vagina before reaching sexual climax.
- May develop physiological and psychological problems to both the partners.

(b) Periodic abstinence: It involves avoiding of coitus from days 10 to 17 of the menstrual cycle, when ovulation could be expected. The chances of fertilization are very high in this period. It is called fertile period. A week before and a week after the menstrual phase are supposed to be safe periods for sexual intercourse. It reduces the chances of pregnancy by about 80 percent.

(c) Lactational amenorrhea: It involves the prevention of conception by breastfeeding the child. Ovulation and the cycle do not occur during the period of lactation. It has no side effect. However, this is effective up to 6 months following parturition. A chance of failure of this method is high.

2. Artificial Methods: This involves mechanical or barrier methods.

(a) Condoms: These are rubber or latex sheaths which are put on penis before coitus (copulation). These are popularly called 'Nirodh'. These check pregnancy by preventing deposition of sperms in the vagina. These can be self-inserted so as to give privacy to the user. These also prevent the spread of sexually transmitted diseases (STDs) including AIDS, syphilis etc. Female condoms are also available called femidoms.

(b) Diaphragms and cervical caps: These are mechanical barriers made of rubber and fitted in vagina of female to check the entry of sperms in uterus. These are reusable.

(c) Intra Uterine Devices (IUDs): These are inserted by doctors or expert nurses in the uterus through vagina. These include:

- Non-medicated IUDs (e.g., Lippes loop)
- Copper releasing IUDs (e.g., Copper T): The Cu ions suppress motility and fertilising capacity of sperms.
- Hormone releasing IUDs (e.g., Progestasert, LNG-20): Make the uterus unsuitable for implantation and the cervix hostile to the sperms.
- **IUDs increase phagocytosis of sperms.**
- **IUDs are ideal contraceptives for the females who want to delay pregnancy or spacing children.**

3. Chemical Methods: These are of the following types:

(a) Spermicidal tablets, jellies, paste and creams introduced in the vagina before coital activity. These kill sperms. Common spermicidal chemicals used are lactic acid, citric acid, potassium permanganate, zinc sulphate etc.

(b) Physiological (Oral) Devices: These are the hormonal preparation in the form of pills for females.

- The pills are usually small doses of progestogens or progestogen–estrogen combinations in the form of tablets (pills).
- Pills are taken daily for 21 days starting within the first five days of menstrual cycle. After a gap of 7 days (during which menstruation occurs) it has to be repeated in the same pattern as long as the female desires to prevent conception.
- They inhibit ovulation and implantation as well as alter the quality of cervical mucus to prevent /retard entry of sperms.
- Pills are very effective with lesser side effects.
- **Saheli:** It is a new oral contraceptive for the females. It was developed by **Central Drug Research Institute** (CDRI) Lucknow. It contains a non-steroidal preparation. It is a 'once a week' pill with very few side effects and high contraceptive value.
- **Drawbacks of Oral Contraceptives :** Nausea, abdominal pain, breakthrough bleeding, irregular menstrual bleeding, breast cancer, etc.

(c) Injectables/Implants

- Progestogens alone or in combination with oestrogen is used by females as injections or implants under skin.
- Their mode of action is similar to that of pills and their effective periods are much longer. These are also effective within 72 hours of coitus. Thus it has been found to be very effective as emergency contraceptives.

4. Sterilisation or Surgical Methods: These methods block the gamete transport and so prevent conception. These include the following measures:

(a) Male sterilisation: Sterilisation procedure in the male is called 'vasectomy' in which a small part of the vas deferens is removed or tied up through a small incision on the scrotum.

(b) Female sterilisation: Tubectomy is the sterilization procedure in females. In this, a small part of the fallopian tube is removed or tied up through a small incision in the abdomen or through vagina.

Scan to know more about this topic

Surgical Methods

Medical Termination of Pregnancy (MTP)

- Intentional or voluntary termination of pregnancy before full term is called MTP or induced abortion.
- 45 to 50 million MTPs are performed in a year all over the world (i.e. 1/5th of total number of conceived pregnancies).
- MTP helps to decrease the population.
- Because of emotional, ethical, religious and social issues many countries have not legalised MTP.
- Government of India legalised MTP in 1971 with some strict conditions to check indiscriminate and illegal female foeticides which are reported to be high in India.

➢ **Importance of MTP**

- To avoid unwanted pregnancies due to casual intercourse or failure of the contraceptive used during coitus **or rapes.**
- Essential in cases where continuation of the pregnancy could be harmful to the mother or to the foetus or both.

➢ MTPs are safe during the first trimester, (up to 12 weeks of pregnancy). 2nd trimester abortions are very risky.

➢ **Problems Related with MTPs**

- Majority of the MTPs are performed illegally.
- Misuse of amniocentesis (a foetal sex determination test based on the chromosomal pattern in the amniotic fluid).
- If the foetus is female, it is followed by MTP. Such practices are dangerous for the young mother and foetus.
- The Medical Termination of Pregnancy (Amendment) Act, 2017 was enacted by the government of India with the intension of reducing the incidence of illegal abortion and consequent maternal mortality and morbidity.

➢ **Amniocentesis**

- It is a pre-natal diagnostic method to determine the sex of the developing baby. This method has both positive and negative application. This method is legally banned in India.

(a) Positive application

- **It helps to detect any genetically controlled congenital disease or any metabolic disorders in foetus.**

(b) Negative application

- **People use this method for female foeticide, which causes a sex--imbalance in the society.**

MNEMONICS

Concept Name: Sexually Transmitted Diseases (STDs)

Mnemonics: **H**aryana **G**overnment **H**eads **G**irl's **S**chool

Interpretation: Hepatitis B, Genital Herpes, HIV, Gonorrhoea, Syphilis

Sexually Transmitted Diseases (STDs)

- Diseases transmitted through sexual intercourse are called Sexually transmitted diseases (STDs)/Venereal diseases (VD) or Reproductive tract infections (RTI). e.g., Gonorrhoea, syphilis, genital herpes, chlamydiasis, genital warts, trichomoniasis, hepatitis-B and AIDS.
- Except Hepatitis B, genital herpes, HIV and other diseases are completely curable if detected early and treated properly.
- **Early symptoms:** Itching, fluid discharge, slight pain, swellings, etc., in the genital region.
- Absence or less significant early symptoms and the social stigma deter the infected persons to consult a doctor. This leads to pelvic inflammatory diseases (PID), abortions, still births, ectopic pregnancies, infertility, cancer of the reproductive tract etc.
- All persons are vulnerable to STDs. These are very high among persons in the age group of 15-24 years.
- **Prevention:**

(a) Avoid sex with unknown partners/multiple partners.
(b) Always use condoms during coitus.
(c) In case of doubt, go to a qualified doctor for early detection and get complete treatment.

➢ **Infertility**

- It is the inability of couple to produce baby even after unprotected intercourse.
- The reasons for this may be physical, congenital, diseases, drugs, immunological or even psychological.

➢ **Assisted Reproductive Technologies (ART)**

Scan to know more about this topic — *In vitro* fertilisation

(1) In *vitro* fertilisation (IVF– test tube baby programme): In this method, ova from the wife/donor and sperms from the husband/donor are collected and are induced to form zygote under simulated conditions in the laboratory. This is followed by Embryo transfer (ET). It is of 2 types:

(a) Zygote Intra Fallopian Transfer (ZIFT) : Transfer of zygote or early embryos (with up to 8 blastomeres) into fallopian tube.

(b) Intra Uterine Transfer (IUT): Transfer of embryos with more than 8 blastomeres into the uterus. Embryo formed by *in vivo* fertilisation (fertilisation within the female) is also used for such transfer to assist those females who cannot conceive.

(2) Gamete Intra Fallopian Transfer (GIFT) : Transfer of an ovum from a donor into the fallopian tube of another female who cannot produce ovum, but can provide suitable environment for fertilisation and development.

(3) Intra cytoplasmic sperm injection (ICSI): It is a laboratory procedure in which a single sperm (from male partner) is injected directly into an egg (from female partner). Then the fertilised egg is implanted into the woman's uterus.

(4) Artificial insemination (AI)technique: It is the method of transferring semen (sperm) collected from the husband or a healthy donor into the vagina or the uterus (IUI – intra-uterine insemination) of the recipient female.

This technique is useful for the male partner having inability to inseminate female or has low sperm counts.

(5) Surrogacy: Here, a woman (surrogate mother) bears a child for a couple unable to produce children, because the wife is infertile or unable to carry.

The surrogate is impregnated either through artificial insemination or through implantation of an embryo produced by in vitro fertilisation.

➢ **Problems of ART**

- It requires high precision handling by specialised professionals and expensive instrumentation. Therefore, these facilities are available only in very few centres and are affordable to only a limited number of people.
- Emotional, religious and social problems.

➢ Legal adoption is one of the best methods for couples looking for parenthood.

NCERT CORNER

Exercise Questions

Q. 1. What do you think is the significance of reproductive health in a society?

[NCERT Ex. Q.1, Page 50]

Ans. (i) Reproductive health may be defined as a condition of overall human well-being which includes social, physical, emotional and behavioural aspects of reproduction.

(ii) The significance of reproductive health in society lies in several key aspects:

(a) Reproductive health programs educate individuals and couples about birth control methods and the advantages of maintaining small families.

(b) It initiatives also raise awareness about sexually transmitted diseases and promote safe sexual practices to prevent their transmission.

(c) It encompasses the importance of maternal and child health. It emphasizes the significance of proper prenatal care, safe childbirth practices, and postnatal care for both mothers and infants..

(d) Reproductive health programs address issues such as sexual abuse and sex-related crimes, promoting awareness and prevention strategies.

Q. 2. Suggest the aspects of reproductive health which needs to be given special attention in the present scenario. **[NCERT Ex. Q.2, Page 50]**

Ans. The aspects of reproductive health, which needs to be given special attention in the present scenario, are following:

(i) Creating awareness amongst people about various reproduction-related aspects. It can be done through governmental and non-governmental agencies, sex-education in the schools, parents and other relatives, teachers, etc.

(ii) Creating awareness on providing and improving existing medical facilities and attention to the problems, like menstrual irregularities, pregnancy-related aspects, delivery, medical termination of pregnancy (MTP), STDs, birth control and infertility.

(iii) Post-natal care of mother and child is another important aspect of the reproductive and child health-care programme in the present scenario.

Q. 3. Is sex education necessary in schools? Why?

[NCERT Ex. Q.3, Page 50]

Ans. Yes, sex education is necessary in school. Because,

(i) It provides right information about sex-related problems and also protect them from the myths and misconceptions regarding sex-related issues.

(ii) It also helps them to lead an important and healthy reproductive life by providing proper information on reproductive organs, adolescence-related changes, safe and hygienic sexual practices.

(iii) At school level, children from age group of 12 years and above should be counselled about reproductive system, processes and practices and importance of safe and responsible sex.

(iv) It creates awareness on child sexuality whether it is valuable or detrimental; the use of birth control, such as condoms and hormonal contraception, and the impact of such use on pregnancy, and the transmission of STDs and AIDS.

Q. 4. Do you think that reproductive health in India has improved in the past 50 years? If yes, mention some such areas of improvement.

[NCERT Ex. Q.4, Page 50]

Ans. (i) Yes, in the last 50 years, reproductive health in India has tremendously improved.

(ii) Areas of such improvement are given below:

(a) Massive child immunisation which has led to decrease in child or infant mortality.

(b) Maternity and child health due to better post-natal care of mother and baby.

(c) Increasing use of contraceptives which resulted in decrease in the rate of transmission of STDs.

(d) Family planning which created awareness of having small and healthy family.

Q. 5. What are the suggested reasons for population explosion? **[NCERT Ex. Q.5, Page 50]**

Ans. (i) Population explosion may be defined as a sudden and rapid rise in population growth.

(ii) Probable factors that contribute to population explosion in India are the following:

(a) A rapid decline in death rate.

(b) Decline in Maternal Mortality Rate (MMR) and Infant Mortality Rate (IMR).

(c) An increase in number of people in reproducible age.

(d) Increased rate of immigration.

(e) Low living standards, poverty and poor health due to improper food and nutrition for such large populations.

Q. 6. Is the use of contraceptives justified? Give reasons.

[NCERT Ex. Q.6, Page 50]

Ans. (i) Yes, the use of contraceptives is justified.

(ii) Because,

(a) It helps to overcome the population growth rate.

(b) It will help in bringing birth rate down and subsequently control population growth.

(c) With the rapid spread of HIV/AIDS in the country, there is now a growing realisation about the need to know about contraception and condoms.

(d) They are also helpful in preventing unwanted pregnancies.

(e) They do not interfere with sexual desire of sexual act.

Q. 7. Removal of gonads cannot be considered as a contraceptive option. Why? **[NCERT Ex. Q.7, Page 50]**

Ans. (i) Contraceptives devices (such as natural, barrier, oral and surgical methods) are used to prevent unwanted pregnancies and spreading of STDs.

(ii) Gonads (testes and ovary) are the reproductive organs of male and female respectively. They play an important role in sexual reproduction, as they are responsible for the secretion of sex hormones and production of sex gametes.

(iii) Removal of gonads or its parts cannot be considered as a contraceptive option because it will lead to permanent infertility and also stop the secretions of essential sex hormones that are required for the normal functioning of the accessory reproductive parts.

Q. 8. Amniocentesis for sex determination is banned in our country. Is this ban necessary? Comment. [NCERT Ex. Q.8, Page 50]

Ans. (i) Yes, the statutory ban on amniocentesis in India is necessary.

(ii) Amniocentesis is a surgical procedure, which is carried out to diagnose the sex and foetal defects, in the early second trimester of pregnancy.

(iii) In this procedure, amniotic fluid is removed from the uterus for testing or treatment. Amniotic fluid is the fluid that surrounds and protects a baby during pregnancy. This fluid contains foetal cells and various chemicals produced by the baby.

(iv) Amniocentesis was developed to determine genetic disorder but now-a-days it can be used to detect the sex of the foetus before birth and the female foetus is then aborted. Therefore, to prevent illegal termination of female foetus by using amniocentesis it is necessary to ban in India.

(v) The solution to this problem is not passing more laws, such as banning sex determination ultrasound, etc., but raising the social and economic status of women.

Q. 9. Suggest some methods to assist infertile couples to have children. [NCERT Ex. Q.9, Page 50]

Ans. Infertility is the inability of a sexually active, non-contracepting couple to achieve pregnancy in 1 year. Specialised health-care units (Infertility Clinics) could help in diagnosis and corrective treatment of some of these disorders and enable these couples to have children. However, where such corrections are not possible, the couples could be assisted to have children through certain special techniques commonly known as ART.

Methods to assist infertile couples to have children are:

(a) *In vitro* fertilisation: It is a medical procedure whereby an egg is fertilised by sperm in a test tube or elsewhere outside the body. IVF is followed by embryo transfer. ET is a method to treat infertility and commonly known as the 'Test-tube baby' programme.

(b) Zygote Intra-Fallopian transfer: In this technique, eggs are retrieved from a woman, mixed with sperm and early embryos (upto 8 blastomeres) could then be transferred into fallopian tube of a woman, who is unable to produce eggs but has the ability to conceive.

Q. 10. What are the measures one has to take to prevent from contracting STDs? [NCERT Ex. Q.10, Page 50]

Ans. STD is a sexually transmitted disease which can be prevented by the following measures:

(i) Avoiding sex with multiple or unknown partners.

(ii) Use of condoms during intercourse.

(iii) In case of doubt, go for medical professional for early detection and get complete treatment if diagnosed with disease.

(iv) Education and counselling of persons at risk on ways to adopt safer sexual behaviour.

Q. 11. State True/False with explanation.

(a) Abortions could happen spontaneously too. (True/False)

(b) Infertility is defined as the inability to produce a viable offspring and is always due to abnormalities/defects in the female partner. (True/False)

(c) Complete lactation could help as a natural method of contraception. (True/False)

(d) Creating awareness about sex-related aspects is an effective method to improve reproductive health of the people. (True/False)

[NCERT Ex. Q.11, Page 50]

Ans. (a) True. Due to internal factors, like incompatibility, abortion could happen spontaneously.

(b) False. Infertility is defined as the inability to produce a viable offspring even after unprotected sexual co-habitation. It is due to abnormalities/defects in either male or female or both the partners.

(c) True. Complete lactation could help as a natural method of contraception, but it is limited to period up to 6 months after parturition.

(d) True. Creating awareness about sex-related aspects removes the myths and misconceptions about these problems.

Q. 12. Correct the following statements.

(a) Surgical methods of contraception prevent gamete formation.

(b) All sexually transmitted diseases are completely curable.

(c) Oral pills are very popular contraceptives amongst the rural women.

(d) In E. T. technique, embryos are always transferred into the uterus. [NCERT Ex. Q.12, Page 50]

Ans. (a) Surgical methods of contraception prevent the flow of gamete during the coitus thereby preventing conception.

(b) Except for hepatitis B, genital herpes and human immunodeficiency virus (HIV) infections, other STDs are completely curable if detected early and treated properly.

(c) Oral pills are very popular contraceptives amongst the educated urban women.

(d) In embryo transfer (ET) techniques, an embryo of 8 cell stage or lesser is transferred to the fallopian tube while that of more than 8 blastomere stage is transferred to the uterus.

□□

PRINCIPLES OF INHERITANCE AND VARIATION

CHAPTER 4

Introduction

- **Genetics** is the branch of biology which deals with the study of inheritance.
- The word "genetics" is derived from Greek word genesis, which means " to grow into " or "to become".
- The term Genetics was coined by W. Bateson in 1905.
- Living beings produce offsprings of their own kinds. The similarities are due to inherited characters or heredity.
- **Inheritance** is the process by which characters are passed on from parent to progeny; it is the basis of heredity.
- **Variation** is the degree by which progeny differ from their parents.

Mendel's Laws of Inheritance

- Johann Gregor Mendel, also known as the 'father of genetics' started a decade long research project in 1856 to study the patterns of inheritance.
- Mendel conducted experiments for the first time to understand the pattern on inheritance and variations in living organisms.
- During Mendel's investigations into inheritance patterns it was for the first time that statistical analysis and mathematical logic were applied to problems in biology.
- His experiments had a large sampling size, which gave greater credibility to the data that he collected.
- The confirmation of his inferences from experiments on successive generations of his test plants, proved that his results pointed to general rules of inheritance rather than being unsubstantiated ideas.
- Gregor Mendel, conducted hybridisation experiments on garden peas for seven years (1856-1863) and proposed the laws of inheritance in living organisms.
- Mendel conducted artificial/cross–pollination experiments by performing **emasculation (Removal of anther)** on several true-breeding pea lines.
- A true-breeding line refers to one that have undergone continuous self-pollination and show stable trait inheritance and expression for several generations.

➢ **Hybridisation Experiments on Garden Peas (*Pisum sativum*)**

- He carried out his experiments on inheritance with the common pea plant taking 7 features of the plant which included;

S. No.	Characters	Dominant	Recessive
1.	Height of the stem	Tall (T)	Dwarf (t)
2.	Colour of the flower	Violet/Red (R)	White (r)
3.	Position of the flower	Axial (A)	Terminal (a)
4.	Shape of pod	Full/Inflated (I)	Constricted(i)
5.	Colour of pod	Green (G)	Yellow (g)
6.	Shape of seed	Round (R)	Wrinkled (r)
7.	Colour of seed/ cotyledons	Yellow (Y)	Green (y)

Inheritance of One Gene

➢ **Monohybrid Cross:**

- It is a cross involving two plants differing in one pair of contrasting characters. e.g., Mendel crossed tall and dwarf pea plants to study the inheritance of one gene.

➢ **Steps in Making a Cross of Pea:**

- Selection of two pea plants with contrasting characters
- Removal of anthers (emasculation) of one plant to avoid self pollination. This is female parent.
- Collection of pollen grains from the other plant (male parent) and transfer to female parent (pollination).
- Collection of seeds produced as a result of this cross and grew them to generate plants of the first hybrid generation called the filial$_1$ progeny or the F_1.
- Mendel observed that all the F_1 progeny plants were tall, like one of its parents; none were dwarf.
- Mendel made similar observations for other pairs of traits and proposed that factors were inherited from parent to offspring. Later these factors were called genes.

➢ **Mendel Observations:**

- The F_1 hybrid always showed one of the parental forms of the trait.

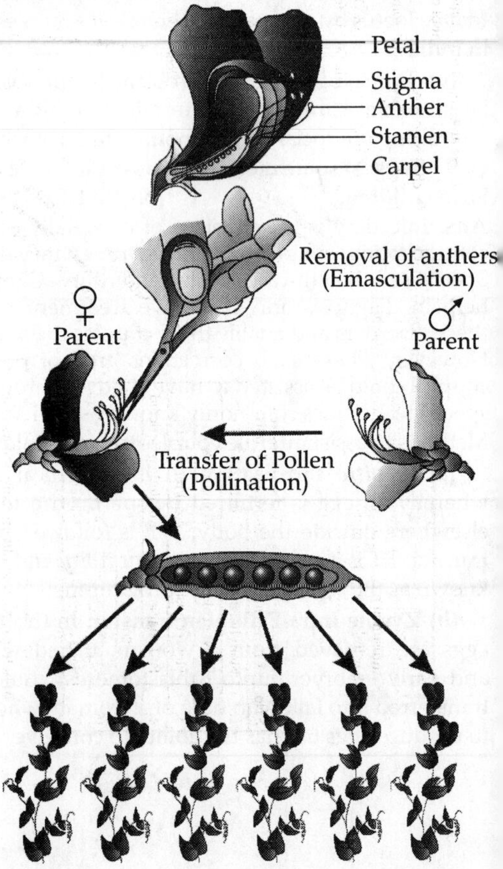

Fig. 4.1 Steps in making a cross in pea

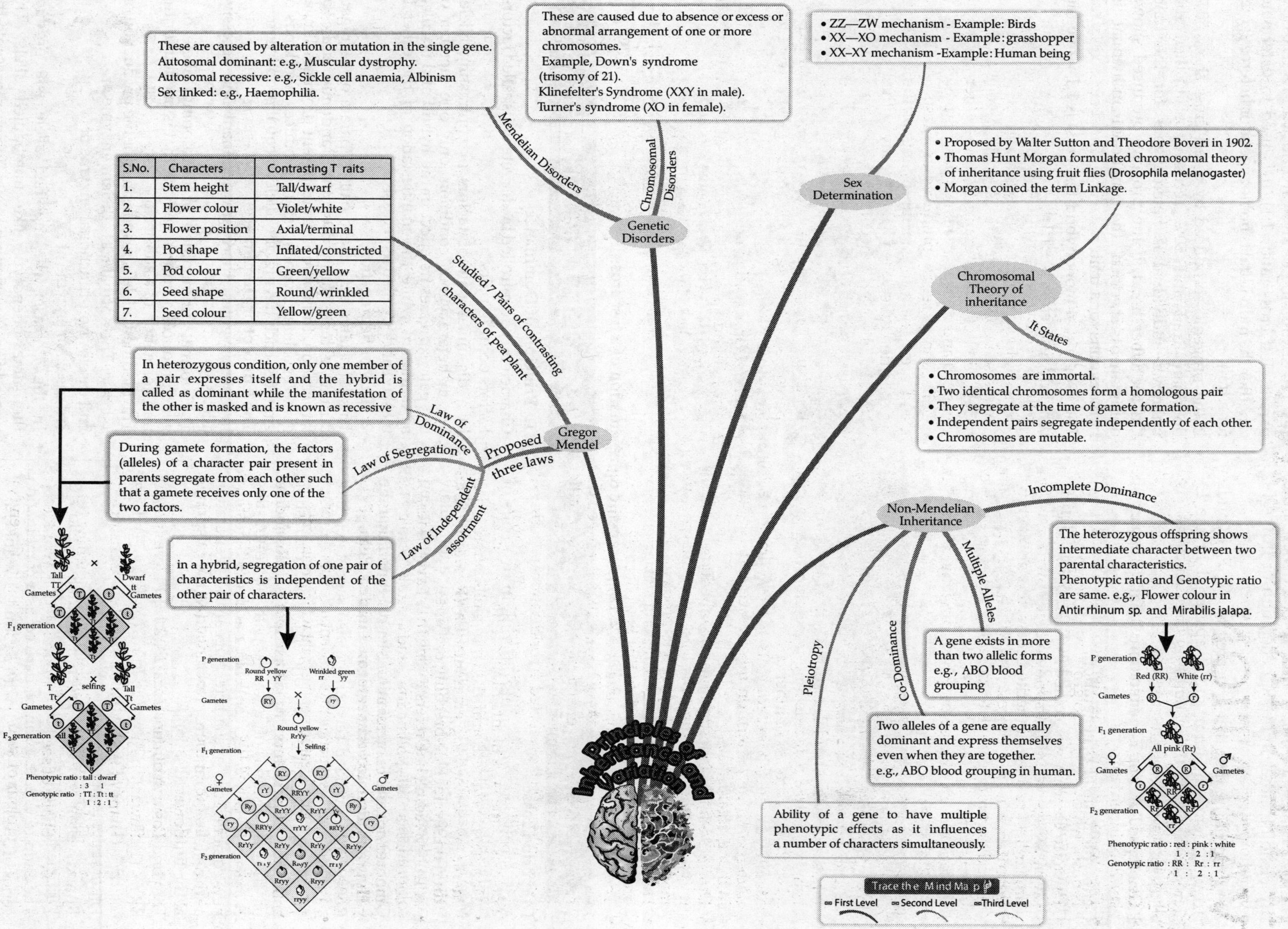

S.No.	Characters	Contrasting Traits
1.	Stem height	Tall/dwarf
2.	Flower colour	Violet/white
3.	Flower position	Axial/terminal
4.	Pod shape	Inflated/constricted
5.	Pod colour	Green/yellow
6.	Seed shape	Round/ wrinkled
7.	Seed colour	Yellow/green

- Both the parental forms of the trait (contrasting forms of the trait) appeared without any change in the F_2 generation.
- The two contrasting forms in a trait did not show any blending either in the F_1 generation or in the F_2 generation.
- The form of the trait that appeared in the F_2 hybrids is called dominant form and it appeared in the F_2 generation about three times in frequency as its alternate (recessive) form.

➤ **Phenotypic Ratio of F_2 generation:** 3 Tall: 1 Dwarf = 3: 1

➤ **Genotypic Ratio of F_2 generation:**

- Homozygous tall (TT): 1, Heterozygous tall (Tt): 2, Homozygous dwarf (tt): 1= 1: 2: 1

➤ **Back cross and Test cross**

- **Back cross:** Crossing of F_1 hybrid with either of its parent.
- **Test cross:** Crossing of an F_1 hybrid with its recessive parent (Test cross ratio=1:1). It is used to determine whether the individual is homozygous or heterozygous for a trait.
- If the progenies produced by a test cross show 50% dominant trait and 50% recessive trait, then the unknown individual is heterozygous for the trait. On the other hand, if the progeny produced shows dominant trait, then the unknown individual is homozygous for a trait.

The progeny of monohybrid test cross is 1:1 while the dihybrid tests cross is 1:1:1:1.

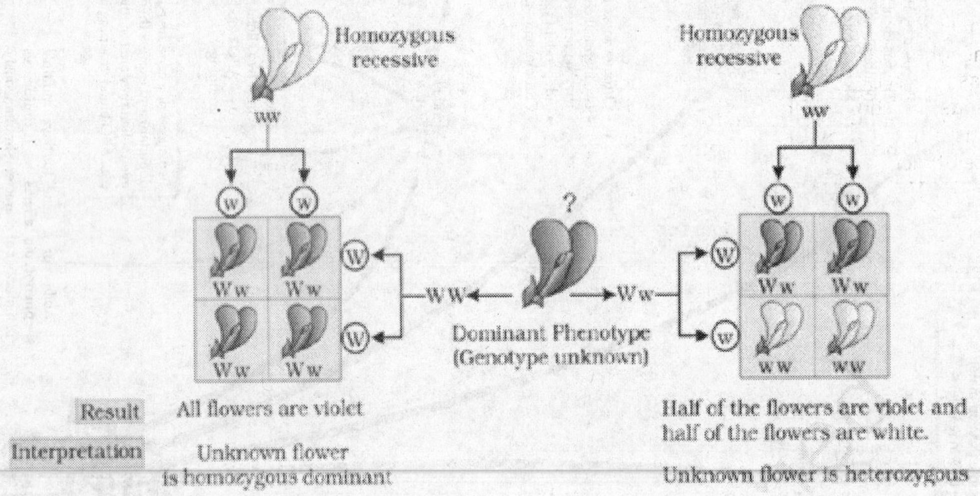

Fig. 4.2. Diagrammatic representation of a test cross

Inheritance of Two Genes

➤ **Dihybrid Cross**

- A cross between two parents differing in two pairs of contrasting characters.
- Mendel made some dihybrid crosses, e.g., Cross between pea plant with round shaped and yellow coloured seeds (RRYY) and wrinkled shaped and green coloured seeds (rryy).
- On observing the F_2, generation Mendel found that the yellow and green colour segregated in a 3:1 ratio.
- Round and wrinkled seed shape also segregated in a 3:1 ratio.
- Thus, the segregation of one pair of contrasting characters (Round and wrinkled shape) is independent of the segregation of another pair of contrasting character (yellow and green) colour and also that some new combinations of character appear in F_2 generation as the alleles get randomly rearranged in the offsprings at the time of fertilisation.
- Dihybrid genotypic ratio: 1:2:1:2:4:2:1:2:1
  RRYY (1): RRYy (2): RRyy (1): RrYY (2): RrYy (4): Rryy (2): rrYY (1): rrYy (2): rryy (1).
- Dihybrid Phenotypic ratio:
- Round yellow 9: Round green 3: Wrinkled yellow 3: Wrinkled green 1, i.e., 9: 3: 3: 1
- The ratio of 9: 3: 3: 1 can be derived as a combination series of 3 yellow: 1 green, with 3 round: 1 wrinkled.
  i.e., (3: 1) (3: 1) = 9: 3: 3: 1

Mendel's Law of Inheritance

1. **Principle of Dominance**

- Characters are controlled by discrete units called factors.
- Factors occur in pairs.
- In a dissimilar pair of factors or contrasting alleles i.e., in heterozygous condition, only one member of the pair expresses its effect in the hybrid and is called as dominant while the manifestation of the other is masked and is called as recessive.

2. **Law of Segregation**

- This law states that allelic pairs separate or segregate during gamete formation and randomly unite at fertilisation, thus homozygous parent produces similar gametes. Heterozygous parent produces two kinds of gametes, each having one allele in equal proportion.

➤ **The Concept of Dominance**

- In heterozygotes, there are dominant and recessive alleles.
- The normal (unmodified or functioning) allele of a gene produces a normal enzyme that is needed for the transformation of a substrate.
- The modified allele is responsible for the production of:
  1st case: The normal/less efficient enzyme or
  2nd case: A non-functional enzyme or
  3rd case: No enzyme at all
- **In the 1st case:** The modified allele will produce the same phenotype like unmodified allele. The unmodified (functioning) allele, which represents the original phenotype is the dominant allele.

- **In 2nd and 3rd cases:** Here,the modified allele becomes recessive. The recessive trait is seen due to non-functional enzyme or because no enzyme is produced.

3. Mendel's Law of Independent Assortment:

- The law states that, when two pairs of traits are combined in a hybrid, segregation of one pair of characters is independent of the other pair of characters'.

➢ **Non-recognition of Mendel's work**

- **Mendel's work remained unrecognised till 1900 because,**

(a) Communication was not easy.
(b) Non recognition of Mendel as a scientist.
(c) His mathematical approach was new and unacceptable.
(d) He used statistical calculations which were beyond the comprehension of the biologists of his time.
(e) Chromosomes, mitosis and meiosis were not known in Mendel's time.
(f) The concept of genes (factors) as a stable and discrete units was not accepted. (Mendel could not explain the continuous variations seen in nature).
(g) Mendel could not provide any physical proof for the existence of factors.
(h) In 1900, de Vries of Holland, Correns of Germany and Von Tschermak of Austria independently rediscovered. Mendel's results on the inheritance of characters.

MNEMONICS

Concept Name: Non-Mendelian inheritance

Mnemonics: I Can Manage Physics

Interpretation: Incomplete dominance, Co-dominance, Multiple alleles, Pleiotropy

Non-Mendelian Inheritance

➢ **Incomplete Dominance**

- It is an inheritance in which heterozygous offspring shows intermediate character between two parental characteristics. e.g., Flower colour in Snapdragon (dog flower or *Antirrhinum sp.*) and *Mirabilis jalapa* (4'O clock plant).
- Here, phenotypic and genotypic ratios are same.
- Phenotypic ratio = 1 Red: 2 Pink: 1 White
- Genotypic ratio = 1 (RR): 2 (Rr): 1(rr)
- This means that 'R' was not completely dominant over 'r'.

➢ **Co-dominance**

- It is the inheritance in which both alleles of a gene are expressed equally and independently in a hybrid i.e., both the alleles are dominant, e.g., ABO blood grouping in humans.
- ABO blood groups are controlled by the gene *I*.
- The gene (*I*) has three alleles I^A, I^B and *i*. However a person can have any two of these three alleles. I^A and I^B both are dominant alleles while *i* is a recessive allele.
- The alleles I^A and I^B produce antigen A and antigen B respectively on the RBC surface while allele *i* doesn't produce any antigen.
- When I^A and I^B are present together they both express their own types of surface antigen A and B. This is due to co-dominance.

➢ **Multiple Allelism**

- Here more than two alleles govern the same character.
- Since in an individual only two alleles are present, multiple alleles can be found only when population studies are made. e.g., ABO blood grouping (3 alleles: I^A, I^B & *i*). Skin colour and height of humans are also examples of multiple alleles.

➢ **Pleiotropy**

- Pleiotropy is the phenomenon in which one gene controls many traits. For example, the gene in pea plants that controls the round and wrinkled texture of seeds also influences the phenotypic expression of starch grain size.
- So, if starch grain size is considered as the phenotype, then from this angle, the alleles show incomplete dominance.
- Therefore, dominance is not an autonomous feature of a gene or the product that it has information for. It depends as much on the gene product and the production of a particular phenotype.

Polygenic Inheritance

➢ Some traits controlled by three or more genes and these traits are called polygenic traits. Besides the involvement of multiple genes, polygenic inheritance also takes into account the influence of environment. **Example:** Colour of Human Skin.

➢ In polygenic traits, each allele expresses itself phenotypically.

➢ **Example:**

- A, B, C are three dominant alleles for dark skin colour. While a, b, c are three recessive alleles responsible for light skin colour.
- AABBCC Genotype will result in dark skin colour.
- aabbcc genotype will result in light skin colour.
- It is expected that genotype having dominant and recessive alleles will have an intermediate skin colour.
- Thus, the number of each type of alleles in a genotype would determine the skin colour in humans.

Chromosomal Theory (1902)

- The chromosomal Theory was proposed independently by Walter Sutton and Theodore Boveri in 1902.
- Walter Sutton & Theodore Boveri proposed that the pairing and separation of a pair of chromosomes during meiosis lead to segregation of pair of factors.
- Sutton united chromosomal segregation with Mendelian principles and called it as Chromosomal Theory of Inheritance.

Scan to know more about this topic

Chromosomal Theory of Inheritance

- **It states that—**

(a) Chromosomes are vehicles of heredity i.e., they are transmitted from parents to offspring.
(b) Two identical chromosomes form a homologous pair. Genes are present in a linear fashion on chromosomes.
(c) They segregate at the time of gamete formation.
(d) Independent pairs segregate independently of each other.
(e) Chromosomes are mutable.
(f) Sex chromosomes determine sex of an individual.

➤ **Parallelism between genes (Mendelian factors) & Chromosomes:**

- Mendelian factors as well as chromosomes are transferred from generation to generation.
- The chromosomes occurs in homologous pairs. The genes also occurs in pairs (allele pairs).
- Both chromosomes and genes segregate at the time of gamete formation in such a way that gametes receive only one chromosome & similarly one allele of each pair.
- Different pairs of chromosomes segregate independently of each other. Similarly one pair of alleles segregate independently of another pair.
- Fusion of two (male & female) gametes brings about the diploid chromosome number as well as the allelic pairs in the offsprings.

➤ **Experimental verification of chromosomal theory:**

- Thomas Hunt Morgan proved Chromosomal Theory of Inheritance using fruit flies (*Drosophila melanogaster*).
- **He took fruit flies suitable for his experiments because:**
  (a) It breeds very quickly.
  (b) Short life cycle (life cycle: 12-14 days).
  (c) Breeding can be done throughout the year.
  (d) Hundreds of progenies are produced per mating.
  (e) They can grow on simple synthetic medium.
  (f) Male and female flies are easily distinguishable.

➤ **Linkage and Recombination**

- **Recombination:** It is a process by which pieces of DNA are broken and recombined to produce new combination of alleles.
- **Linkage:** Physical association of two or more genes on a chromosome, which show tendency to inherit together. They do not show independent assortment.
- Morgan *et.al* crossed yellow body and white eyed females with wild type brown body and red eyed males and inter-crossed F_1 offsprings. He found that the two genes did not segregate independently, resulted in deviation from normal dihybrid ratio 9: 3: 3: 1 in F_2 generation because the appearance of parental combinations were higher than the non-parental and new recombinations.

➤ **Morgan's Experiment**

- Morgan carried out several dihybrid test crosses in *Drosophila* to study sex-linked genes.
  Cross A: Yellow-bodied, white-eyed females (yw/yw) X Brown-bodied, red-eyed males (y'w'/yw) (wild type).
  Cross B: Double recessive White-eyed, miniature winged (wm/wm) X Hybrid Red eyed, large winged (w'm/ wm) (wild type).
- **Morgan in the above crosses found that**

(a) The two genes did not segregate independently of each other and the F_2 ratio deviated from the 9: 3: 3: 1 ratio.
(b) Genes were located on the X chromosome.
(c) When two genes were situated on the same chromosome, the proportion of parental gene combinations was much higher than the non-parental type. This is due to linkage.
(d) Genes for white and yellow were very tightly linked and showed only 1.3% new recombination while white and miniature wings showed 37.2% recombination (loosely linked).
(e) Tightly linked genes show low recombination.
(f) Loosely linked genes show high recombination.

- Strength of linkage is inversely proportional to the distance between two linked genes. Thus, the linkage between y and w alleles is stronger than the linkage between w and m alleles.
- **Linkage groups:** All the genes present together on a single chromosome make up a linkage group. The total number of linkage groups in an organism is equal to its haploid number of chromosomes or number of homologous pairs in diploid organisms.
- Alfred Sturtevant used the recombination frequency between gene pairs as a measure of the distance between genes and 'mapped' their position on the chromosome.
- Recombination frequency or the cross over value (COV) can be calculated by the following formula.

$$\text{COV} = \frac{\text{Number of recombinants}}{\text{Total number of offsprings}} \times 100$$

- Genetic maps are used as a starting point in the sequencing of genomes and was done in Human Genome.

Sex Determination

Scan to know more about this topic

Sex Determination

- The method by which the distinction between male and female is established in a species is called sex determination.
- Sex of an individual is finalised at the time of zygote formation.

➤ **Autosomes and Sex chromosomes (allosomes)**

- Autosomes are chromosomes other than sex chromosomes. They contain genes which determine somatic characteristics.
- Number of autosomes is same in males and females.
- Sex chromosomes (X & Y) are the chromosomes which are involved in sex determination.

➤ **Henking (1891)** studied spermatogenesis in some insects and observed that 50% of sperm received a nuclear structure after spermatogenesis, whereas other 50% sperm did not receive it. Henking called this structure as the **X body** (later it was called as **X-chromosome**).

➤ **Mechanism of Sex Determination**

(i) Chromosomal sex determination: It is based on heterogamety, i.e., occurrence of two types of gametes in one of the two sexes. It is of following types:

(a) **ZZ-ZW mechanism:** Male is homogametic (ZZ) and female is heterogametic (Z & W). e.g., Birds.

(b) Sex Determination in honey bee is based on the number of sets of chromosomes an individual receives. An offspring formed from the union of a sperm and an egg develops as a female (queen or worker), and an unfertilised egg develops as a male (drone) by means of parthenogenesis. The males have half the number of chromosomes (16) than that of a female (32). This is called as haplodiploid sex-determination system.

(c) **Sex Determination in Humans (XX-XY type)**

- Human has 23 pairs of chromosomes (22 pairs are autosomes and 1 pair is sex chromosomes).
- A pair of X-chromosomes (XX) is present in the female, whereas X and Y chromosomes are present in male.
- During spermatogenesis, males produce 2 types of gametes i.e., 50 % with X-chromosome and 50 % with Y-chromosome.
- Females produce only ovum with an X-chromosome.
- There is an equal probability of fertilisation of the ovum with the sperm carrying either X or Y chromosome.
- The sperm determines whether the offspring will be male or female.

(ii) **Environmental Sex-determination:** Determination of sex depends upon the environmental condition. The environmental factors like temperature etc. determine whether the zygote will develop into male or female. e.g., in turtles and crocodile.

(iii) **Genic balance mechanism of sex determination:** Sex of the individual is decided by the ratio of X-chromosome and autosome as is found in *Drosophila*.

(iv) **Cytoplasmic Sex-determination:** Cytoplasmic or fertility factor called as F^+ factor located in plasmid determines the sex as is found in some bacteria.

Mutation

- Mutuation is a phenomenoin which research in alteration of DNA sequences and consequency results in changes in the genotype and the phenotype of an organism.
- In addition to recombination, mutation is another phenomenon that leads to variation in DNA.

Genetic Disorders

- There are two types of genetic disorders namely, Mendelian disorders and Chromosomal disorders.

➢ **Mendelian Disorders**

- It is caused by alteration or mutation in the single gene.
- The pattern of inheritance of Mendelian disorders can be traced in a family by the pedigree analysis. e.g., Haemophilia, Cystic fibrosis, Colour blindness, Thalassemia, etc.
- Mendelian disorders may be dominant or recessive. By pedigree analysis one can easily understand whether the trait is dominant or recessive.

➢ **Colour Blindness**

- It is a sex-linked recessive disorder due to defect in either red or green cone of eye resulting in failure to discriminate between red and green colour.
- This defect is due to mutation in certain genes present in the X chromosome.
- It occurs in about 8 percent of males and only about 0.4 per cent of females. This is because the genes that lead to red-green colour blindness are on the X chromosome. Males have only one X chromosome and females have two.

➢ **Haemophilia**

- Sex linked recessive disease.
- In this, a protein involved in the blood clotting is affected.
- A simple cut results in non-stop bleeding.
- The heterozygous female (carrier) for haemophilia may transmit the disease to sons.
- The possibility of a female becoming a haemophilic is very rare because mother has to be at least carrier and father should be haemophilic (unviable in the later stage of life).
- Queen Victoria was a carrier of the disease. So her family pedigree shows a number of haemophilic descendents.

➢ **Thalassemia**

- This is also an autosome-linked recessive blood disease transmitted from parents to the offspring when both the partners are unaffected carrier for the gene (or heterozygous).
- The defect could be due to either mutation or deletion which ultimately results in reduced rate of synthesis of one of the globin chains (α and β chains) that make up haemoglobin.
- This causes the formation of abnormal haemoglobin molecules resulting into anaemia which is characteristic of the disease.
- Thalassemia can be classified according to which chain of the haemoglobin molecule is affected. In α Thalassemia, production of α globin chain is affected while in β Thalassemia, production of β globin chain is affected.
- Thalassemia differs from sickle-cell anaemia in that the former is a quantitative problem of synthesising few globin molecules while the latter is a qualitative problem of synthesising an incorrectly functioning globin.

➢ **Chromosomal Disorders**

Scan to know more about this topic

Chromosomal Disorders

- They are caused due to absence or excess or abnormal arrangement of one or more chromosomes.
- These are of two types namely,
  (a) Aneuploidy
  (b) Euploidy.

➢ **Aneuploidy**

- The gain or loss of chromosomes due to failure of segregation of chromatids during cell division. It includes,

(a) **Nullisomy (2n-2):** A complete homologous pair is lost from diploid set.

(b) **Monosomy (2n-1):** One chromosome is lost from diploid set.

(c) **Trisomy (2n+1):** One chromosome is added to diploid set, so that one chromosome occurs in triplicate.

(d) **Tetrasomy (2n+2):** Two chromosomes are added to diploid set, so that a chromosome is found in **Polyploidy (Euploidy).**

- It is an increase in number of chromosomes sets beyond diploid X condition (2n). Failure of cytokinesis after telophase stage of cell division results in an increase in a whole set of chromosomes. This is often seen in plants.
- On the basis of number of chromosome sets, the polyploids are of following types: triploids (3n), tetraploids (4n), pentaploids (5n), hexaploids (6n), etc.

(a) **Autopolyploidy:** It is a process of having two or more sets of chromosomes, from same parental species. e.g., AAA (autotriploid), AAAA (autotetraploid), etc.

(b) **Allopolyploidy:** It is the increase in number of sets of chromosome due to coming together of diploid genomes of two or more than two individuals of different species. e.g., AABB, AABBDD. Bread wheat is allohexaploid (AABBDD). Triticale is the man made cereal formed by hybridisation between durum wheat and rye. It is allohexaploid.

- **Chromosomal aberrations:** These are the changes in morphology and structure of chromosome resulting in the change in number and sequence of genes on them without any change in ploidy. They are of following types:

(1) **Deletion:** It is the loss of a terminal segment of a chromosome or from within the chromosome (interstitial segment) followed by reunion of its remaining parts.

(2) **Inversion:** It is a change in a chromosome architecture due to breaking up, rotation through 180° of a segment and its reunion so that sequence of genes is reversed in the inverted region.

(3) **Duplication:** It is a change in chromosome structure in which a part of chromosome breaks up and unites with another homologous chromosome. This process repeats the chromosome segments because the same block of genes is present more than once in a haploid component.

(4) **Translocation:** It is a change in chromosome architecture which is due to breaking up of segment of chromosome and its union with another non-homologous chromosome. It may also be due to mutual exchange of chromosomal segments between non-homologous chromosomes.

➢ **Examples for Chromosomal Disorders**

(a) **Down's Syndrome (Mongolism):**

- It is the presence of an additional copy of chromosome number 21 (trisomy of 21).
- Genetic constitution: 45 A + XX or 45 A + XY (i.e., 47 chromosomes).
- **Features:**

(a) They are short statured with small round head.
(b) Broad flat face.
(c) Furrowed big tongue and partially open mouth.
(d) Many "loops" on finger tips.
(e) Palm is broad with characteristic palm crease.
(f) Retarded physical, psychomotor & mental development.
(g) Congenital heart disease.

(b) **Klinefelter's Syndrome:**

- It is the presence of an additional copy of X-chromosome in male.
- Genetic constitution: 44 A + XXY (i.e., 47 chromosomes).
- **Features:**

(a) Overall masculine development however the feminine development is also expressed. e.g., development of breast (Gynaecomastia).
(b) Sterile.
(c) Mentally retarded.

(c) **Turner's Syndrome:**

- This is due to the absence of one of the X chromosomes in female.
- Genetic constitution: 44 A + XO (i.e., 45 chromosomes).
- **Features:**

(a) Sterile, Ovaries are rudimentary.
(b) Lack of other secondary sexual characters.
(c) Dwarf.
(d) Mentally retarded.

MNEMONICS

Concept Name: Chromosomal disorders

Mnemonics: **D**river **K**nowledge **T**est

Interpretation: Down's syndrome, Klinefelter's syndrome, Turner's syndrome

NCERT CORNER

Exercise Questions

Q. 1. Mention the advantages of selecting pea plant for experiment by Mendel. [NCERT Ex. Q.1, Page 78]

Ans. Mendel selected pea plants to carry out his study on the inheritance of characters from parents to offspring. He selected pea plant because of the following features:

- Peas have many visible contrasting characters such as tall/dwarf plants, round/wrinkled seeds, green/yellow pod, purple/white flowers, etc.
- Peas have bisexual flowers and therefore undergo self pollination easily. Thus, pea plants produce offsprings with same traits generation after generation.
- In pea plants, cross pollination can be easily achieved by emasculation in which the stamen of the flower is removed without affecting the pistil.
- Pea plants have a short life span and produce many seeds in one generation.

Q. 2. Differentiate between the following:

(a) Dominance and Recessive

(b) Homozygous and Heterozygous

(c) Monohybrid and Dihybrid.[NCERT Ex. Q.2, Page 78]

Ans. (a) Dominance and Recessive

Characters	Dominance/trait/ allele	Recessive/trait/ allele
Definition	It expresses itself even in the presence of recessive allele.	Recessive allele fails to express its effect in presence of dominant allele.
Polypeptide chain	Dominant allele forms complete polypeptide chain or enzyme to express its effect.	Recessive allele forms incomplete defective polypeptide chain or enzyme as a result, it fails to express its effects.

(b) Homozygous and Heterozygous

Characters	Homozygous	Heterozygous
Definition	Homozygous individuals bear similar alleles i.e., TT or tt for height	Heterozygous individuals bear dissimilar alleles e.g., Tt for height.
Type of alleles	Bear either dominant or recessive alleles, never both.	Always with both dominant and recessive alleles.
Gametes	• It produces only one type of gametes i.e., T,T or t, t. • It breeds true, i.e., gives rise to parental type of offspring on self breeding.	• It produces both types of gametes T and t. • It does not breed true, i.e., produces offspring with different genotypes on self breeding.

Extra vigour	Such individuals do not show extra vigour	The individuals can show extra vigour (hybrid and vigour or heterosis)

(c) Monohybrid and Dihybrid

Characters	Monohybrid	Dihybrid
Definition	When only one allelic pair is considered in cross breeding, it is called monohybrid cross.	When two allelic pairs are used in crossing, it is called dihybrid cross.
Example	Inheritance of tall and dwarf characters is a monohybrid cross	Inheritance of yellow and round seed characters and green wrinkled characters is a dihybrid cross.

Q. 3. A diploid organism is heterozygous for 4 loci, how many types of gametes can be produced?

[NCERT Ex. Q.3, Page 78]

Ans. Locus is a fixed position on a chromosome, which is occupied by a single or more genes. Heterozygous organisms contain different alleles for an allelic pair. Hence, a diploid organism, which is heterozygous at four loci, will have four different contrasting characters at four different loci. For example, if an organism is heterozygous at four loci with four characters, say Aa, Bb, Cc, Dd, then during meiosis, it will segregate to form 8 separate gametes.

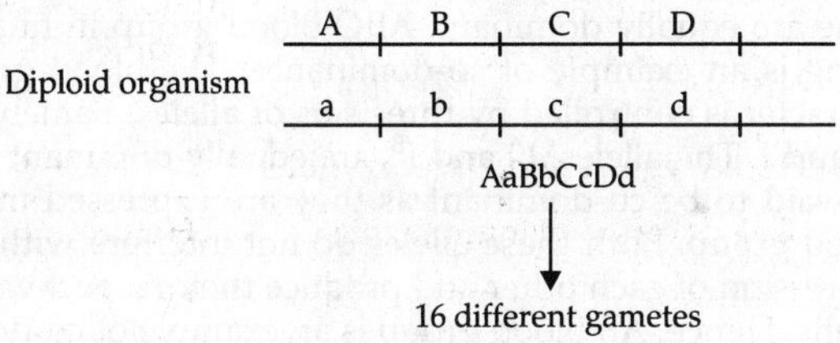

If the genes are not linked, then the diploid organism will produce 16 different gametes. However, if the genes are linked, the gametes will reduce their number as the genes might be linked and the linked genes will be inherited together during the process of meiosis.

Q. 4. Explain the Law of Dominance using a monohybrid cross. [NCERT Ex. Q.4, Page 78]

Ans. Mendel's law of dominance states that a dominant allele expresses itself in a monohybrid cross and suppresses the expression of recessive allele. However, this recessive allele for a character is not lost and remains hidden or masked in the progenies of F_1 generation and reappears in the next generation. For example, when pea plants with round seeds (RR) are crossed with plants with wrinkled seeds (rr), all seeds in F_1 generation were found to be round (Rr). When these round seeds were self-fertilised, both the round and wrinkled seeds appeared in F_2 generation in 3: 1 ratio. Hence, in F_1 generation, the dominant character (round seeds) appeared and the recessive character (wrinkled seeds) got suppressed, which reappeared in F_2 generation.

Q. 5. Define and design a test-cross.

[NCERT Ex. Q.5, Page 78]

Ans. Test cross is a cross between an organism with unknown genotype and a recessive parent. It is used to determine whether the individual is homozygous or heterozygous for a trait. If the progenies produced by a test cross show 50% dominant trait and 50% recessive trait, then the unknown individual is heterozygous for a trait. On the other hand, if the progeny produced shows dominant trait, then the unknown individual is homozygous for a trait.

Q. 6. Using a Punnett square, work out the distribution of phenotypic features in the first filial generation after a cross between a homozygous female and a heterozygous male for a single locus. [NCERT Ex. Q.6, Page 78]

Ans. In guinea pigs, heterozygous male with black coat colour (Bb) is crossed with the female having white coat colour (bb). The male will produce two types of gametes, B and b, while the female will produce only one kind of gamete, r. The genotypic and phenotypic ratio in the progenies of F_1 generation will be same i.e., 1:1.

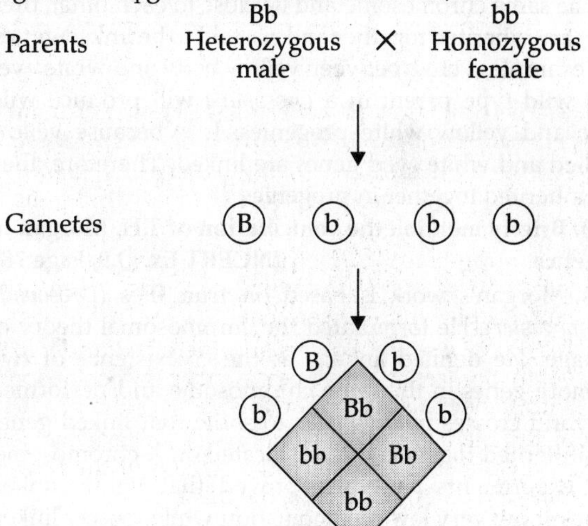

F_1 generation Black coat : White coat
2 : 2

Q. 7. When a cross in made between tall plants with yellow seeds (TtYy) and tall plant with green seed (Ttyy), what proportions of phenotype in the offspring could be expected to be

(a) Tall and green.

(b) Dwarf and green. [NCERT Ex. Q.7, Page 78]

Ans. A cross between tall plant with yellow seeds and tall plant with green seeds will produce

(a) Three tall and green plants

(b) One dwarf and green plant

Parents Tall Yellow × Tall Green
Tt Yy Tt yy

Gametes TY, Ty, tY, ty Ty, ty

	Ty	ty
TY	TTYy Tall Yellow	TTYy Tall Yellow
Ty	TTYy Tall Yellow	TTYy Tall Yellow
tY	TTYy Tall Yellow	TTYy Tall Yellow
ty	TTYy Tall Yellow	TTYy Tall Yellow

Phenotypes: Tall and Yellow = 3
Tall and Green = 3
Dwarf and Green = 1
Dwarf and Yellow = 1
Total = 8

Thus, (a) Proportion of tall and green is 3/8
(b) Proportion of dwarf and green is 1/8

Q. 8. Two heterozygous parents are crossed. If the two loci are linked what would be the distribution of phenotypic features in F_1 generation for a dihybrid cross? **[NCERT Ex. Q.8, Page 78]**

Ans. Linkage is defined as the coexistence of two or more genes in the same chromosome. If the genes are situated on the same chromosome and lie close to each other, then they are inherited together and are said to be linked genes. For example, a cross between yellow body and white eyes and wild type parent in a *Drosophila* will produce wild type and yellow white progenies. It is because yellow bodied and white eyed genes are linked. Therefore, they are inherited together in progenies.

Q. 9. Briefly mention the contribution of T.H. Morgan in genetics. **[NCERT Ex. Q.9, Page 78]**

Ans. Morgan's work is based on fruit flies (*Drosophila melanogaster*). He formulated the chromosomal theory of linkage. He defined linkage as the co-existence of two or more genes in the same chromosome and performed dihybrid crosses in *Drosophila* to show that linked genes are inherited together and are located on X-chromosome. His experiments have also proved that tightly linked genes show very low recombination while loosely linked genes show higher recombination.

Q.10. What is pedigree analysis? Suggest how such an analysis, can be useful. **[NCERT Ex. Q.10, Page 78]**

Ans. Pedigree analysis is a method used to study the inheritance of traits within a family over multiple generations. It involves creating a family tree that represents the inheritance of specific traits, abnormalities, or diseases. This tool is valuable for tracing how certain characteristics or genetic conditions are passed down through generations.

The primary purpose of pedigree analysis is to gain insights into the inheritance patterns of traits and diseases within a family. By studying these patterns, genetic counselors can offer guidance to help prevent the occurrence of certain genetic disorders, such as haemophilia or sickle cell anemia, in future generations of the same family.

Q.11.How is sex determined in human beings? **[NCERT Ex. Q.11, Page 78]**

Ans. Human beings exhibit male heterogamy. In humans, males (XY) produce two different types of gametes, X and Y. The human female (XX) produces only one type of gametes containing X chromosomes. The sex of the baby is determined by the type of male gamete that fuses with the female gamete. If the fertilising sperm contains X chromosome, then the baby produced will be a girl and if the fertilising sperm contains Y chromosome, then the baby produced will be a boy. Hence, it is a matter of chance that determines the sex of a baby. There is an equal probability of the fertilising sperm being an X or Y chromosome. Thus, it is the genetic makeup of the sperm that determines the sex of the baby.

Q.12.A child has blood group O. If the father has blood group A and mother blood group B, work out the genotypes of the parents and the possible genotypes of the other offsprings. **[NCERT Ex. Q.12, Page 78]**

Ans. The blood group characteristic in humans is controlled by three set of alleles, namely, I^A, I^B, and i. The alleles, I^A and I^B , are equally dominant whereas allele, *i*, is recessive to the other alleles. The individuals with genotype, $I^A I^A$ and I^A *i*, have blood group A whereas the individuals with genotype, $I^B I^B$ and I^B *i*, have blood group B. The persons with genotype $I^A I^B$ have blood group AB while those with blood group O have genotype *ii*. Hence, if the father has blood group A and mother has blood group B, then the possible genotype of the parents will be, father- $I^A I^A$ and mother- $I^B I^B$ or I^B *i*. A cross between homozygous parents will produce progeny with AB blood group. While a cross between heterozygous parents will produce progeny with 'AB' or 'O' or 'A' or 'B' blood group.

Q.13. Explain the following terms with example:
(a) Co-dominance
(b) Incomplete dominance **[NCERT Q. No. 13, Page 78]**

Ans. (a) Co-dominance: Co-dominance is the phenomenon in which both the alleles of a contrasting character are expressed in heterozygous condition. Both the alleles of a gene are equally dominant. ABO blood group in human being is an example of co-dominance. The blood group character is controlled by three sets of alleles, namely, I^A, I^B, and i. The alleles, I^A and I^B, are equally dominant and are said to be co-dominant as they are expressed in AB blood group. Both these alleles do not interfere with the expression of each other and produce their respective antigens. Hence, AB blood group is an example of co-dominance.

(b) Incomplete dominance: Incomplete dominance is a phenomenon in which one allele shows incomplete dominance over the other member of the allelic pair for a character. For example, a monohybrid cross between the plants having red flowers and white flowers in *Antirrhinum* species will result in all pink flower plants in F_1 generation. The progeny obtained in F_1 generation does not resemble either of the parents and exhibits intermediate characteristics. This is because the dominant allele, R, is partially dominant over the other allele, r. Therefore, the recessive allele, r, also gets expressed in the F_1 generation resulting in the production of intermediate pink flowering progenies with Rr genotype.

Q.14. What is point mutation? Give one example. **[NCERT Ex. Q.14, Page 78]**

Ans. When a mutation occurs in a single base pair of DNA, it is termed as a point mutation. E.g. Sickle cell anaemia.

Q.15. Who had proposed the chromosomal theory of inheritance? [NCERT Ex. Q.15, Page 78]

Ans. Sutton and Boveri proposed the chromosomal theory of inheritance in 1902.

Q. 16. Mention any two autosomal genetic disorders with their symptoms. [NCERT Ex. Q.16, Page 78]

Ans. Two autosomal genetic disorders are as follows: Thalassemia: It is an autosomal recessive blood disorder that can be inherited from parents when both are carriers of the gene. The defect could be due to either mutation or deletion which ultimately results in reduced rate of synthesis of one of the globin chain (α and β) that make up haemoglobin.

Symptoms: Facial deformities, abdominal swelling, slow growth and pale or yellowish skin are some common symptoms of thalassemia.

Down's syndrome: It is an autosomal disorder that is caused by the trisomy of chromosome 21.

Symptoms: The individual is short statured with round head, open mouth, protruding tongue, short neck, slanting eyes, and broad short hands. The individual also shows retarded mental and physical growth.

□□

CHAPTER 5

MOLECULAR BASIS OF INHERITANCE

Nucleic Acids

- DNA and RNA are the two types of nucleic acids.
- DNA is the genetic material in all the organisms except some viruses.
- RNA acts as a genetic material in some viruses but mostly functions as a messenger. It has additional roles as well: functions as adapter, structural molecule, and in some cases as a catalytic molecule.

DNA

- DNA is a long polymer of deoxyribonucleotides.
- The length of DNA is usually defined as number of nucleotides present in it.

➢ **Structure of Polynucleotide Chain**

- Polynucleotides are the polymers of nucleotides.
- DNA and RNA are examples of polynucleotides.
- **Nucleotide:** A nucleotide has 3 components: **1.** A nitrogenous base **2.** A pentose sugar (ribose in RNA and deoxyribose in DNA) **3.** A phosphate group.

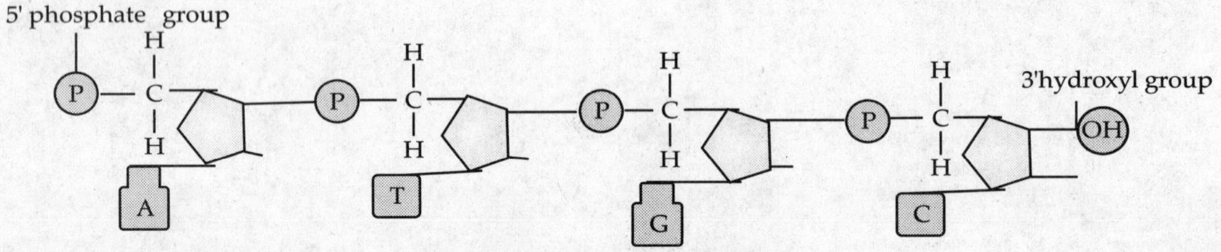

Fig 5.1: A polynucleotide Chain

- A nitrogenous base is linked to the pentose sugar through a N-glycosidic linkage to form nucleoside.
- **Nitrogenous bases are of 2 types:**

(a) Purines: It includes Adenine (A) and Guanine (G).

(b) Pyrimidines: It includes Cytosine (C), Thymine (T) and Uracil (U). Thymine (5-methyl Uracil) present only in DNA and Uracil only in RNA (In place of Thymine).

Scan to know more about this topic

Genetic material and Historical Background

MNEMONICS

1. Concept Name: 5 Nitrogenous Bases

Mnemonics: CUT AGAIN

Interpretation: Cytosine, Uracil, Thymine, Adenine, Guanine

2. Concept Name: NUCLEOTIDE

Mnemonics: SuPer maN

Interpretation: **S**ugar + **P**hosphate+ **N**itrogen base = **N**ucleotide

- According to the nature of pentose sugar, two types of nucleosides are formed ribonucleoside and deoxyribonucleotides.

Nucleosides in RNA (Ribonucleosides)	Nucleosides in DNA (Deoxyribonucleosides)
Adenosine	*Deoxyadenosine*
Guanosine	*Deoxyguanosine*
Cytidine	*Deoxycytidine*
Uridine	*Deoxythymidine*

- **Nucleotide (deoxynucleotide):** Nitrogen base + sugar + phosphate group.
- In RNA, every nucleotide residue has an additional –OH group present at 2′-position in the ribose.
- 2 nucleotides are linked through **3′ – 5′ phosphodiester** bond to form dinucleotide.
- When series of nucleotides are linked together, it forms polynucleotide.

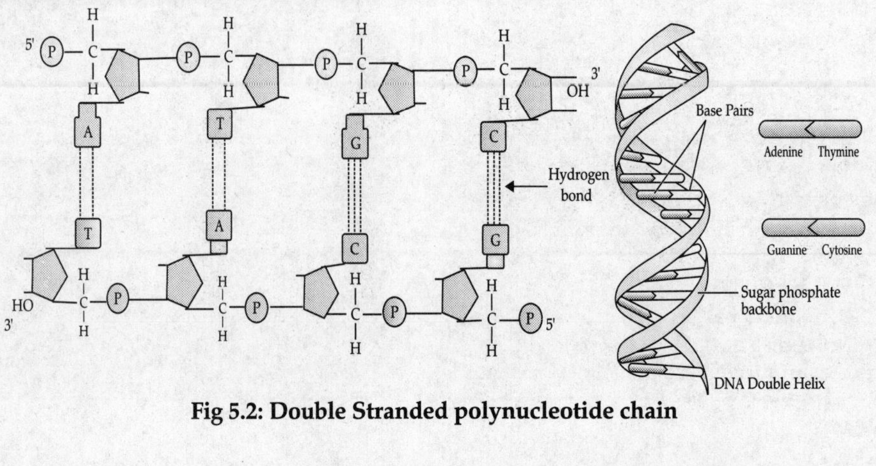

Fig 5.2: Double Stranded polynucleotide chain

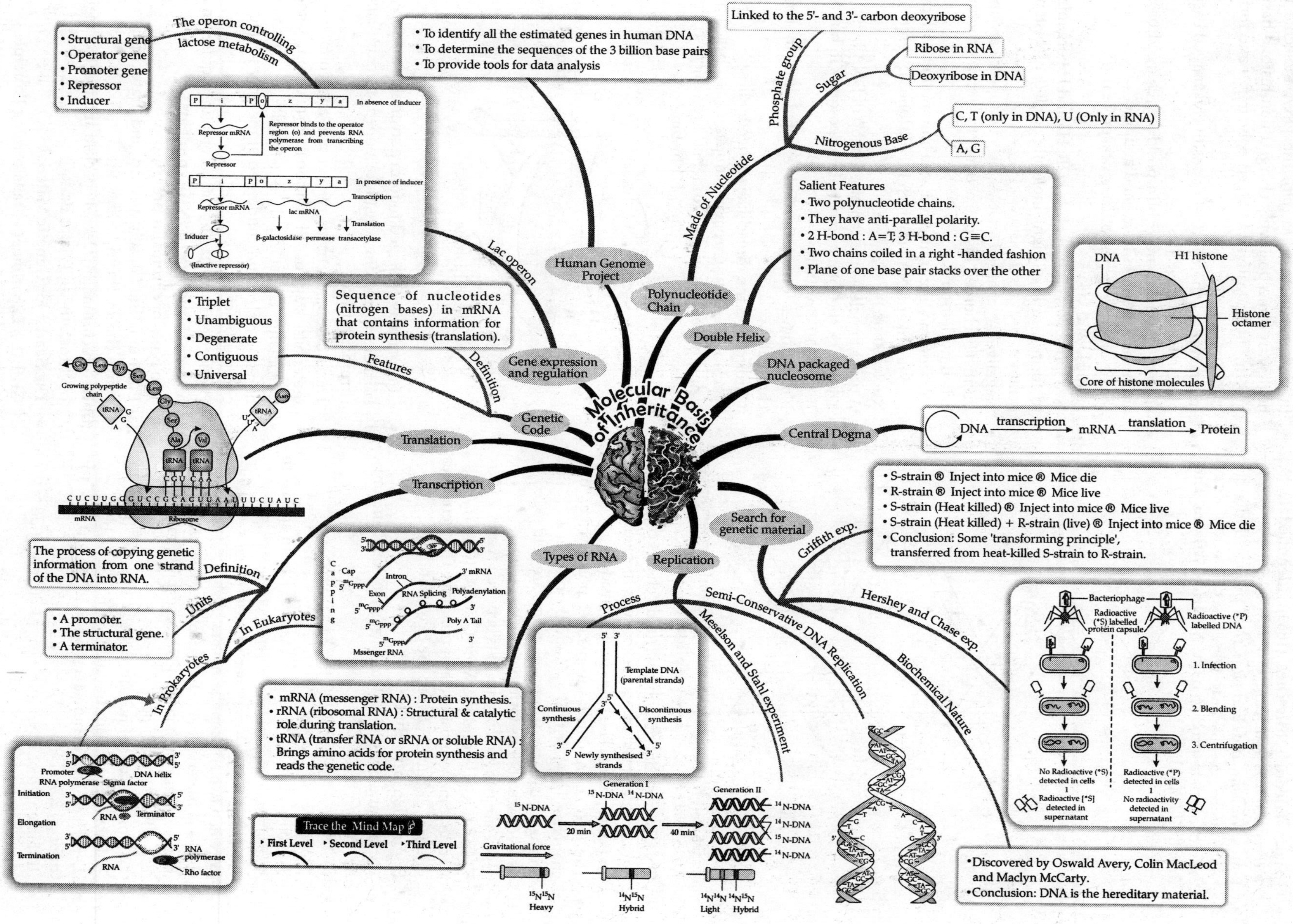
Molecular Basis of Inheritance
Human Genome Project
• To identify all the estimated genes in human DNA
• To determine the sequences of the 3 billion base pairs
• To provide tools for data analysis
Polynucleotide Chain
Made of Nucleotide
Phosphate group
Linked to the 5'- and 3'- carbon deoxyribose
Sugar
Ribose in RNA
Deoxyribose in DNA
Nitrogenous Base
C, T (only in DNA), U (Only in RNA)
A, G
Double Helix
Salient Features
• Two polynucleotide chains.
• They have anti-parallel polarity.
• 2 H-bond : A=T; 3 H-bond : G≡C.
• Two chains coiled in a right -handed fashion
• Plane of one base pair stacks over the other
DNA packaged nucleosome
DNA
H1 histone
Histone octamer
Core of histone molecules
Central Dogma
DNA transcription mRNA translation Protein
Search for genetic material
Griffith exp.
• S-strain ® Inject into mice ® Mice die
• R-strain ® Inject into mice ® Mice live
• S-strain (Heat killed) ® Inject into mice ® Mice live
• S-strain (Heat killed) + R-strain (live) ® Inject into mice ® Mice die
• Conclusion: Some 'transforming principle', transferred from heat-killed S-strain to R-strain.
Hershey and Chase exp.
Bacteriophage
Radioactive (*S) labelled protein capsule
Radioactive (*P) labelled DNA
1. Infection
2. Blending
3. Centrifugation
No Radioactive (*S) detected in cells
Radioactive [*S] detected in supernatant
Radioactive (*P) detected in cells
No radioactivity detected in supernatant
Biochemical Nature
•Discovered by Oswald Avery, Colin MacLeod and Maclyn McCarty.
•Conclusion: DNA is the hereditary material.
Replication
Semi-Conservative DNA Replication
Meselson and Stahl experiment
15N-DNA
Generation I
15N-DNA 14N-DNA
Generation II
14N-DNA
14N-DNA
15N-DNA
14N-DNA
20 min
40 min
Gravitational force
15N15N Heavy
14N15N Hybrid
14N14N Light
14N15N Hybrid
Process
Template DNA (parental strands)
Continuous synthesis
Discontinuous synthesis
Newly synthesised strands
Types of RNA
• mRNA (messenger RNA) : Protein synthesis.
• rRNA (ribosomal RNA) : Structural & catalytic role during translation.
• tRNA (transfer RNA or sRNA or soluble RNA) : Brings amino acids for protein synthesis and reads the genetic code.
Transcription
Definition
The process of copying genetic information from one strand of the DNA into RNA.
Units
• A promoter.
• The structural gene.
• A terminator.
In Eukaryotes
Capping
Cap
Intron
Exon
RNA Splicing
Polyadenylation
Poly A Tail
Messenger RNA
In Prokaryotes
Promoter
DNA helix
RNA polymerase
Sigma factor
Initiation
Elongation
Terminator
Termination
RNA polymerase
Rho factor
RNA
Translation
Growing polypeptide chain
tRNA
Ribosome
mRNA
CUCUUGGGUCCGCAGUUAAUUUCUAUC
Genetic Code
Features
• Triplet
• Unambiguous
• Degenerate
• Contiguous
• Universal
Definition
Sequence of nucleotides (nitrogen bases) in mRNA that contains information for protein synthesis (translation).
Gene expression and regulation
Lac operon
The operon controlling lactose metabolism
• Structural gene
• Operator gene
• Promoter gene
• Repressor
• Inducer
In absence of inducer
Repressor mRNA
Repressor
Repressor binds to the operator region (o) and prevents RNA polymerase from transcribing the operon
In presence of inducer
Transcription
lac mRNA
Translation
Inducer
(Inactive repressor)
β-galactosidase permease transacetylase
Trace the Mind Map
First Level
Second Level
Third Level

➢ **Structure of DNA**

- **Johann Friedrich Miescher (1869):** Identified DNA and named it as 'Nuclein'.
- **James Watson and Francis Crick** proposed double helix model of DNA. It was based on the X-ray diffraction data produced by **Maurice Wilkins and Rosalind Franklin.**

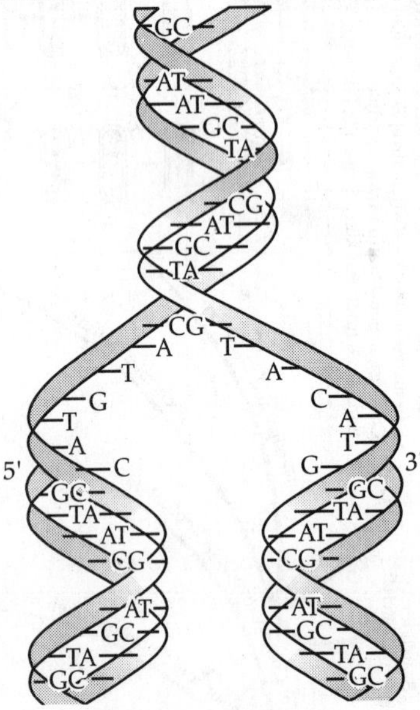

Fig 5.3: Watson Crick model of Semi-conservative DNA replication

- DNA is made of two polynucleotide chains coiled in a right handed fashion. Its backbone is formed of sugar and phosphates. The bases project inside.
- The two chains have anti-parallel polarity, i.e., one chain has the polarity 5′ → 3′ and the other has 3′ → 5′.
- Nitrogenous bases of opposite chains are held together by hydrogen bonds forming base pairs (bp).
- There are two hydrogen bonds between A and T (A = T) and three H-bonds between C and G (C ≡ G).
- Purine comes opposite to a pyrimidine. This generates uniform distance between the two strands.

➢ **Erwin Chargaff's Rule**

- Purines and pyrimidines are always in equal amounts, i.e., A + G = T + C.
- In DNA, the proportion of A is equal to T and the proportion of G is equal to C, i.e., A = T and G ≡ C.
- The base ratio A + T/G + C may vary from species to species but constant for a given species.
- Length of DNA = number of base pairs × distance between two adjacent base pairs.
- Φ 174 (a bacteriophage) has 5386 nucleotides.
- Bacteriophage lambda has 48502 base pairs (bp).
- *E. coli* has 4.6×10^6 bp.
- Haploid content of human DNA = 3.3×10^9 bp.
- Number of base pairs in human = 6.6×10^9 bp.
- Length of DNA in humans = 6.6×10^9 bp × 0.34×10^{-9} m/bp = 2.2 m.
- If the length of DNA in *E. coli* = 1.36 mm (1.36×10^{-3} m).

  ∴ The number of base pairs = 1.36×10^{-3} m/0.34×10^{-9} m/bp = 4×10^6 bp.

➢ **Packaging of DNA Helix**

- In prokaryotes (e.g., *E. coli*), the DNA molecule is held with some positively charged non-histone basic proteins like negatively charged polyamines and form 'nucleoid'.
- In eukaryotes, there is a set of positively charged basic proteins called histones.
- Histones proteins are rich in positively charged basic amino acid residues lysine and arginine.
- There are five types of histones proteins-H1, H2A, H2B, H3 and H4.
- Two molecules each of H2A, H2B, H3 and H4 organize to form a unit of eight molecules called as histone octamer.
- Negatively charged DNA is wrapped around positively charged histone octamer to form a structure called nucleosome.
- Nucleosomes are connected with one another with the help of linker DNA on which H1 Histone is present.

➢ **Nucleosome**

- A typical nucleosome contains 200 bp of DNA helix.
- Therefore, the total number of nucleosomes in human = 6.6×10^9 bp/200 bp = 3.3×10^7.
- Nucleosomes constitute the repeated unit to form chromatin.
- Chromatin is the thread-like stained bodies.
- Nucleosomes in chromatin appears as "beads-on-string" when it is viewed under electron microscope.

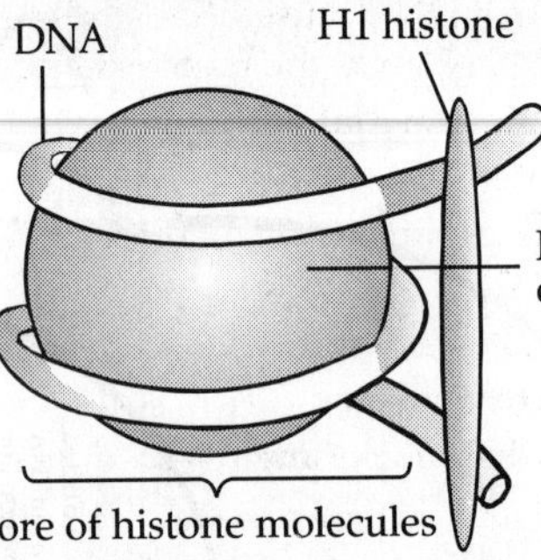

Fig 5.4: Nucleosome

- Chromatin is packaged to form a solenoid structure.
- Further supercoiling constitute looped structure called **chromatin fibre.**

  These chromatin fibres further coil and condense at metaphase stage of cell division to form chromosomes.
- Chromatin is packaged → solenoid → chromatin fibres → coiled and condensed at metaphase stage → chromosomes.
- Higher level packaging of chromatin requires **non-histone chromosomal (NHC) proteins.**
- Two types of chromatin are:

(a) Euchromatin: Loosely packed and transcriptionally active chromatin and stains light.

(b) Heterochromatin: Densely packed and inactive region of chromatin and stains dark.

➢ **The Search for Genetic Material**

Griffith's Experiment - Transforming Principle

- **Griffith** (1928) used mice and a bacterial strain, *Streptococcus pneumoniae*.

- *Streptococcus pneumoniae* has two strains:

(a) Smooth (S) strain (Virulent): Has polysaccharide mucous coat. Causes pneumonia.

(b) Rough (R) strain (Non-virulent): No mucous coat. Does not cause pneumonia.

➢ **Experiment**

- S-strain → Inject into mice → Mice die
- R-strain → Inject into mice → Mice live
- S-strain (Heat killed) → Inject into mice → Mice live
- S-strain (Heat killed) + R-strain (live) → Inject into mice → Mice die
- He concluded that there exists some 'transforming principle', that is transferred from heat-killed S-strain to R-strain. It enabled R-strain to synthesise smooth polysaccharide coat and become virulent. This must be due to the transfer of genetic material.

➢ **Biochemical Characterisation of Transforming Principle**

- Oswald Avery, Colin MacLeod & Maclyn McCarty in 1944 worked to determine the biochemical nature of 'transforming principle' in Griffith's experiment.
- They purified biochemicals (proteins, DNA, RNA, etc.) from heat killed S cells using suitable enzymes.
- They discovered that —

(a) Digestion of protein and RNA (using Proteases and RNases) did not affect transformation. So, the transforming substance was not a protein or RNA.

(b) Digestion of DNA with DNase inhibited transformation. It means that DNA caused transformation of R cells to S cells, i.e., DNA was the transforming substance.

➢ **The Genetic Material is DNA**

- The fact that DNA is the genetic material also came from the experiments of **Alfred Hershey** and **Martha Chase (1952)**.
- They worked with viruses that infect bacteria and are called **bacteriophages**.

➢ **Hershey-Chase Experiment—Blender Experiment**

- Hershey and Chase made two preparations of bacteriophage - In one, proteins were labelled with ^{35}S by putting in medium containing radioactive sulphur (^{35}S). In the second, DNA was labelled with ^{32}P by putting in a medium containing radioactive Phosphorous (^{32}P).
- These preparations were used separately to infect *E. coli*.
- After infection, the *E. coli* cells were gently agitated in a blender to separate the phage particles from the bacteria.
- Then the culture was centrifuged. Heavier bacterial cells were formed as a pellet at the bottom. Lighter viral components outside the bacterial cells remained in the supernatant.
- They found that,

(a) Supernatant contains viral protein labelled with ^{35}S, i.e., the viral protein had not entered the bacterial cells.

(b) The bacterial pellet contains radioactive ^{32}P. This shows that viral DNA labelled with ^{32}P had entered the bacterial cells. This proves that DNA is the genetic material.

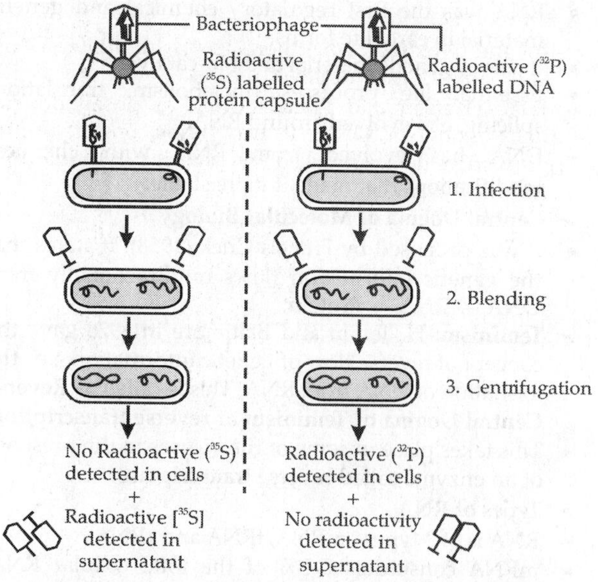

Fig 5.5: Hershey and Chase Experiment

➢ **Properties of Genetic Material**

- A molecule that can act as a genetic material must fulfil the following criteria:

(a) Be able to generate its replica by the process of Replication.

(b) Chemically and structurally be stable.

(c) Allows slow changes, mutations, that are required for evolution.

(d) It should be able to store genetic information which can be inherited.

(e) Be able to express itself as 'Mendelian Characters'.

➢ **DNA is a Better Genetic Material than RNA due to following reasons:**

- DNA is chemically less reactive and structurally more stable. It has the capacity to undergo repair.
- Due to unstable nature of RNA, RNA viruses (e.g., *bacteriophage, Tobacco Mosaic Virus, etc.*) mutate and evolve faster.
- For the storage of genetic information DNA is better due to its stability. But for the transmission of genetic information, RNA is better.
- RNA can directly code for the protein synthesis, hence can easily express the characters. DNA is dependent on RNA for protein synthesis.

Reasons for stability (less reactivity) of DNA	Reasons for mutability (high reactivity) of RNA
Double stranded	*Single stranded*
Presence of thymine	*Presence of Uracil*
Absence of 2′-OH	*Presence of 2′-OH*

- The two DNA strands are complementary. On heating, they separate. When appropriate conditions are provided they come together. (In Griffith's experiment, when the bacteria were heat killed, some properties of DNA did not destroy).

RNA

- RNA is a single stranded structure but it is often folded back upon itself forming helices. Nitrogenous bases are like those of DNA except that there is **uracil** in place of **thymine**.

- RNA was the first regulatory chemical and genetic material in early life forms.
- It acts as genetic material and bio-catalyst.
- Essential life processes (metabolism, translation, splicing, etc) evolved around RNA.
- DNA has evolved from RNA with chemical modifications that made it more stable.

➢ **Central Dogma of Molecular Biology**

- It was proposed by Francis Crick (1958). It states that the genetic information flows unidirectionally from **DNA → RNA → Protein.**

➢ **Teminism:** H. Temin and Baltimore in 1978 gave the concept of reverse flow of genetic information, i.e., the formation of DNA from RNA. This is called as **Reverse Central Dogma or Teminism or reverse transcription**. This takes place in some of the viruses in the presence of an enzyme called **reverse transcriptase.**

➢ **Types of RNA**

- RNA is of 3 types –mRNA, tRNA and rRNA.
- mRNA constitutes 2–5% of the total cellular RNA. tRNA is about 15% and rRNA is about 70–80%.
- **mRNA (messenger RNA):** Provides template for translation (protein synthesis) and is transcribed from DNA.
- **rRNA (ribosomal RNA):** Structural and catalytic role during translation. e.g., 23S rRNA in bacteria acts as ribozyme. It is the component of ribosome and is the most stable type of RNA.
- **tRNA (transfer RNA or sRNA or soluble RNA or adaptor RNA):** Brings amino acids for protein synthesis and reads the genetic code.
- tRNA are smallest amongst all the RNA and is made up of 70–80 nucleotides only.

DNA Replication

- Replication is the copying of DNA from parental DNA.
- **Watson & Crick** proposed Semi-conservative mode of replication.
- It suggests that the parent DNA strands act as template for the synthesis of new complementary strands. After the completion of replication, each DNA molecule would have one parental and one new strand.

➢ **Experimental Proof**

- **Mathew Meselson and Franklin Stahl (1958)** experimentally proved Semi-conservative mode.
- **Meselson & Stahl's Experiment:** They cultured *E. coli* in a medium containing $N^{15}H_4Cl$ (N^{15}: heavy isotope of N). N^{15} was incorporated into both strands of bacterial DNA and the DNA became heavier.
- Another preparation containing N salts labelled with N^{14} was also made. N^{14} was also incorporated in both strands of DNA and became lighter.
- These two types of DNA can be separated by centrifugation in a CsCl density gradient.

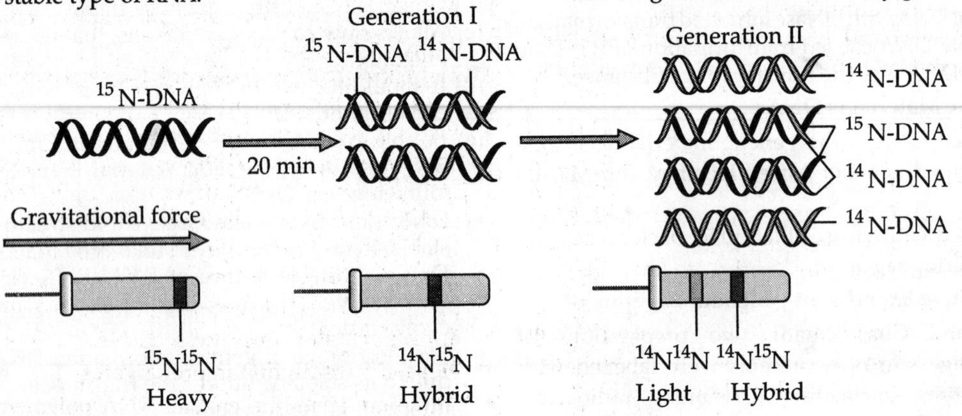

➢ **Separation of DNA by centrifugation**

- They took *E. coli* cells from N^{15} medium and transferred to ^{14}N medium.
- After one generation (i.e. after 20 minutes), they isolated and centrifuged the DNA. Its density was intermediate (hybrid) between ^{15}N DNA and ^{14}N DNA. This showed that in the newly formed DNA, one strand is old (^{15}N type) and one strand is new (^{14}N type). This confirms semi-conservative mode of replication.
- After II generation (i.e., after 40 minutes), there was an equal amounts of hybrid DNA and light DNA.
- **Taylor *et. al* (1958)** performed similar experiments on *Vicia faba* (faba beans) using radioactive thymidine to detect distribution of newly synthesised DNA in the chromosomes. It proved that the DNA in chromosomes also replicate semi-conservatively.

Scan to know more about this topic

DNA Replication Part – 2

➢ **The Machinery and Enzymes for Replication**

- DNA replication starts at a point called origin (ori).
- A unit of replication with one origin is called a replicon.
- During replication, the two strands unwind and separate by breaking H-bonds in the presence of an enzyme, *Helicase*.
- Unwinding of the DNA molecule at a point forms a 'Y'-shaped structure called replication fork.
- The separated strands act as templates for the synthesis of new strands.

Scan to know more about this topic

DNA Replication Part – 3

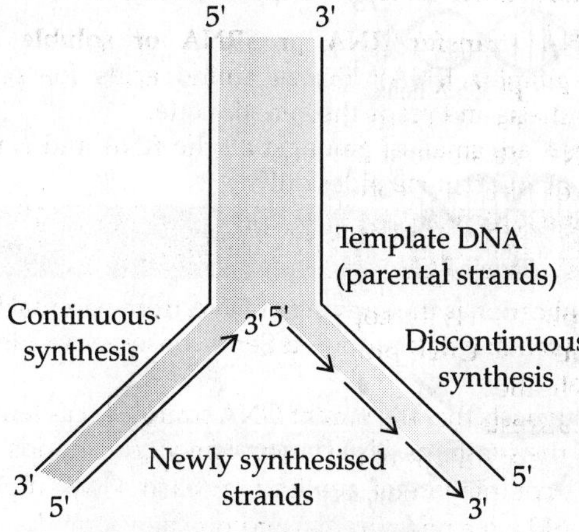

Fig 5.7: Replicating Fork

- DNA replicates in the 5′→3′ direction.
- Deoxyribonucleoside triphosphates (dATP, dGTP, dCTP & dTTP) act as substrate and also provide energy for polymerisation.
- Firstly, a small RNA primer is synthesised in presence of an enzyme, primase.
- In the presence of an enzyme, DNA dependent DNA polymerase, many nucleotides join with one another to primer strand and form a polynucleotide chain (new strand).
- The DNA polymerase forms one new strand (leading strand) on a continuous stretch in the 3′→5′ direction of template strand (Continuous synthesis).
- The other new strand is formed in small stretches (Okazaki fragments) in 5′→3′ direction (Discontinuous synthesis).
- The **Okazaki fragments** are then joined together to form a new strand by an enzyme, DNA ligase. This new strand is called **lagging strand**.
- If a wrong base is introduced in the new strand, DNA polymerase can do proofreading.
- *E. coli* completes replication within 38 minutes, i.e., 2000 bp per second.
- In eukaryotes, the replication of DNA takes place at S-phase of the cell cycle. Failure in cell division after DNA replication results in polyploidy.

➢ **Transcription**

- It is the process of copying genetic information from one strand of the DNA into RNA.
- Here, adenine pairs with uracil instead of thymine.
- Both strands are not copied during transcription, because:

Scan to know more about this topic

Transcription

(a) The code for protein is different in both strands. This complicates the translation.

(b) If two RNA molecules are produced simultaneously they would be complimentary to each other, hence form a double stranded RNA. This prevents translation.

➢ **Transcription Unit**

- It is the segment of DNA between the sites of initiation and termination of transcription.
- It consists of 3 regions:

(a) A promoter (Transcription start site): Binding site for RNA polymerase.

(b) Structural gene: The region between promoter and terminator where transcription takes place.

(c) A terminator: The site where transcription stops.

- The DNA- dependent RNA polymerase catalyzes the polymerisation only in 5′→3′ direction.
- 3′→5′ acts as template strand. 5′→3′ acts as coding strand.
- 3′–ATGCATGCATGCATGCATGCATGC–5′ Template strand.

  5′–TACGTACGTACGTACGTACGTACG–3′ Coding strand.

➢ **Transcription Unit and the Gene**

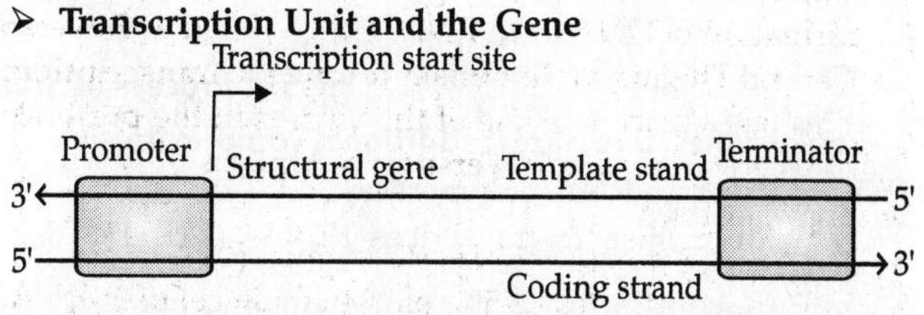

Fig 5.8: Schematic structure of a transcription unit

- **Gene:** Functional unit of inheritance. It is the DNA sequence coding for RNA molecule.
- **Cistron:** A segment of DNA coding for a polypeptide.
- Structural gene in a transcription unit is of two types:

(a) Monocistronic structural genes (split genes): It is seen in eukaryotes. Here, the coding sequences (expressed sequences or exons) are interrupted öby introns (intervening sequences).

(b) Polycistronic structural genes: It is seen in prokaryotes. Here, there are no split genes.

- **Exons and Introns:** In eukaryotes, the monocistronic structural genes have interörupted coding sequences, i.e., the genes in eukaryotes are split. The coding sequences or expressed sequences are called as exons. Exons are said to be those sequences that appear in mature or processed RNA. The **exons** are interrupted by introns. Introns or intervening sequences do not appear in mature or processed RNA.

➢ **Steps of transcription in prokaryotes**

- **Initiation:** Here, the enzyme RNA polymerase binds at the promoter site of DNA. This causes the local unwinding of the DNA double helix. An initiation factor (σ factor) present in RNA polymerase initiates the RNA synthesis.
- **Elongation:** The RNA chain is synthesised in the 5′-3′ direction. In this process, activated ribonucleoside triphosphates (ATP, GTP, UTP & CTP) are added. This is complementary to the base sequence in the DNA template.
- **Termination:** A termination factor (ρ *factor*) binds to the RNA polymerase and terminates the transcription.
- In bacteria (Prokaryotes), transcription and translation can be coupled (Translation can begin before mRNA is fully transcribed) because mRNA requires no processing to become active.
- Transcription and translation take place in the same compartment (no separation of cytosol and nucleus).

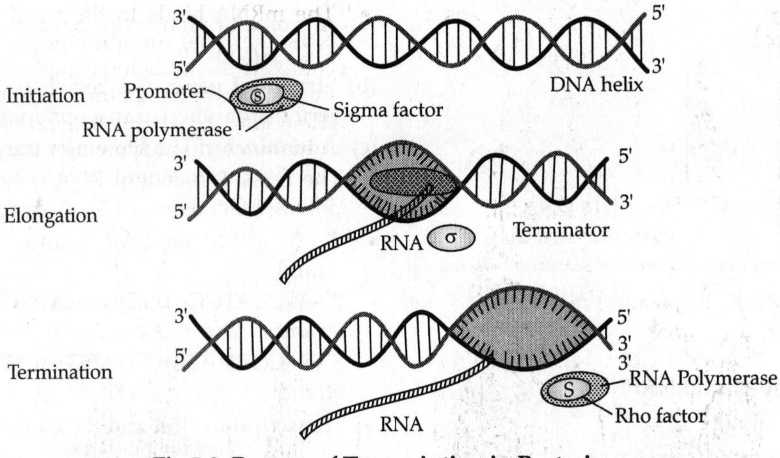

Fig 5.9: Process of Transcription in Bacteria

➢ **In eukaryotes, there are 2 additional complexities:**

(a) There are three RNA polymerases:

- **RNA polymerase I:** Transcribes rRNAs (28S, 18S & 5.8S).
- **RNA polymerase II:** Transcribes the heterogeneous nuclear RNA (hnRNA). It is the precursor of mRNA.
- **RNA polymerase III:** Transcribes tRNA, 5S rRNA and snRNAs (small nuclear RNAs).

(b) The primary transcripts (hnRNA): They contain both the exons and introns and are non-functional. Hence introns have to be removed. For this, it undergoes the following processes:

- **Splicing:** From hnRNA, introns are removed (by the spliceosome) and exons are spliced (joined) together.
- **Capping:** Here, a nucleotide methyl guanosine triphosphate (cap) is added to the 5′ end of hnRNA.
- **Tailing (Polyadenylation):** Here, adenylate residues (200-300) are added at 3′-end. It is the fully processed hnRNA, now called mRNA.

Genetic Code

➢ It is the sequence of nucleotides in mRNA that contains information for protein synthesis (translation). There are 22 amino acids that are involved in translation.

- **George Gamow** suggested that for coding 20 amino acids, the code should be made up of 3 consecutive nucleotides.
- **Har Gobind Khorana** developed the chemical method involved in synthesising RNA molecules with defined combinations of bases (homopolymers and co-polymers).
- **Marshall Nirenberg** developed cell-free system for protein synthesis.
- Severo Ochoa (polynucleotide phosphorylase) enzyme is used to polymerise RNA with defined sequences in a template independent manner.

MNEMONICS

Concept Name: Genetic Code

Mnemonics: DU CUT

Interpretation: Degeneracy, **U**nambiguous, **C**omma less, **U**niversal, **T**riplet

➢ **Salient Features of Genetic Code**

- The genetic code is a triplet code (three-letter code) where three adjacent nitrogen bases code for a single amino acid.
- 61 codons code for amino acids. 3 codons (UAA, UAG and UGA) do not code for any amino acids. They function as **stop codons** (Termination codons or non-sense codons).
- Genetic code is universal and non-overlapping, e.g., from bacteria to human UUU codes for Phenylalanine. Some exceptions are found in mitochondrial codons and in some protozoans.
- No punctuations between adjacent codons (comma less code). The codon is read in mRNA in a contiguous fashion.
- A single amino acid is represented by many codons (except AUG for methionine and UGG for tryptophan). Such codons are called **degenerate codons.**
- Genetic code is unambiguous and specific, i.e., one codon specifies only one amino acid.
- The codon is read in 5' → 3' direction.
- AUG has dual functions. It codes for Methionine (met) and also acts as initiator codon. In eukaryotes, methionine is the first amino acid and formyl methionine in prokaryotes.

➢ **Mutations and Genetic Code**

- The relationships between genes and DNA are best understood by mutation studies.
- Effects of large deletions and rearrangements in a segment of DNA may result in loss or gain of a gene and so a function.
- A classical example of point mutation is a change of single base pair in the gene for beta globin chain of haemoglobin that results in the change of amino acid residue glutamate to valine. It results into a diseased condition called as **sickle cell anaemia.**
- Insertion or deletion of one or two bases changes the reading frame from the point of insertion or deletion.
- When there is shifting of the reading frame due to insertion or deletion of the nucleotide, such mutation is known as **frame shift mutation.**
- This forms the genetic basis of proof that codon is a triplet and it is read in a contiguous manner.

➢ **The Adapter Molecule – tRNA**

- The tRNA is a molecule which has about 60% of its part double stranded and the rest single stranded which has unpaired bases. Fig 5.10

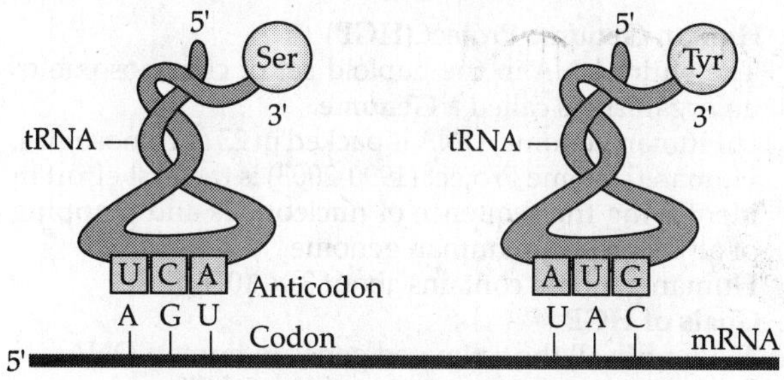

Fig 5.10: tRNA- the adapter molecule

- The tRNA has

(a) An anticodon (NODOC) loop that has bases complementary to the CODON with which it gets attached in mRNA.

(b) An amino acid acceptor end to which amino acid binds. This end or site lies at the 3' end & CCA–OH group. The 5' end bears G.

(c) **T Ψ C loop:** This is the site for attaching with ribosome. This has some unusual bases like Ψ (pseudouridine) and ribothymidine.

(d) **DHU-Loop:** It is the binding site for the enzyme aminoacyl synthetase. It is the largest loop and has Dihydrouridine.

(e) **Extra arm:** It is a variable side arm lying between T Ψ C and anticodon loop.

- tRNA is called adapter molecule because it picks up amino acids from cytoplasm and transfers them to ribosomes during protein synthesis.
- For initiation, there is another tRNA called **initiator tRNA**.
- There are no tRNAs for stop codons.
- 2-D structure of tRNA looks like a clover-leaf according to Robert Holly (1965). 3-D structure looks like inverted 'L' according to Klug (1974).

Translation

➢ Protein Synthesis takes place in ribosomes. It includes 4 steps:

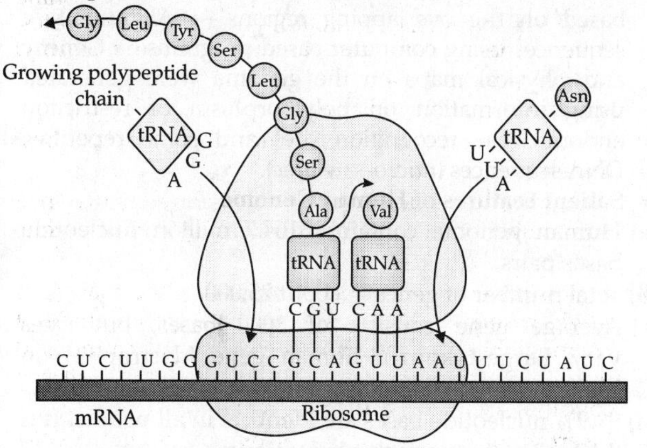

Fig 5.11: Translation

1. **Charging of tRNA (aminoacylation of tRNA)**

- Formation of peptide bond requires energy obtained from ATP.
- For this, amino acids are activated (amino acid + ATP) and linked to their cognate tRNA in the presence of aminoacyl tRNA synthetase. So, the tRNA becomes charged.

2. **Initiation**

- It begins at the 5′-end of mRNA in the presence of an initiation factor.
- The mRNA binds to the small subunit of ribosome. Now the large subunit binds to the small subunit to complete the initiation complex.
- Large subunit has 2 binding sites for tRNA: aminoacyl tRNA binding site (A site) and peptidyl site (P site).
- Initiation codon for methionine is AUG. So,methionyl tRNA complex would have UAC at the Anticodon site.

3. **Elongation**

- At the P-site, the first codon of mRNA binds with anticodon of methionyl tRNA complex.
- Another aminoacyl tRNA complex with an appropriate amino acid enters the ribosome and attaches to A site.
- Its anticodon binds to the second codon on the mRNA and a peptide bond is formed between first and second amino acids in presence of an enzyme, peptidyl transferase.
- The uncharged tRNA moves from P site to E site and the peptidyl-tRNA moves to the P site. This is called translocation.
- Then 3rd codon comes into A site and a suitable tRNA with 3rd amino acid binds at the A site. This process is repeated.
- A group of ribosomes associated with a single mRNA for translation is called a polyribosome (polysomes).
- A ribozyme is a ribonucleic acid (RNA) enzyme that catalyses a chemical reaction. The ribozyme catalyses specific reactions in a similar way to that of protein synthesis. Also called catalytic RNA, ribozyme are found in ribosome where they join amino acids together to form protein chains.

4. **Termination**

- When aminoacyl tRNA reaches the termination codon like UAA, UAG & UGA, the termination of translation occurs. The polypeptide and tRNA are released from the ribosomes.
- The ribosome dissociates into large and small subunits at the end of protein synthesis.
- An mRNA has additional sequences that are not translated (untranslated regions or UTR). UTRs are present at both 5′-end (before start codon) and 3′-end (after stop codon). They are required for efficient translation process.

➢ **Regulation of Gene Expression**

Gene expression results in the formation of a polypeptide. In eukaryotes, the regulation includes the following levels:

- Transcriptional level (formation of primary transcript).
- Processing level (regulation of splicing).
- Transport of mRNA from nucleus to the cytoplasm.
- Translational level.

➢ **Importance of regulation of gene expression:**

- Gene regulation is the process to switch off or switch on the genes as per the requirement of the organism.
- Gene regulation is required so that there is no waste of energy in expressing the genes which is not required at the time.
- However, there are housekeeping genes which are always expressed in the cell.
- The metabolic, physiological and environmental conditions regulate expression of genes.
- In *E. coli*, the enzyme beta-galactosidase hydrolyses lactose into galactose and glucose. In the absence of lactose, the synthesis of beta-galactosidase stops.
- The development and differentiation of embryo into adult are result of the regulation of several set of genes.

➢ **Operon Concept:** This is a regulatory system that is observed in bacteria.

- "Each metabolic reaction is controlled by a set of genes".
- All the genes regulating a metabolic reaction constitute an *Operon*. e.g., *lac* operon, *trp* operon, *ara* operon, *his* operon, *val* operon, etc.
- When a substrate is added to growth medium of bacteria, a set of genes is switched on to metabolise it. This is called induction.
- When a metabolite (product) is added, the genes to produce it are turned off. This is called repression.

➢ **The *Lac* Operon**

- ***Lac* operon in *E. coli*:** The operon controlling lactose metabolism. It consists of a regulator gene, 3-structural genes, an operator gene, promoter gene, a repressor and an inducer.

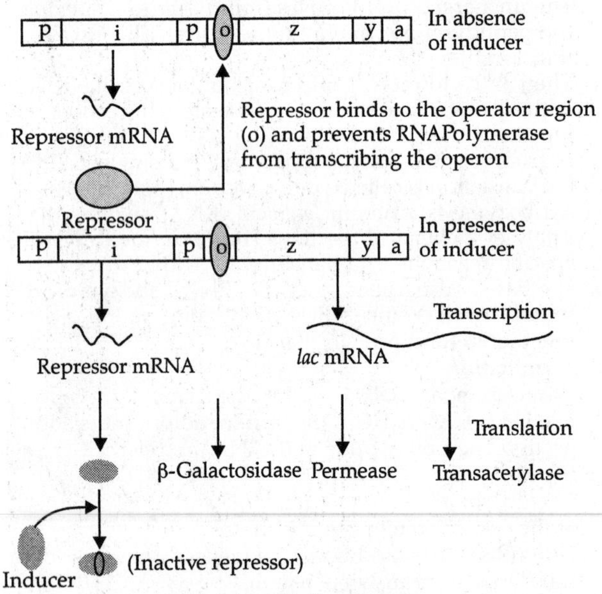

Fig 5.12: The *lac* Operon

(a) A regulatory or inhibitor (i) gene: Codes for the repressor.

(b) 3 structural genes:

(i) ***z* gene:** Codes for β-galactosidase (hydrolyse lactose to galactose and glucose).

(ii) ***y* gene:** Codes for permease (increase permeability of the cell to lactose).

(iii) ***a* gene:** Codes for a transacetylase.

- The genes present in the operon function together in the same or related metabolic pathway. There is an **operator** region for each operon.
- If there is no lactose (inducer), *lac* operon remains switched off. In the absence of inducer, repressor gene is active. The regulator gene synthesises mRNA to produce the **repressor protein**, this protein binds to the operator genes and blocks RNA polymerase movement. So the structural genes are not expressed.
- In the absence of glucose, if lactose is provided in the growth medium, the lactose is transported into the *E. coli* cells by the action of permease. Lactose (inducer) binds with repressor protein.
- So, repressor protein cannot bind to **operator gene**. The operator gene becomes free and induces the RNA polymerase to bind with **promoter gene** then transcription starts. Regulation of *lac* operon by repressor is called negative regulation.

➢ **Human Genome Project (HGP)**

- The entire DNA in the haploid set of chromosome of an organism is called a **Genome.**
- In Human genome, DNA is packed in 23 chromosomes.
- Human Genome Project (1990-2003) is the first effort in identifying the sequence of nucleotides and mapping of all the genes in human genome.
- Human genome contains about 3×10^9 bp.

➢ **Goals of HGP**

(a) To identify all the estimated genes in human DNA.

(b) To determine the sequences of the 3 billion chemical base pairs that make up human DNA.

(c) To store this information in databases.

(d) To improve tools for data analysis.

(e) To transfer related technologies developed during the project of society to other sectors of society.

(f) To address the ethical, legal and social issues (ELSI) that may arise from the project.

➢ **HGP was Closely Associated with Bioinformatics**

Application of computer science and information technology to the field of biology and medicine helps in analysing DNA sequence data.

➢ **Methodologies of HGP**

There are two major approaches namely, ESTs and sequence annotation.

- **Expressed Sequence Tags (ESTs):** Focused on identifying all the genes that are expressed as RNA and sequencing the same.
- **Sequence annotation:** Sequencing whole set of genome containing all the coding & non-coding regions and later assigning functions to different regions.

➢ **Procedure:**

Isolate total DNA from a cell → Convert into random fragments of smaller size → Clone in suitable host (e.g. BAC – bacterial artificial chromosomes & YAC – yeast artificial chromosomes) for amplification through PCR (polymerase chain reaction) → Fragments are sequenced using Automated DNA sequencers (using Frederick Sanger method) → Sequences are arranged based on the overlapping regions → Alignment of sequences using computer based programs → Genetic and physical maps on the genome were generated using information on polymorphism of restriction endonuclease recognition sites and some repetitive DNA sequences (micro-satellites).

➢ **Salient Features of Human Genome**

(a) Human genome contains 3164.7 million nucleotide bases pairs.

(b) Total number of genes = about 25,000.

(c) Average gene consists of 3000 bases, but sizes vary. Largest known human gene (dystrophin on X-chromosome) contains 2.4 million bases.

(d) 99.9% nucleotide bases are identical in all people. It is 0.1% what makes each of us unique.

(e) Functions of over 50% of discovered genes are unknown.

(f) Chromosome 1 has most genes (2968) and Y has the fewest (231).

(g) Less than 2% of the genome codes for proteins.

(h) Repeated sequences make up very large portion of human genome. Repetitive sequences are stretches of DNA sequences that are repeated many times. They have no direct coding functions but they shed light on chromosome structure, dynamics and evolution.

(i) About 1.4 million locations where single-base DNA differences (SNPs- Single nucleotide polymorphism or 'snips') occur in humans.

➢ **Rice Genome Project**

- Rice is one of the most largely consumed foods in India. Also, the population is increasing with a rapid pace, so, to meet this requirement, Rice genome project has been launched to increase the production of rice. Rice has the smallest genome of 430Mb nucleotides located on chromosome 12
- **Rice Genome:** It is a joint project of National Institute of Aerobiological Sciences (NIAS), forestry and fisheries (STAFF), Ministry of Agriculture, Forestry and Fisheries (NAFF), Society for Techno-innovation of Agriculture genome research program.
- *Arabidopsis* is an experiment plant of rice genome because it has fast life cycle and can be easily grown. It has smaller genome and high diversity and helps in enhancing the molecular products.

➢ **Need for sequencing rice genome:**

- To know the functioning of genes by accurate gene sequencing.
- It is important for agronomic traits which requires mapping of genomic sequences.
- Improvement of other cereals will become easier.

➢ **DNA Fingerprinting (DNA profiling)**

- It is the technique to compare the DNA fragments of two individuals.
- Developed by **Alec Jeffreys (1985)**. He is considered as the father of DNA fingerprinting. **Lalji Singh** is the Father of Indian DNA fingerprinting.

➢ **Basis of DNA Fingerprinting**

- DNA carries some non-coding sequences called **repetitive sequence [Variable Number Tandem Repeats (VNTR)]**.
- Number of repeats is specific. It varies from person to person and is specific to a person.
- The size of VNTR varies from 0.1 to 20 kb.
- Repetitive DNA are separated from bulk genomic DNA as different peaks during density gradient centrifugation.
- The bulk DNA forms a major peak and the other small peaks are called as satellite DNA.
- Satellite DNA is classified into many categories (micro-satellites, mini-satellites etc) based on base composition (A: T rich or G: C rich), length of segment and number of repetitive units.
- An inheritable mutation observed in a population at high frequency is called DNA polymorphism (variation at genetic level).
- Polymorphism is higher in non-coding DNA sequence. This is because mutations in these sequences may not have any immediate effect in an individual's reproductive ability.
- These mutations accumulate generation after generation and cause polymorphism. For evolution & speciation, polymorphisms play important role.

➢ **Steps of DNA Fingerprinting (Southern Blotting Technique)**

Scan to know more about this topic

DNA Finger Printing

(a) Isolate DNA (from any cells like blood stains, semen or hair roots).

(b) Make copies (amplification) of DNA by Polymerase Chain Reaction (PCR) if the amount of isolated DNA is small.

(c) Digest DNA by restriction endonucleases.

(d) Separate DNA fragments by gel electrophoresis over agarose polymer gel.

(e) Treat with alkali solution (NaOH) to denature DNA bonds so as to split them into single stranded DNAs in the gel.

(f) Transfer (blotting) single stranded DNA fragments to synthetic membranes such as nitrocellulose or nylon, and then baked in a vacuum oven at 80°C for 3-5 hours (to fix the DNA fragment on the membrane).

(g) Nitrocellulose filter membrane is placed in a solution containing radioactive labelled single stranded DNA probe. The DNA probes are small radioactive synthetic DNA segments of known sequences of nitrogen bases. These DNA probe binds with the complimentary sequences of the DNA fragment on the membrane to form a hybridised DNA.

(h) The filter paper is washed to remove unbound probe.

(i) The hybridised DNA is photographed on to an X-ray film by autoradiography. The image (in the form of dark and light bands) obtained is called DNA fingerprint. This gives the characteristic pattern of an individual's DNA.

➢ **Applications of DNA Fingerprinting are:**

- Forensic tool to solve paternity, rape, murder, etc.
- For the diagnosis of genetic diseases.
- To determine phylogenetic status of animals.

NCERT CORNER

Exercise Questions

Q. 1. Group the following as nitrogenous bases and nucleosides:

Adenine, Cytidine, Thymine, Guanosine, Uracil and Cytosine. **[NCERT Ex. Q.1, Page 109]**

Ans. (i) Nitrogenous bases : Adenine, thymine, uracil and cytosine.

(ii) Nucleosides: Cytidine and guanosine.

Q. 2. If a double-stranded DNA has 20 percent of cytosine, calculate the percentage of adenine in the DNA. **[NCERT Ex. Q.2, Page 109]**

Ans. (i) According to Chargaff's rule, the DNA molecule should have an equal ratio of pyrimidine (cytosine and thymine) and purine (adenine and guanine). It means that the number of adenine molecules is equal to thymine molecules and the number of guanine molecules is equal to cytosine molecules.

$$\% A = \% T \text{ and } \% G = \% C$$

(ii) If double-stranded DNA (*ds*DNA) has 20% of cytosine, then according to the law, it would have 20% of guanine. Thus, percentage of G + C content = 40%.

(iii) The remaining 60% represents both A + T molecule. Since adenine and guanine are always present in equal numbers, the percentage of adenine molecule is 30%.

Q. 3. If the sequence of one strand of DNA is written as follows:

5′-ATGCATGCATGCATGCATGCATGCATGC-3′

Write down the sequence of complementary strand in 5′→3′ direction. [NCERT Ex. Q.3, Page 109]

Ans. The DNA strands are complementary to each other with respect to base sequence. Hence, if the sequence of one strand of DNA is:

5′-ATGCATGCATGCATGCATGCATGCATGC-3′

Then, the sequence of complementary strand in direction will be:

3′-TACGTACGTACGTACGTACGTACGTACG-5′

Therefore, the sequence of nucleotides on DNA polypeptide in direction is:

5′-GCATGCATGCATGCATGCATGCATGCAT-3′

Q. 4. If the sequence of the coding strand in a transcription unit is written as follows:

5′-ATGCATGCATGCATGCATGCATGCATGC-3′

Write down the sequence of *m*RNA. [NCERT Ex. Q.4, Page 109]

Ans. If the coding strand in a transcription unit is 5′-ATGCATGCATGCATGCATGCATGCATGC-3′

Then, it is known that the sequence of mRNA is same as the coding strand of DNA. However, in RNA, thymine is replaced by uracil. Hence, the sequence of mRNA will be, 5′-AUGCAUGCAUGCAUGCAUGCAUGCAUGC-3′

Q. 5. Which property of DNA double helix led Watson and Crick to hypothesise semi-conservative mode of DNA replication? Explain. [NCERT Ex. Q.5, Page 109]

Ans. (i) Watson and Crick observed that the two strands of DNA are anti-parallel and complementary to each other with respect to their base sequences. This type of arrangement in DNA molecule led to the hypothesis that DNA replication is semi-conservative.

(ii) It means that the double-stranded DNA molecule separates and then, each of the separated strand acts as a template for the synthesis of a new complementary strand. As a result, each daughter DNA molecule would have one parental strand and a newly synthesised daughter strand.

(iii) Since only one parental strand is conserved in each daughter molecule, it is known as semi-conservative mode of replication.

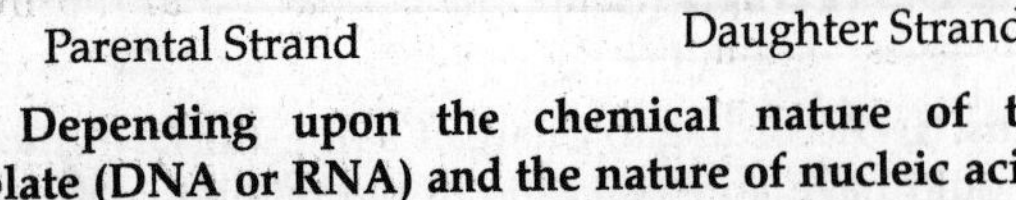

Q. 6. Depending upon the chemical nature of the template (DNA or RNA) and the nature of nucleic acids synthesised from it (DNA or RNA), list the types of nucleic acid polymerases. [NCERT Ex. Q.6, Page 109]

Ans. There are two different types of nucleic acid polymerases.

(i) DNA-dependent DNA polymerases.

(ii) DNA-dependent RNA polymerases.

The DNA-dependent DNA polymerases use a DNA template for synthesising a new strand of DNA, whereas DNA-dependent RNA polymerases use a DNA template strand for synthesising RNA.

Q. 7. How did Hershey and Chase differentiate between DNA and protein in their experiment while proving that DNA is the genetic material? [NCERT Ex. Q.7, Page 109]

Ans. (i) Hershey and Chase worked with bacteriophage and *E. coli* to prove that DNA is the genetic material. They used different radioactive isotopes to label DNA and protein coat of the bacteriophage.

(ii) They grew some bacteriophages on a medium containing radioactive phosphorus (^{32}P) to identify DNA and some on a medium containing radioactive sulphur (^{35}S) to identify protein. Then, these radioactive-labelled phages were allowed to infect *E. coli* bacteria. After infecting, the protein coat of the bacteriophage was separated from the bacterial cell by blending and then subjected to the process of centrifugation.

(iii) Since the protein coat was lighter, it was found in the supernatant while the infected bacteria got settled at the bottom of the centrifuge tube. In case I, supernatant was found radioactive which shows protein did not enter in bacterial cell during infection. While in case II, bacterial cells were radioactive as they have radioactive DNA. Hence, it was proved that DNA is the genetic material as it was transferred from virus to bacteria.

For Diagram: Refer to Revision notes/ Fig 5.5 Page 126.

Q. 8. Differentiate between the followings:

(a) Repetitive DNA and Satellite DNA

(b) mRNA and tRNA

(c) Template strand and Coding strand.

[NCERT Ex. Q.8, Page 109]

Ans. (a) Repetitive DNA and satellite DNA

Repetitive DNA	Satellite DNA
Repetitive DNA are DNA sequences that contain small segments, which are repeated many times.	Satellite are DNA sequences that contain highly repetitive DNA.
The repeat units may be few base pairs long or hundreds to thousands of base pairs long.	It has short sequence repeats (upto 10 bp long).
It appears as light bands during CsCl density gradient analysis.	In CsCl density gradient analysis, it appears as small dark bands.
Repetitive DNAs are separated from the bulk genome DNA at different peaks during density gradient centrifugation.	It gets separated from repetitive DNA as small peaks.

(b) mRNA and tRNA

mRNA	tRNA
It is straight chain molecule.	It has a looped structure that appear clover leaf like.

It has a series of codon each of which codes for a particular amino acid.	It has an amino acid binding site and anti-codon (a sequence of 3 bases complementary to a codon).
It dictates the sequence of amino acids on the polypeptide chain.	It carries a specific amino acid to the site of protein synthesis.

(c) Template strand and coding strand

Template strand	Coding strand
It is the DNA strand that has polarity 3'→5', and acts as template for transcription.	It is the DNA strand that has polarity 5'→3', and does not code for anything.
It transcribes RNA with complementary base sequence.	It's base sequence is the same as in the transcript (RNA) except of thymine in place of uracil.

Q. 9. List two essential roles of ribosome during translation. [NCERT Ex. Q.9, Page 109]

Ans. The important functions of ribosome during translation are:

(i) Ribosome acts as the site where protein synthesis takes place from individual amino acids. It is made up of two subunits. The smaller subunit comes in contact with mRNA and forms a protein synthesising complex whereas the larger subunit acts as an amino acid binding site.

(ii) Ribosome acts as a catalyst for forming peptide bond. For example, 23 S *r*-RNA in bacteria acts as a ribozyme.

Q.10. In the medium where *E. coli* was growing, lactose was added, which induced the *lac* operon. Then, why does lac operon shut down some time after addition of lactose in the medium? [NCERT Ex. Q.10, Page 109]

Ans. (i) *Lac* operon is a segment of DNA which works in a co-ordinated manner to metabolise lactose into glucose and galactose.

(ii) In *lac* operon, lactose acts as an inducer. It binds to the repressor and inactivates it. Once the lactose binds to the repressor, RNA polymerase binds to the promoter region. Hence, three structural genes express their product and respective enzymes are produced. These enzymes act on lactose so that lactose is metabolised into glucose and galactose.

(iii) After sometime, when the level of inducer decreases as it is completely metabolised by enzymes, it causes synthesis of the repressor from regulator gene. The repressor binds to the operator gene and prevents RNA polymerase from transcribing the operon. Hence, the transcription is stopped. This type of regulation is known as negative regulation.

For Diagram: Refer to Revision notes/ Fig 5.12.

Q.11. Explain (in one or two lines) the function of the followings :

(a) Promoter , (b) *t*RNA , (c) Exons

[NCERT Ex. Q.11, Page 109]

Ans. (a) Promoter : This is a region of DNA which helps in initiating the process of transcription. It serves as the binding site for RNA polymerase.

(b) *t*RNA : Transfer RNA (*t*RNA) is a small RNA that reads the genetic code present on *m*RNA. It carries specific amino acid to *m*RNA on ribosome during translation of proteins.

(c) Exons : They are coding sequences of DNA in eukaryotes that transcribe for proteins.

Q. 12. Why is the Human Genome project called a mega project? [NCERT Ex. Q.12, Page 109]

Ans. (i) Human genome project was considered to be a mega project because it had a specific goal to sequence every base pair present in the human genome.

(ii) It took around 13 years for its completion and got accomplished in year 2005. It was a large scale project, which aimed at developing new technology and generating new information in the field of genomic studies.

(iii) As a result of it, several new areas and avenues have opened up in the field of genetics, biotechnology, and medical sciences. It provided clues regarding the understanding of human biology.

Q. 13. What is DNA fingerprinting? Mention its application. [NCERT Ex. Q.13, Page 109]

Ans. DNA fingerprinting is a technique used to identify and analyse the variations in various individuals at the level of DNA. It is based on variability and polymorphism in DNA sequences.

Applications:

- It is used in forensic science to identify potential crime suspects.
- It is used to establish paternity and family relationships.
- It is used to identify and protect the commercial varieties of crops and livestock.
- It is used to find out the evolutionary history of an organism and trace out the linkages between groups of various organisms.

Q.14. Briefly describe the following:

(a) Transcription, (b) Polymorphism, (c) Translation

(d) Bioinformatics [NCERT Ex. Q.14, Page 109]

Ans. (a) Transcription: Transcription is the process of synthesis of RNA from DNA template. A segment of DNA gets copied into mRNA during the process.

- The process of transcription starts at the promoter region of the template DNA and terminates at the terminator region. The segment of DNA between these two regions is known as transcription unit.
- The transcription requires RNA polymerase enzyme, a DNA template, four types of ribonucleotides, and certain cofactors such as Mg^{2+} .
- The three important events that occur during the process of transcription are:
  (i) Initiation
  (ii) Elongation
  (iii) Termination
- The DNA-dependent RNA polymerase and certain initiation factors (σ) bind the double stranded DNA at the promoter region of the template strand and initiate the process of transcription.
- RNA polymerase moves along the DNA and leads to the unwinding of DNA duplex into two separate strands. Then, one of the strands, called sense strand, acts as template for mRNA synthesis.

- The enzyme, RNA polymerase, utilises nucleoside triphosphates (dNTPs) as raw material and polymerises them to form mRNA according to the complementary bases present on the template DNA.
- This process of opening of helix and elongation of polynucleotide chain continues until the enzyme reaches the terminator region.
- As RNA polymerase reaches the terminator region, the newly synthesised mRNA transcripted along with enzyme is released. Another factor called terminator factor (ρ) is required for the termination of the transcription.

For diagram: Refer to Revision notes/ Fig 5.9.

(b) Polymorphism: Polymorphism is a form of genetic variation in which distinct nucleotide sequence can exist at a particular site in a DNA molecule.

- This heritable mutation is observed at a high frequency in a population. It arises due to mutation either in somatic cell or in the germ cells.
- The germ cell mutation can be transmitted from parents to their offsprings.
- This results in accumulation of various mutations in a population, leading to variation and polymorphism in the population. This plays a very important role in the process of evolution and speciation.
- Since, polymorphism is the basis of genetic mapping of human genome, it forms the basis of DNA fingerprinting too.

(c) Translation: Translation is the process of polymerising amino acid to form a polypeptide chain.

- The triplet sequence of base pairs in mRNA defines the order and sequence of amino acids in a polypeptide chain.
- The process of translation involves three steps: Initiation, Elongation and Termination.
- During the initiation of the translation, tRNA gets charged when the amino acid binds to it using ATP.
- The start (initiation) codon (AUG) present on mRNA is recognised only by the charged tRNA.
- The ribosome acts as actual site for the process of translation and contains two separate sites in a large subunit for the attachment of subsequent amino acids.
- The small subunit of ribosome binds to mRNA at the initiation codon (AUG) followed by the large subunit. Then, it initiates the process of translation.
- During the elongation process, the ribosome moves one codon downstream along with mRNA so as to leave the space for binding of another charged tRNA.
- The amino acid brought by tRNA gets linked with the previous amino acid through a peptide bond and this process continues resulting in the formation of a polypeptide chain.
- When the ribosome reaches one or more Stop codon (UAA, UAG, and UGA), the process of translation gets terminated. The polypeptide chain is released and the ribosomes get detached from mRNA.

For Diagram: Refer to Revision notes/ Fig 5.11.

(d) Bioinformatics: Bioinformatics is the application of computational and statistical techniques to the field of molecular biology.

- It solves the practical problems arising from the management and analysis of biological data. The field of bioinformatics developed after the completion of human genome project (HGP).
- This is because an enormous amount of data has been generated during the process of HGP that has to be managed and stored for easy access and interpretation for future use by various scientists.
- Hence, bioinformatics involves the creation of biological databases that store the vast information of biology. It develops certain tools for easy and efficient access to the information and its utilisation.
- Bioinformatics has developed new algorithms and statistical methods to find out the relationship between the data, to predict protein structure and their functions, and to cluster the protein sequences into their related families.

□□

CHAPTER 6

EVOLUTION

Introduction

- Evolution is an orderly change from one form to another.
- **Evolutionary Biology:** Study of history of life forms on earth.

Origin of Life

- Big Bang Theory states that universe originated about 20 billion years ago by a thermonuclear explosion (big bang) of a dense entity.
- The earth was formed about 4.5–5 billion years ago.
- There was no atmosphere on early earth.
- Water vapours, CH_4, CO_2 and NH_3 released from molten mass covered the surface.

$$H_2O \rightarrow H_2 + O_2$$
$$NH_3 + O_2 \rightarrow NO + H_2O$$
$$CH_4 + O_2 \rightarrow CO_2 + H_2O$$

- Then the ozone layer was formed.
- As it cooled, the water vapour condensed to fall as rain and helped to form oceans.

> **MNEMONICS**
>
> **Concept Name:** Theories of Origin of life
>
> **Mnemonics: A**ll **B**oys **C**ome in **S**chool it's **C**ompulsory
>
> **Interpretation: Abiogenesis, Biogenesis, Cosmic theory, Special creation theory, Chemical evolution theory**

➢ **Theories of Origin of Life**

(i) Abiogeneses states that life originated from non-living things.

- It states that life came out of decaying and rotting matter like straw, mud, etc.
- **Louis Pasteur** (1864) demonstrated that life comes only from pre-existing life and dismissed abiogenesis theory.
- He showed that in pre-sterilised flasks, life did not come from killed yeast while in another flask open to air, new living organisms arose.

(ii) Biogeneses

- It was proposed by **Francisco Redi, Spallanzani** and **Louis Pasteur**.
- It states that life originates from pre-existing life.

(iii) Cosmic Theory (Theory of Panspermia)

- It states that the units of life (spores) were transferred to different planets including earth.

(iv) Theory of Special Creation

- It states that living and non-living things are created by some supernatural power (God).

(v) Theory of Chemical Evolution of life

- It was proposed by **Oparin** and **Haldane**.
- It states that the first form of life was originated from non-living inorganic and organic molecules such as CH_4, NH_3, H_2O, sugars, proteins, nucleic acids, etc.
- "Abiogenesis first, but biogenesis ever since".
- **Two hypothetical proposals of Oparin-Haldane's theory are:**

(i) Chemical evolution from inorganic to organic molecules.

(ii) First life formed by assembly and interaction of organic molecules.

- This theory is also known as primary abiogeneses.

Urey-Miller Experiment

- **Harold Urey** and **Stanley Miller** conducted an experiment to prove theory of chemical evolution.
- They created a condition similar to that of primitive earth (i.e. high temperature, volcanic storms, reducing atmosphere, devoid of oxygen but containing compounds of carbon, hydrogen, nitrogen and water.
- They made electric discharge in a closed flask containing CH_4, NH_3, H_2 and water vapour at 800° C.
- As a result, some amino acids were formed.
- In similar experiments, others observed formation of sugars, nitrogen bases, pigments and fats.
- First non-cellular form of life originated 3 billion years ago.
- They were RNA, proteins, polysaccharide, etc.
- The first cellular form of life did not possibly originate till about 2000 million years ago. These were probably single-cells. All life forms were in water environment only.

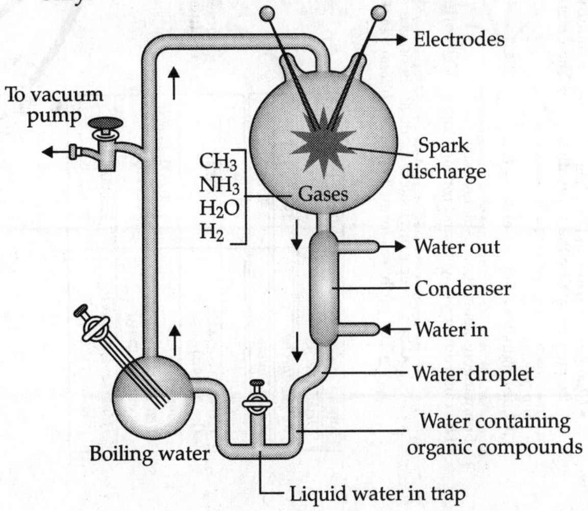

Fig 6.1: Miller and Urey's Experiment

Evolution

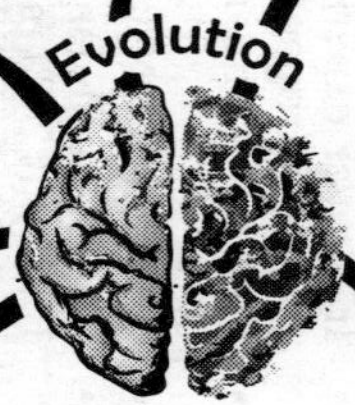

Theories

- Modern synthetic theory
  - Changes occurring in the allele frequencies within the population
- Biogenesis
  - Life originates from pre-existing life.
- Spontaneous generation (Abiogenesis)
  - Life came out of decaying and rotting matter
- Cosmic theory/Panspermia
  - The units of life (spores) were transferred to earth.
- Special creation theory
  - Living and non–living things were created by God.
- Chemical evolution theory
  - Life originated from non-living inorganic & organic molecules

Origin of Life

- The universe originated about 20 billion years ago.
- The earth was formed about 4.5 billion years ago.

Origin of Life-Urey and Miller's Experiment

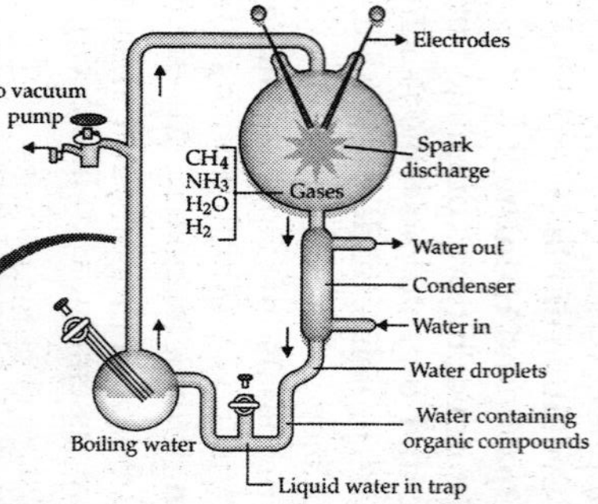

Human Evolution

Human ancestors	Origin period
Dryopithecus	20-25 mya
Ramapithecus	14-15 mya
Australopithecus	3-4 mya
Homo habilis	2 mya
Homo erectus (Java man)	1.5 mya
Homo sapiens neanderthalensis (primitive man)	1,00,000-40,000 years ago
Homo sapiens sapiens (modern man)	75,000-10,000 years ago

Hardy Weinberg Principle

Factors affecting
- Gene Migration
- Genetic drift
- Mutation
- Genetic recombination
- Natural Selection

Theory of Mutation

- Proposed by Hugo de Vries
- Single step large mutation.
- Mutation caused speciation

Theory of Biological Evidences

Darwinism
- Natural Selection
- Heritable minor variations.
- Over production by organisms.
- Limited natural resources.
- Struggle for existence.
- Survival of the fittest.

Evidences

Palaeontological Evidence
- By study of fossils
- Fossils help to study phylogeny, connecting link and about extinct animals.

Morphological & Anatomical

Homologous Organs
- Human hand, Whale's flippers, Bat's wing, and Cheetah's foot.
- Thorns of *Bougainvillea* and tendrils of *Cucurbita*.

Analogous Organs
- Wings of insects and wings of birds.
- Eyes of Octopus and mammals
- Flipper of Penguins and Dolphins.
- Sweet potato (modified root) and Potato (modified stem).

Bio-Geographical

Adaptive Radiation
- Darwin Finches

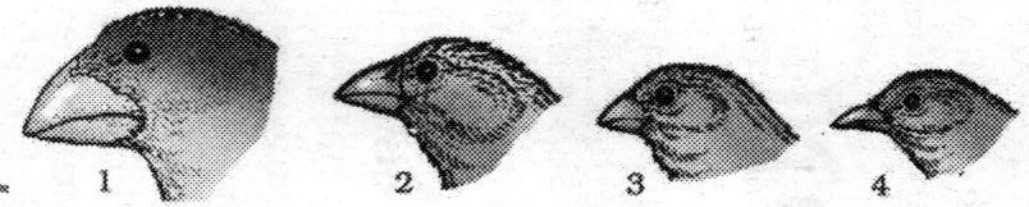

- Marsupial Radiation

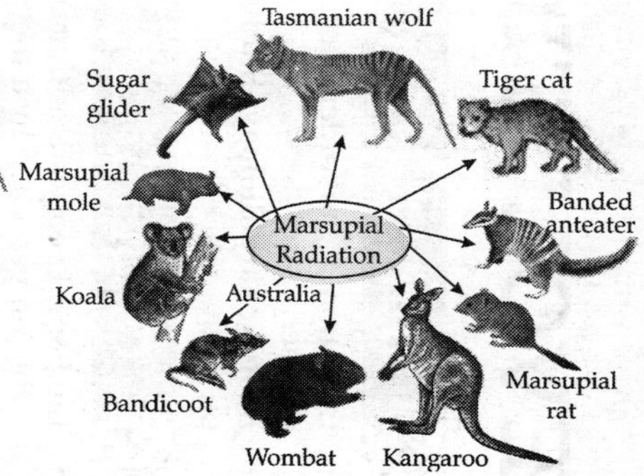

- Placental Mammals
  - e.g., Placental wolf and Tasmanian wolf-marsupial.

Bio-Chemical
- Similarities in proteins and genes.

Embryological
- Similarities in embryo development.

Natural Selection
- Dark-coloured peppered moth *Biston betularia*, (var. *carbonaria*) preferred over the white moth.
- By anthropogenic action

Trace the Mind Map
- First Level
- Second Level
- Third Level

➢ Evolution of Life Forms – Various Theory

- Based on observations made during a sea voyage in a survey ship called H.M.S. Beagle round the world, **Charles Darwin** concluded that existing living forms share similarities to varying degrees not only among themselves but also with life forms that existed millions of years ago.
- There had been extinctions of different life forms in the years gone by just as new forms of life, arose at different periods of history of earth.
- There has been gradual evolution of life forms due to variation in characteristics.
- Those characteristics which enable some to survive better in natural conditions (climate, food, physical factors etc.) would out-breed others that are less-endowed to survive under such natural conditions or fitness of the individual or population.
- The fitness, according to Darwin, refers ultimately and only to reproductive fitness. Hence, those who are better fit in an environment, leave more progeny than others.
- Therefore, they will survive more and hence are selected by nature.
- He called it natural selection and implied it as a mechanism of evolution.
- **Alfred Wallace**, a naturalist who worked in Malay Archipelago also came to similar conclusions around the same time.
- All the existing life forms share similarities and share common ancestors.
- However, these ancestors were present at different periods in the history of earth.
- The geological history of earth closely correlates with the biological history of earth.

➢ Evidences for Evolution

1. Paleontological Evidences

- The study of fossils is known as paleontology.
- Fossils are remnants of life forms or the parts found, which are preserved in rocks (earth crust).
- Fossils are written documents of evolution.

Scan to know more about this topic

Evidences of Evolution

- **Significance of Fossils**

(a) To study phylogeny (evolutionary history or race history) e.g., Horse evolution.

(b) To study the connecting link between two groups of organisms e.g. *Archaeopteryx* having reptilian and avian characteristics.

(c) To study about extinct animals e.g., Dinosaurs.

(d) To study about geological period by analysing fossils in different sedimentary rock layers. The study showed that life forms varied over time and certain life forms are restricted to certain geological time spans.

2. Morphological and Anatomical Evidences

- Comparative anatomy and morphology evidences showed that different forms of animals have some common structural features. This can be explained as follows:

(a) Homologous Organs and Homology

- Homologous organs are the organs having fundamental similarity in structure and origin but different in functions. This phenomenon is called homology. e.g., Human hand, Whale's flippers, Bat's wings, and Cheetah's foot.
- All these perform different functions but are constructed on the same fundamental plan.
- Homology can be seen in skeleton (e.g., humerus, radius, ulna, carpals, metacarpals & phalanges), heart, blood vessels, excretory system, brain, etc.
- **Homology in Plants:**

(i) The thorns of *Bougainvillea* and tendrils of *Cucurbita*.

(ii) The origin of homologous organs is due to divergent evolution.

(iii) The divergent evolution is the process by which related species become less similar in order to survive and adapt in different environmental conditions.

(iv) Homology indicates common ancestry.

(b) Analogous Organs and Analogy

- Analogous organs are the organs having similar function but different structure and origin. This phenomenon is called analogy.
- **Examples**

(i) Wings of insects (formed of a thin flap of chitin) and wings of birds (modified forelimbs).

(ii) Eyes of Octopus (retina from skin) and mammals (retina from embryonic brain).

(iii) Flipper of Penguins and Dolphins.

(iv) Sweet potato (modified root) and Potato (modified stem).

(v) Trachea of insects (from ectoderm) and lungs of vertebrates (from endoderm).

- The origin of analogous organs is due to convergent evolution.
- The convergent evolution is the process by which unrelated species become more similar in order to survive and adapt in similar environmental conditions.

3. Adaptive Radiation (Biogeographical Evidences)

- Adaptive radiation (evolution by adaptation) is the evolution of closely related species in a given geographical area starting from a point.

Examples

(a) Darwin's finches (seen in Galápagos Islands).

(b) Australian marsupials.

(c) Placental mammals in Australia.

- When more than one adaptive radiation occur in an isolated geographical area, this leads to convergent evolution, e.g., Australian Marsupials and Placental mammals.

4. Biochemical Evidences

- Similarities in proteins and genes.
- Similarities in other bio-molecules and metabolism.

5. Evidences for Evolution by Natural Selection

- Natural selection is the process that results in the adaptation of an organism to its environment by means of selectively reproducing changes in its genotype, or genetic constitution.
- Examples of natural selection: Industrial Melanism (In England).

➢ Before Industrialisation (1850s):

- There were more white winged moths (*Biston betularia*) on trees than dark winged or melanised moths (*Biston carbonaria*).
- **Reason:** White coloured lichen covered the trees. In that background the white winged moths survived

but the dark coloured moths were easily spotted out and picked out by predators.

➢ **After industrialisation (1920):**

- More dark winged moths and less white winged moths.
- **Reason:** The tree trunks became dark due to pollution by industrial smoke and soot. No growth of lichens. Under this condition the white winged moth did not survive because the predators identified them easily against dark background. Dark winged moth survived because of suitable dark background.
- Excess use of herbicides, pesticides, antibiotics or drugs, etc. resulted in selection of resistant varieties (Natural selection by anthropogenic action).

Theories of Biological Evolution

➢ **Darwinism (Theory of Natural Selection)**

- It was proposed by **Charles Darwin (1859)** in his book "**Origin of Species**".
- It is based on two key concepts namely,

(a) Branching Descent (Adaptive radiation)

- It explains that all organisms are modified descendants of previous life forms.

(b) Natural Selection

- Consider a bacterial colony (say A) growing on a given medium.
- If the medium composition is changed, only a part of the population (say B) can survive under new conditions. This variant population outgrows the others and appears as new species, i.e., B is better than A under new condition.
- Nature selects for fitness.
- The work of **Thomas Malthus** on principle of populations (1798) was influenced by **Darwin.**
- **Natural selection is based on the following facts:**

(a) Heritable minor variations.

(b) Overproduction by organisms.

(c) Limited natural resources.

(d) Struggle for existence for food and space.

(e) Survival of the fittest.

- Population size grows exponentially if everybody reproduces maximally (e.g., bacterial population).
- In fact, population size is limited due to competition for resources (Struggle for existence).
- Only some survives (Survival of the fittest).
- Darwin said that the organisms with heritable variations make resource utilisation better.
- They reproduce and leave more progeny.
- It leads to a change in population characteristics and new forms appear.

➢ **The modern synthetic theory**

The modern synthetic theory is also known as Neo-Darwinian theory which merges the theory of Darwinian evolution with Mendelian genetics given by many evolutionary biologists such as such as T. Dobzhansky, Sewall Wright, G.L. Stebbins, Ernst Mayr. This theory provided a new definition of evolution as "the changes occurring in the allele frequencies within the populations" which emphasizes the genetic basis of evolution.

➢ **Factors of modern synthetic theory**

- Mutation
- Genetic recombination
- Genetic drift
- Natural selection
- Isolation

➢ **Mechanism of Evolution**

- Darwin ignored about origin of variation and mechanism of speciation.

Scan to know more about this topic

Mechanism of Evolution

➢ **Mutation Theory**

- **Hugo de Vries** (1901) proposed Mutation Theory of evolution in his book "Mutation theory".
- He conducted some experiments on *Oenothera lamarckiana* (evening primrose) and believed that evolution takes place through mutation and not by minor variation.
- Evolution for Darwin was gradual while for deVries it is a sudden / spontaneous process. He believed mutation caused speciation and hence called it **saltation** (single step large mutation).

➢ **Differences between Darwinian Variation & Mutation**

Darwinian Variation	Mutation
It shows minor variation.	It shows large variation.
It is slow and directional.	It is random, sudden and direction less.
It showed gradual evolution.	It showed discontinuous evolution and speciation by saltation.
It is caused by reshuffling of genes.	It is caused by change in the genetic material.

Hardy - Weinberg Principle

- It says that allele frequencies in a population are stable and constant from generation to generation.
- The gene pool (total genes and their alleles in a population) remains constant. This is called genetic equilibrium (Hardy-Weinberg equilibrium).
- Sum total of all the allelic frequencies = 1. e.g., in a diploid, p and q are the frequencies of alleles A and a respectively.
- The frequency of AA = p^2 (i.e. the probability of an allele A with frequency p is the product of the probabilities, i.e. p^2)
- The frequency of aa = q^2
- The frequency of Aa = 2pq
- Hence $p^2 + 2pq + q^2 = 1$ [binomial expansion of $(p+q)^2$]
- Change of frequency of alleles in a population causes disturbance in genetic equilibrium. This is due to evolution.

➢ **Factors Affecting Hardy-Weinberg Equilibrium:** There are fine basic processes which may bring about the change in Hardy Weinberg equilibrium and bring about the variations at the genetic level as follows:

(a) Gene Migration

- Gene flow from one population to another.

- Here, gene frequencies change in both populations.
- There would be a gene flow, if migration happens multiple times.

(b) Genetic Drift
- The accidental gene flow causing change in frequency.
- Sometimes, the change in frequency is so different in the new sample of population, that they become a different species.
- The original drifted population becomes founders and the effect is called founder effect.

(c) Mutation
- Mutations result in formation of new phenotypes.
- Over few generations, this leads to speciation.

(d) Genetic Recombination
- It is the reshuffling of gene combinations during crossing over resulting in genetic variation.

(e) Natural Selection: It is the major factor which adds variations in the population, change the gene frequencies in the gene pool resulting in the formation new gene pool. Three types of natural selection are namely, Stabilising selection, Directional selection and Disruptive selection.

(i) **Stabilising Selection:** Here, more individuals acquire average character value and variation is reduced.

(ii) **Directional Selection:** Here, individuals of one extreme are more favoured.

(iii) **Disruptive Selection:** Individuals of both the extremes are favoured. It produces two peaks, that may lead to the development of two different populations.

➢ **Origin and Evolution of Man (Human ancestry)**

(i) ***Dryopithecus* & *Ramapithecus* (15 mya)**

(a) Hairy.

(b) Walked like gorillas and chimpanzee.

(c) *Dryopithecus:* ape-like.

(d) *Ramapithecus:* man-like.

(e) Fossils of man-like bones found in Ethiopia and Tanzania.

(f) Man-like primates (3-4 mya): Height up to 4 feet.

(ii) ***Australopithecus* (2 mya)**
- In East African grasslands.
- Hunted with stone weapons.
- Ate fruits.

(iii) ***Homo habilis***
- First human-like being (hominid).
- Brain capacity: 650-800 cc.
- Did not eat meat.

(iv) ***Homo erectus* (1.5 mya)**
- Large brain (900 cc): Ate meat.

(v) **Neanderthal man: 40,000 - 1 lakh yrs ago:**
- Brain 1400 cc.
- Lived in East and Central Asia.
- Used hides to protect their body.
- Buried their dead.

(vi) ***Homo sapiens* (Modern man):** Evolution took place during 10,000 to 75,000 years ago.
- Prehistoric cave art developed about 18,000 years ago.
- Agriculture and settlements: 10,000 years ago.

MNEMONICS

Concept Name: Human Evolution

Mnemonics: Dr. **R**am **A**nd **H**anuman **J**b **P**ahunche **N**ew **C**ar **S**e

Interpretation:
Dryopithecus
Ramapithecus
Australopithecus
Homo habilis
Java Man
Peking Man
Neanderthal
Cro - Magnon
Homo sapiens sapiens

NCERT CORNER

Exercise Questions

Q. 1. Explain antibiotic resistance observed in bacteria in light of Darwinian selection theory.
[NCERT Ex. Q.1, Page 126]

Ans. (i) Darwinian selection theory states that individuals with favourable variations are better adapted than individuals with less favourable variations. It means that nature selects the individuals with useful variations which are better evolved to survive in the existing environment.

(ii) An example of such selection is antibiotic resistance in bacteria.

(iii) When bacterial population was grown on an agar plate, containing antibiotic penicillin, the colonies that were sensitive to penicillin died, whereas one or few bacterial colonies that were resistant to penicillin survived. This is because these bacteria had undergone chance mutation, which resulted in the evolution of a gene that made them resistant to penicillin drug.

(iv) Hence, the resistant bacteria multiplied quickly as compared to non-resistant (sensitive) bacteria, thereby increasing their number. Hence, the advantage of an individual over other helps in the struggle for existence.

Q. 2. Find out from newspapers and popular science articles any new fossil discoveries or controversies about evolution. **[NCERT Ex. Q.2, Page 126]**

Ans. (i) Fossils of dinosaurs have revealed the evolution of reptiles in Jurassic period.

(ii) As a result of this, evolution of other animals such as birds and mammals has also been discovered.

(iii) However, two unusual fossils recently unearthed in China have ignited a controversy over the evolution of birds.

(iii) *Confuciusornis* is one such genus of primitive birds that were crow-sized and lived during the *Cretaceous* period in China.

Q. 3. Attempt giving a clear definition of the term "species." **[NCERT Ex. Q.3, Page 126]**

Ans. Species can be defined as a group of organisms, which have the capability to inter-breeding in order to produce fertile offspring.

Q. 4. Try to trace the various components of human evolution.
(Hint : brain size and function, skeletal structure, dietary preference, etc.). [NCERT Ex. Q.4, Page 126]

Ans. The various components of human evolution are:

S. No.	Name	Brain capacity	Posture	Food	Features
(i)	*Dryopithecus africanus*		Knuckle walker, walked similar to gorillas and chimpanzees (was more apelike)	Soft fruit and leaves	• Canines are large. • Arms and legs are of equal size.
(ii)	*Ramapithecus*		Semi-erect (more man like)	Seeds, nuts	• Canines were small. • Molars were large.
(iii)	*Australopithecus africanus*	450 cc	Full erect posture, height (1.05 m)	Herbivorous (ate fruits)	• Hunted with stone weapons. • They lived at trees. • Their canines and incisors were small.
(iv)	*Homo habilis*	735 cc	Fully erect posture, height (1.5 m)	Carnivorous Do not eat meat.	• Canines were small. • They were the first tool makers.
(v)	*Homo erectus*	800–1,100 cc	Fully erect posture, height (1.5–1.8 m)	Omnivorous	They used stone and bone tools for hunting games.
(vi)	*Homo neanderthalensis*	1,300–1,600 cc	Fully erect posture, height (1.5–1.66 m)	Omnivorous	• They are cave dwellers • They used to hide to protect themselves. • They buried their dead.
(vii)	*Homo sapiens fossilis* *Cro Magnon*	1,650 cc	Fully erect posture with height (1.8 m)	Omnivorous	• They had strong jaw with teeth close together. • They were cave dwellers. • They made paintings and carvings in the caves. • They developed a culture and were called first modern men.
(viii)	*Homo sapiens sapiens*	1,200–1,600 cc	Fully erect posture. height (1.5–1.8 m)	Omnivorous	• They are the living modern men, with high intelligence. • They developed art, culture, language, speech, etc. • They cultivated crops and domesticated animals.

Q. 5. Find out through internet and popular science articles whether animals other than man have self-consciousness. [NCERT Ex. Q.5, Page 126]

Ans. (i) There are many animals other than humans, which have self-consciousness. An example of animal being self-conscious are dolphins.

(ii) Dolphins are highly intelligent mammals. They have a sense of self and they also recognise others among themselves and others. They communicate with each other by whistles, tail-slapping and other body movements.

(iii) Not only dolphins, there are certain other animals such as crow, parrot, chimpanzee, gorilla, orangutan, etc., which exhibit self-consciousness. Apes, like the human beings, have well developed facial muscles for showing facial gestures and also have property of self-consciousness.

Q. 6. List 10 modern-day animals and using the internet resources link it to a corresponding ancient fossil. Name both. [NCERT Ex. Q.6, Page 126]

Ans. The modern-day animals and their ancient fossils are listed in the following table:

S. No.	Animal	Fossils
(i)	Man	*Ramapithecus*
(ii)	Horse	*Eohippus*
(iii)	Dog	*Leptocyon*
(iv)	Camel	*Protylopus*
(v)	Elephant	*Deinotherium*
(vi)	Whale	*Protocetus*
(vii)	Fish	*Arandspis*
(viii)	Tetrapods	*Icthyostega*
(ix)	Bat	*Archaeonycteris*
(x)	Giraffe	*Palaeotragus*

Q. 7. Practice drawing various animals and plants. [NCERT Ex. Q.7, Page 126]

Ans. (i) Ask your teachers and parents to suggest the names of plants and animals and practice to draw them.

(ii) You can also take help from your book and internet to find the names of plants and animals.

Q. 8. Describe one example of adaptive radiation. **[NCERT Ex. Q.8, Page 126]**

Ans. (i) Adaptive radiation is an evolutionary process that produces new species from a single, rapidly diversifying lineage. This process occurs due to natural selection.

(ii) An example of adaptive radiation is Darwin finches, found in Galapagos Island.

(iii) A large variety of finches is present in Galapagos Island that arose from a single species, which reached this land accidentally. As a result, many new species have evolved, diverged and adapted to occupy new habitats. These finches have developed different eating habits and different types of beaks to suit their feeding habits. The insectivorous, blood sucking and other species of finches with varied dietary habits have evolved from a single seed eating finch ancestor.

Q. 9. Can we call human evolution as adaptive radiation? **[NCERT Ex. Q.9, Page 126]**

Ans. (i) No, we cannot call human evolution as adaptive radiation.

(ii) Because, adaptive radiation is an evolutionary process that produces new species from a single, rapidly diversifying lineage, which is not the case with human evolution.

(iii) Human evolution is a gradual process that took place slowly in time. It represents an example of anagenesis.

Q 10. Using various resources such as your school Library or the internet and discussions with your teacher, trace the evolutionary stages of any one animal, say horse. **[NCERT Ex. Q.10, Page 126]**

Ans. The evolution of horse started with Eohippus during Eocene period. It involved the following evolutionary stages:

(i) Gradual increase in body size.

(ii) Elongation of head and neck region.

(iii) Increase in the length of limbs and feet.

(iv) Gradual reduction of lateral digits.

(v) Enlargement of third functional toe.

(vi) Strengthening of the back. Pliohippus gave rise to Equus or the modern horse with one toe in each foot. They have incisors for cutting grass and molars for grinding food.

□□

HUMAN HEALTH AND DISEASES

CHAPTER 7

Health and Diseases

- Health is a state of complete physical, mental and social well-being.
- Health is affected by
  - Genetic disorders
  - Infections
  - Sedentary life style (Junk food, lack of exercise, habits etc).
- A disease can be defined as any condition that may lead to discomfort, distress, health problems or death of the affected person. It is related to the individuals only.

Types of Diseases

- **Congenital Diseases:** These are diseases which are present since birth. For instance, hole in the heart of an infant. They are caused by some genetic abnormalities or metabolic disorder or malfunctioning of an organ.
- **Acquired Diseases:** These are diseases which may occur after birth during one's lifetime. It is divided into two types, based on their ability or inability to spread from one individual to another.

(a) Infectious diseases: These are diseases which can be transmitted from diseased person to healthy person by means of infectious agents (or pathogens). e.g., tuberculosis, measles, malaria, etc. Infectious diseases are also known as communicable diseases.

(b) Non- infectious diseases: These are diseases which cannot be transmitted from an affected individual to a healthy person. For e.g., high blood pressure, cancer, allergy, obesity, etc. These are also known as non-communicable diseases.

Pathogens

- Pathogens are disease causing organisms.
- Parasites are pathogens as they harm the host by living in or on them.
- Pathogens have to adapt to life within the environment of the host.

Common Infectious Disases in Humans

1. Bacterial Diseases:

(a) Typhoid

- **Pathogen:** *Salmonella typhi*
- **Symptoms:** Sustained high fever (39°- 40°C), weakness, stomach pain, constipation, headache and loss of appetite. Intestinal perforation and death may occur.
- **Mode of transmission:** It enters the small intestine through food and water and migrates to other organs through blood.
- **Confirmatory test:** Widal test is used for confirmation of the disease.

(b) Pneumonia

- **Pathogen:** *Streptococcus* or *Diplococcus pneumoniae* and *Haemophilus influenzae.*
- **Symptoms:** Infects lung's alveoli. The alveoli get filled with fluid leading to respiratory problems, fever, chills, cough, and headache. In severe cases, lips and finger nails turn gray to bluish colour.
- **Mode of transmission:** Inhaling the droplets/aerosols released by an infected person. Sharing glasses and utensils with an infected person.

2. Viral Disease:

(a) Common cold

- **Pathogen:** Rhino viruses
- **Symptoms:** Infects nose and respiratory passage. Nasal congestion and discharge, sore throat, hoarseness, cough, headache, tiredness, etc. The disease last for 3-7 days.
- **Mode of transmission:** Inhaling droplets resulting from cough or sneezes of an infected person or transmitted through contaminated objects.

(b) Dengue

- **Pathogen:** DENV-1, DENV-2
- **Symptoms:** Nausea, vomiting, Aches and pain, rashes and most common symptom is fever.
- **Mode of transmission:** Biting of *Aedes sp.*

(c) Chikungunya

- **Pathogen:** Chikungunya virus(CHIKV)
- **Symptoms:** Most common symptoms are fever and joint pain, headache, muscle pain, joint swelling.
- **Mode of transmission:** Biting of *Aedes aegypti* and *A.albopictus.*

3. Protozoan diseases:

(a) Malaria

- **Pathogen:** *Plasmodium sp.* (*P. vivax, P. malariae, P. ovale.* and *P. falciparum*).
- **Symptoms:** Haemozoin causes chill and high fever recurring every 3-4 days.
- **Mode of transmission:** Biting of *Anopheles* mosquito.
- **Prevention:** Eradication of vector and keeping the surrounding clean.
- **Life cycle of *Plasmodium*:**

(a) Life cycle of *Plasmodium* starts with inoculation of sporozoites (infective stage) through the bite of infected female *Anopheles* mosquito.

(b) From the human blood, sporozoites reach the liver cells where they multiply.

(c) The liver cells rupture to liberate the parasites in the blood where they attack the RBCs, multiply and cause their rupture.

(d) The rupture is associated with the release of a toxin called haemozoin, which is responsible for the recurring chill and high fever within 3 - 4 days.

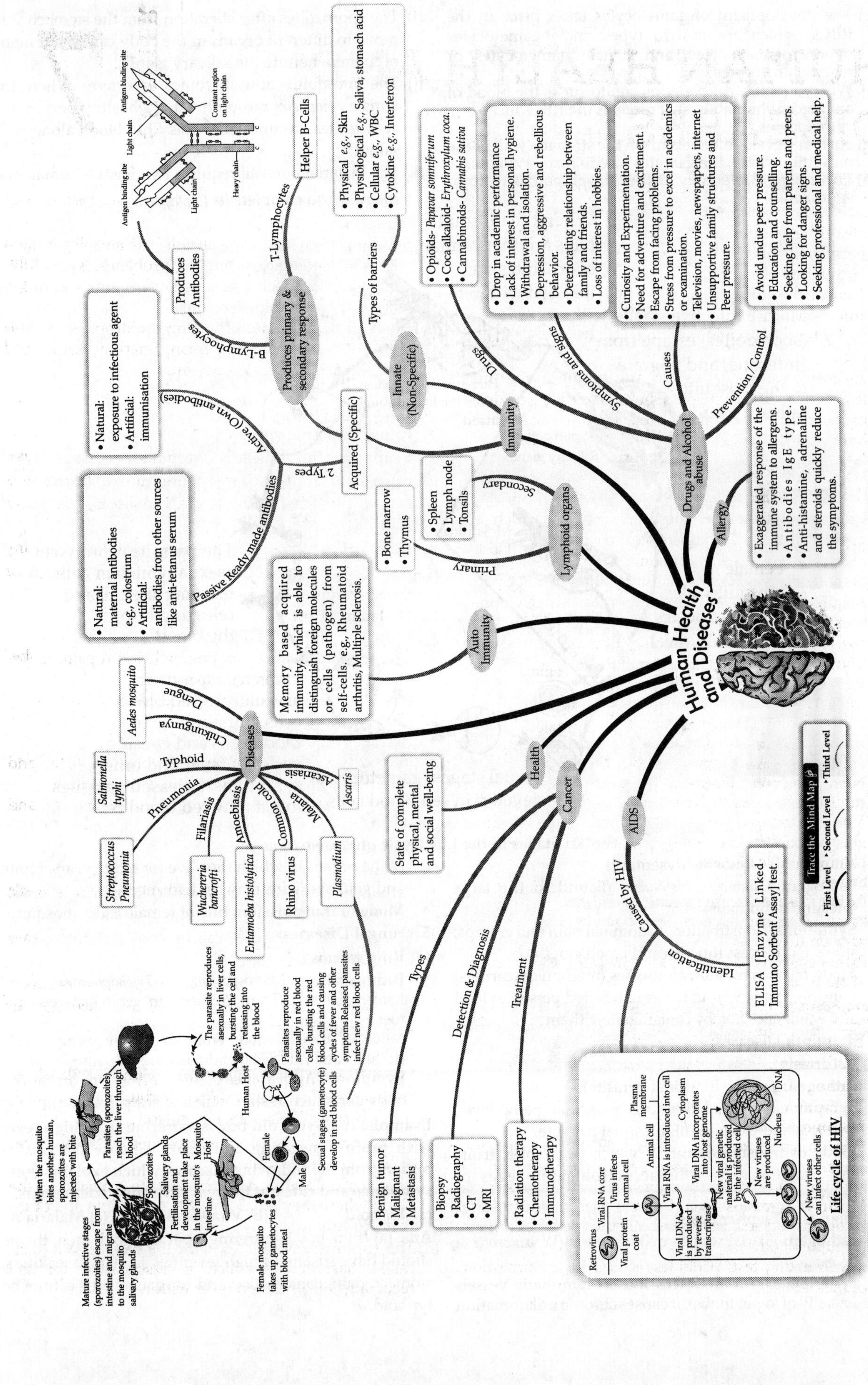
Human Health and Diseases
Immunity
Innate (Non-Specific)
Types of barriers
• Physical e.g., Skin
• Physiological e.g., Saliva, stomach acid
• Cellular e.g., WBC
• Cytokine e.g., Interferon
Acquired (Specific)
Produces primary & secondary response
T-Lymphocytes
Helper B-Cells
B-Lymphocytes
Produces Antibodies
Antigen binding site
Light chain
Heavy chain
Constant region on light chain
2 Types
Active (Own antibodies)
• Natural: exposure to infectious agent
• Artificial: immunisation
Passive Ready made antibodies
• Natural: maternal antibodies e.g., colostrum
• Artificial: antibodies from other sources like anti-tetanus serum
Lymphoid organs
Primary
• Bone marrow
• Thymus
Secondary
• Spleen
• Lymph node
• Tonsils
Auto Immunity
Memory based acquired immunity, which is able to distinguish foreign molecules or cells (pathogen) from self-cells. e.g., Rheumatoid arthritis, Multiple sclerosis.
Drugs and Alcohol abuse
Drugs
• Opioids- Papavar somniferum
• Coca alkaloid- Erythroxylum coca.
• Cannabinoids- Cannabis sativa
Symptoms and signs
• Drop in academic performance
• Lack of interest in personal hygiene.
• Withdrawal and isolation.
• Depression, aggressive and rebellious behavior.
• Deteriorating relationship between family and friends.
• Loss of interest in hobbies.
Causes
• Curiosity and Experimentation.
• Need for adventure and excitement.
• Escape from facing problems.
• Stress from pressure to excel in academics or examination.
• Television, movies, newspapers, internet
• Unsupportive family structures and Peer pressure.
Prevention / Control
• Avoid undue peer pressure.
• Education and counselling.
• Seeking help from parents and peers.
• Looking for danger signs.
• Seeking professional and medical help.
Allergy
• Exaggerated response of the immune system to allergens.
• Antibodies IgE type.
• Anti-histamine, adrenaline and steroids quickly reduce the symptoms.
Diseases
Dengue
Chikungunya
Aedes mosquito
Typhoid
Salmonella typhi
Pneumonia
Streptococcus Pneumonia
Filariasis
Wuchereria bancrofti
Amoebiasis
Entamoeba histolytica
Common cold
Rhino virus
Malaria
Plasmodium
Ascariasis
Ascaris
Mature infective stages (sporozoites) escape from intestine and migrate to the mosquito salivary glands
When the mosquito bites another human, sporozoites are injected with bite
Parasites (sporozoites) reach the liver through blood
Sporozoites
Salivary glands
Fertilisation and development take place in the mosquito's intestine
Mosquito Host
Female mosquito takes up gametocytes with blood meal
Human Host
The parasite reproduces asexually in liver cells, bursting the cell and releasing into the blood
Parasites reproduce asexually in red blood cells, bursting the red blood cells and causing cycles of fever and other symptoms Released parasites infect new red blood cells
Female
Male
Sexual stages (gametocyte) develop in red blood cells
Health
State of complete physical, mental and social well-being
Cancer
Types
• Benign tumor
• Malignant
• Metastasis
Detection & Diagnosis
• Biopsy
• Radiography
• CT
• MRI
Treatment
• Radiation therapy
• Chemotherapy
• Immunotherapy
AIDS
Caused by HIV
Identification
ELISA [Enzyme Linked Immuno Sorbent Assay] test.
Retrovirus
Viral RNA core
Viral protein coat
Virus infects normal cell
Animal cell
Plasma membrane
Viral RNA is introduced into cell
Cytoplasm
Viral DNA is produced by reverse transcriptase
Viral DNA incorporates into host genome
DNA
New viral genetic material is produced by the infected cell
Nucleus
New viruses are produced
New viruses can infect other cells
Life cycle of HIV
Trace the Mind Map
First Level
Second Level
Third Level

(e) The development of gametocytes takes place in the RBCs, which are of two types: male gametocytes or microgametocytes, and female gametocytes or macrogametocytes.

(f) When a female *Anopheles* mosquito sucks the blood of an infected human host, it receives the RBCs including gametocytes.

(g) Further development occurs in the stomach wall of the mosquito where, the gametes fuse to form a zygote.

(h) The zygote undergoes further development to form sporozoites.

(i) The sporozoites after liberation from the stomach wall move to different organs in the body cavity, but many of them penetrate the salivary glands.

(j) The mosquito now becomes infective. When the female *Anopheles* mosquito bites a healthy person, the sporozoites are injected in his / her blood along with saliva.

(k) The malarial parasite requires two hosts – human and *Anopheles*, to complete its life cycle.

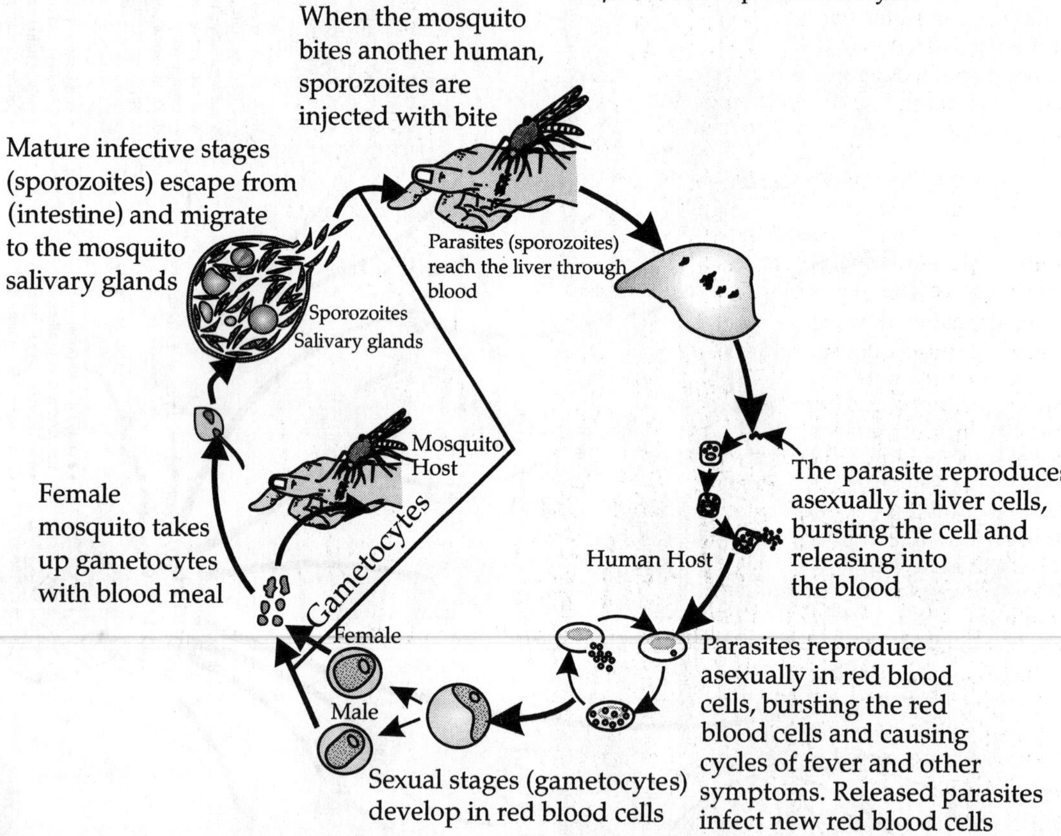

Fig 7.1: Stages in the Life Cycle of *Plasmodium*

(b) Amoebiasis (Amoebic dysentery)

- **Pathogen:** *Entamoeba histolytica* (Found in the large intestine of humans).
- **Symptoms:** Constipation, abdominal pain and cramps, stools with excess mucous and blood clots.
- **Mode of transmission:** Houseflies (mechanical carriers) transmit parasites from faeces of infected person to food and water and thereby contaminating them.

4. Helminth Diseases:

(a) Ascariasis

- **Pathogen:** *Ascaris* (Intestinal parasite).
- **Symptoms:** Internal bleeding, muscular pain, fever, anaemia and blockage of intestinal passage.
- **Mode of transmission:** Soil, water, vegetables, fruits etc. contaminated with faeces containing eggs of parasites.

(b) Filariasis (Elephantiasis)

- **Pathogen:** Filarial worms or *Wuchereria* (*W. bancrofti* & *W. malayi*).
- **Symptoms:** Filarial worms live in lymphatic vessels (usually of lower limbs). It causes chronic inflammation of the organs in which they live for many years. Limbs and genital organs may be deformed.
- **Mode of transmission:** Bite of female *Culex* mosquito.

5. Fungal Diseases:

(a) Ring worms

- **Pathogens:** *Microsporum*, *Trichophyton* and *Epidermophyton*. They are seen in groin between the toes.
- **Mode of transmission:** From soil or by using towels, clothes, comb, etc. Heat and moisture help fungi to grow.
- **Symptoms:** Appearance of dry, scaly lesions on various body parts such as skin, nails and scalp. Intense itching.

Example: A 17-year old boy is suffering from high fever with profuse sweating and chills. Choose the correct option from the following diseases which explains these symptoms and rule out the rest with adequate reasons.

(a) Typhoid **(b) Viral Fever** **(c) Malaria A**

Ans. (a) If the boy is suffering from Typhoid, then, the he should have sustained high fever (39° to 40°C), weakness, stomach pain, constipation and headache. So it cannot be typhoid.

(b) If the boy is suffering from viral fever, he will suffer from high fever, joint pain, weakness, and headache, So it cannot be viral fever.

(c) If the boy is suffering from Malaria, he should have high fever recurring with profuse sweating every three to four days associated with chills and headache. There is a possibility that he is suffering from Malaria because high fever associated with chills is possible with malaria.

Prevention and Control of Diseases

(a) Personal Hygiene: It includes cleanliness of body, drinking clean water, food etc.

(b) Public Hygiene: It includes :

- Proper disposal of wastes and excreta.
- Periodic cleaning and disinfection of water reservoirs, pools, cesspools and tanks (to control water-borne diseases).
- Avoid contact with infected persons or their belongings (to control air-borne diseases).
- Standard practices of hygiene in public catering.

(c) Control and eliminate the vectors (e.g., mosquitoes) and their breeding places by following methods:

- Avoid stagnation of water.
- Regular cleaning of household coolers.
- Use of mosquito nets.
- Introduce larvivorous fishes like *Gambusia* in ponds.
- Spraying insecticides in ditches, drainage and swamps.
- Doors and windows should be provided with wire mesh to prevent entry of mosquitoes.
- These precautions have become more important in the light of recent widespread incidences of the vector-borne (*Aedes* mosquitoes) diseases like dengue and chikungunya in many parts of India.

Immunity

- It is the ability of the immune system of the body to fight against the disease-causing organisms.
- It is divided into two types on the basis of immunity possessed by the body.

Scan to know more about this topic

Immunity and its types

(a) Innate Immunity:

- It is the non-specific defense present at the time of birth. It provides barriers to the entry of foreign agents into our body.
- **The four types of barriers are:**
  - **(i) Physical Barriers:** e.g., Skin covering of the body, mucus coating of the epithelium lining the respiratory, gastrointestinal and urogenital tracts.
  - **(ii) Physiological Barriers:** e.g., Acid in the stomach, saliva in the mouth, tears from eyes.
  - **(iii) Cellular Barriers:** e.g., monocytes and lymphocytes in blood.
  - **(iv) Cytokine Barriers:** e.g., Interferon. Interferons are proteins secreted by virus infected cells, which protect non-infected cells from further viral infection.

(b) Acquired Immunity

- It is a pathogen specific immunity.
- It is not present since birth but develops during the lifetime of an individual.
- It shows two types of responses: primary response and secondary response.
- It is characterised by memory i.e. during first encounter of a pathogen; our body produces a primary response in low intensity. Second encounter with the same pathogen produces a secondary (anamnestic) response in high intensity.
- The primary and secondary immune responses are carried out with B-lymphocytes and T-lymphocytes.

(a) B-lymphocytes: Shows humoral or Antibody Mediated Response/Antibody Mediated Immunity (AMI). In this, antibodies are found in blood plasma. So, it is called as humoral immune response. It includes B-lymphocytes and T-lymphocytes. The latter help the former to produce antibodies.

(b) T-lymphocytes: Shows cell mediated response. It is T-lymphocytes (T-cells) mediated (CMI). CMI causes graft rejection. The body is able to differentiate 'self' and 'non-self'. Tissue matching and blood group matching are essential before undertaking any graft/transplant. After this, the patient has to take immuno suppressants for all his life.

Structure of an antibody molecule

- Antibodies are protein molecules called immunoglobulins.
- In our body, there are different types of antibodies, such as IgG, IgA, IgM, IgE & IgD.
- Each antibody has four polypeptide chains namely, 2 small light chains and 2 large heavy chains. Both are arranged in the shape of 'Y', hence an antibody is represented by H_2L_2.

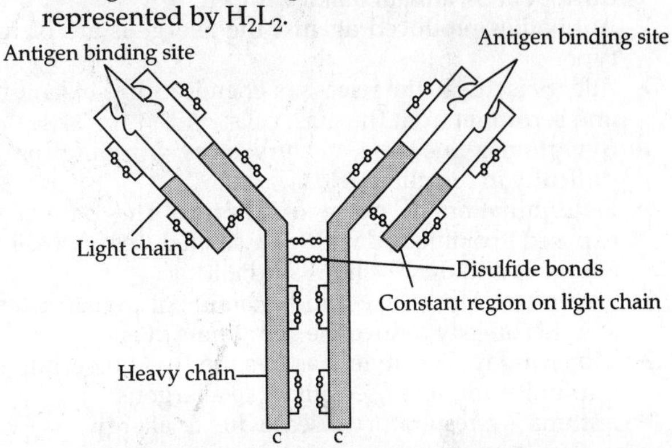

Fig 7.2: Structure of an antibody molecule

- On the basis of production of antibodies, acquired immunity can be further categorised as active and passive immunity.

(a) Active Immunity: In this, body produces its own antibodies against antigens. It is a slow process. It is produced by two ways :

(i) Natural active immunity, during natural infection by microbes.

(ii) Injecting the microbes deliberately during immunisation.

(b) Passive Immunity: Here, readymade antibodies are directly given to protect the body.

Example:

- Natural Passive Immunity : e.g., Antibodies (IgG) from mother → Placenta → Foetus → Antibodies (IgA) in colostrum → infants.
- Artificial Passive Immunity : e.g., Anti-tetanus serum (ATS).

Vaccination and Immunisation

➤ This is based on the property of 'memory' of the immune system.

➤ It is of two types, namely active immunisation and passive immunisation.

(a) Active Immunisation (Vaccination)

- A preparation of vaccine (antigenic proteins of pathogen or inactivated pathogen) is introduced into body.

- The antibodies produced in the body against the antigens neutralise the pathogenic agents during actual infection.
- The vaccines also generate memory B and T-cells that recognise the pathogen quickly on subsequent exposure, e.g., Polio vaccine, Hepatitis B vaccine, DPT vaccine etc.
- Vaccines are produced using DNA recombinant technology (e.g., Hepatitis B vaccine produced from Yeast). Such vaccines are called as second generation vaccines.
- The vaccines produced by conventional methods e.g., small pox-vaccines are called first generation vaccine and those which are synthetic vaccine are the third generation vaccine.

(b) Passive Immunisation

- It is the direct injection of pre-formed antibodies or antitoxin. It is for quick immune response e.g., Immunisation against Tetanus, snake venom, etc.

Allergies

➢ It is the exaggerated or hypersensitive response of the immune system to certain antigens present in the environment.

➢ Allergens are substances causing allergy, e.g., mites in dust, pollens, animal dander, fur, etc.

➢ Antibodies produced against the allergens are of IgE type.

➢ Allergy is due to the release of chemicals like histamine and serotonin from the mast cells.

➢ **Symptoms:** Sneezing, watery eyes, running nose, difficulty in breathing, etc.

➢ **Determination of cause of allergy:** The patient is exposed to or injected with very small doses of possible allergens and the reactions studied.

➢ **Treatment:** Drugs like anti-histamine, adrenaline and steroids quickly reduce the symptoms of allergy.

➢ Modern-day life style has resulted in lowering of immunity and more sensitivity to allergens.

➢ Asthma is a respiratory disease due to allergy.

Auto Immunity

➢ It is caused due to genetic and other unknown reasons. Body attacks self cells which results in damage to the body. This results in auto-immune disease. e.g., Rheumatoid disease.

➢ It is memory-based acquired immunity evolved in higher vertebrates based on the ability to differentiate foreign organisms (e.g., pathogens) from self-cells.

Immune System in the Body

➢ It is the system that gives immunity to the body by recognising, responding and remembering foreign antigens.

➢ It plays an important role in allergic reactions, auto-immune diseases and organ transplantations.

➢ It includes lymphoid organs, tissues, cells and soluble molecules like antibodies.

Scan to know more about this topic

Human Immune System

➢ **Lymphoid Organs:**

- These are the organs where origin, maturation and proliferation of lymphocytes occur.
- These are of two types namely, primary lymphoid organs and secondary lymphoid organs.

(a) Primary Lymphoid Organs

- Here, immature lymphocytes differentiate into antigen-sensitive lymphocytes, e.g., bone marrow and thymus.
- Bone marrow is the main lymphoid organ and is the site of formation of all the blood cells including lymphocytes.
- Thymus is large at the time of birth but keep reducing in size with age and by the time puberty is attained it reduces to a very small size.
- Development and maturation of T-lymphocytes takes place here.

(b) Secondary Lymphoid Organs

- After maturation in primary lymphoid organ, B-cells and T-cells migrate via blood and lymph to the secondary lymphoid organs where they interact with antigens and then proliferate to become effector cells e.g., Spleen, lymph nodes, tonsils, Peyer's patches of small intestine MALT and appendix.
- **Secondary lymphoid organs are:**

(i) Spleen:

- It is a bean-shaped organ.
- It contains lymphocytes and phagocytes.
- It removes worn-out RBCs and microorganisms from blood.
- It is a reservoir of erythrocytes in foetus.

(ii) Lymph Nodes

- These are found in lymphatic system.
- They trap microorganisms or other antigens that enter the lymph and tissue fluid.
- The trapped antigens activate lymphocytes and cause immune response.

(iii) Mucosa Associated Lymphoid Tissue (MALT):

- It is located within the lining of respiratory, digestive and urogenital tracts.
- It constitutes 50% of lymphoid tissue in human body.

AIDS (Acquired Immunodeficiency Syndrome)

➢ AIDS stands for Acquired immunodeficiency Syndrome.

➢ Syndrome means a group of symptoms.

➢ AIDS is the deficiency of immune system.

➢ It is caused by HIV (Human Immunodeficiency Virus), a retrovirus having RNA genome.

Scan to know more about this topic

AIDS

➢ AIDS was first reported in America (1981).

➢ **Mode of Transmission:**

- Sexual contact with infected person.
- Transfusion of contaminated blood and blood products.
- Sharing of infected injections.
- From infected mother to her child through placenta.

➢ **High risk of getting HIV includes:**

- Individuals with multiple sexual partners.
- Drug addicts who take drugs intravenously using infected syringes.
- Individuals who require repeated blood transfusion.
- Children born to an HIV infected mother.

➢ HIV does not spread by touch or physical contact. It spreads only through body fluids.

➢ There is always a time-lag (from few months to 5-10 years) between the infection and appearance of symptoms.

MNEMONICS

1. Concept Name: Primary Lymphoid Organs

Mnemonics: Profit **B**efore **T**ax

Interpretation: Primary : Bone marrow, Thymus

2. Concept Name: Secondary Lymphoid Organs

Mnemonics: Sea **S**urface **L**evel **T**emperature

Interpretation: Secondary : Spleen, Lymph nodes, Tonsils

➢ **Life Cycle of HIV Virus:** HIV enters into body → To macrophages (acts as HIV factory) → RNA genome replicates in presence of *Reverse transcriptase* to form viral DNA → Viral DNA incorporates into host DNA → Infected cells produce virus particles → HIV enters into helper T-cells (T_H) → Replicates and produce progeny viruses → Attack other helper T-cells → T-cells decrease → Weakens immunity.

Retro virus

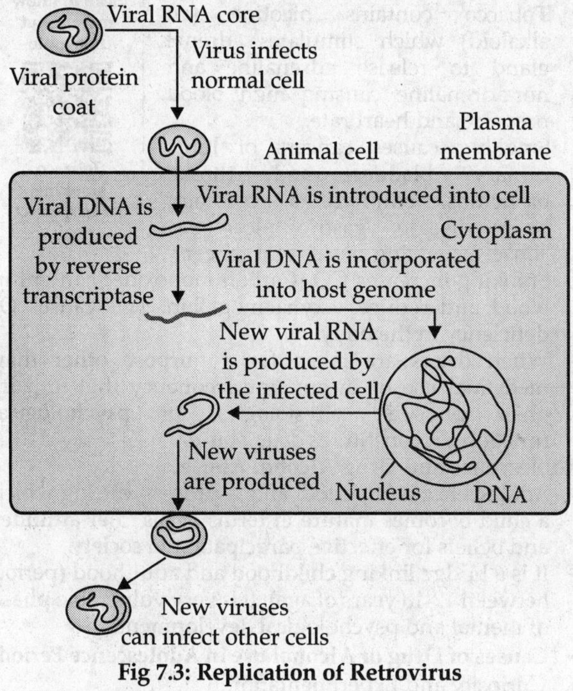

Fig 7.3: Replication of Retrovirus

➢ HIV infected person may be infected with *Mycobacterium*, viruses, fungi and parasites like *Toxoplasma*.

➢ **Diagnosis of AIDS:** ELISA test (Enzyme-Linked Immuno Sorbent Assay)

➢ **Treatment of AIDS**

(i) Anti-viral drugs partially effective.

(ii) They can only prolong the life of the patient.

➢ **Prevention of AIDS**

- Educate peoples about AIDS.
- Making blood (from blood banks) safe from HIV.
- Use of disposable needles and syringes.
- Advocating safe sex and free distribution of condoms.
- Controlling drug abuse.
- Regular check-ups for HIV in susceptible population.

➢ **Example: (i) HIV and Hepatitis-B are STDs. Mention the two other ways by which they can be transmitted to a healthy person.**

(ii) Why is early detection of STD essential? What can it lead to otherwise? Explain.

Ans. (i) HIV can also be transmitted to a healthy person by :

(a) Sharing of infected needles and surgical instruments.

(b) From infected mother to the foetus.

(c) Transfusion of infected blood.

(ii) Leads to complication in life later; pelvic inflammatory disease (PID)/abortion/ infertility/ cancer of reproductive tract, still birth, ectopic pregnancies. STDs are curable if detected early and treated properly otherwise they may lead to death.

Cancer

➢ Cancer is an abnormal and uncontrolled multiplication of cells resulting in the formation of tumor (masses of cells).

➢ Normal cells show a contact inhibition (contact with other cells inhibits their uncontrolled growth). Cancer cells do not have this property.

➢ Tumors are of two types namely, Benign tumour and Malignant tumour.

(a) Benign Tumour

- It remains confined to the place of its origin and do not spread to other parts of the body.
- It is harmless or cause less damage to the body.

(b) Malignant Tumour

- These are a mass of proliferating cells called neoplastic or tumour cells which grow very rapidly to invade and damage the surrounding normal tissues.
- Cells divides and invades new locations by getting transported through blood to distant places.
- It is harmful.

➢ **Metastasis:** It is the property of malignant tumour to invade the distant body parts, thereby initiating formation of new tumours.

➢ Cancer causing agents are called carcinogens.

➢ **Causes of Cancer (Carcinogens):**

(a) Physical agents: Ionising radiations like X-rays and gamma rays and non-ionising radiations like UV rays.

(b) Chemical agents: Tobacco smoke (major cause of lung cancer).

(c) Biological agents: e.g., oncogenic viruses, cellular oncogenes (*c-onc* or proto oncogenes), etc. When *c-onc* in normal cells are activated, the cells become oncogenic.

➢ **Cancer Detection and Diagnosis**

- Cancer detection is based on biopsy and histopathological studies of the tissue and blood and bone marrow tests for increased cell counts in the case of leukemias. In biopsy, a piece of the suspected tissue cut into thin sections is stained and examined under microscope (histopathological studies) by a pathologist.
- Techniques like radiography (use of X-rays), CT (computed tomography) and MRI (magnetic resonance imaging) are very useful to detect cancers

of the internal organs. Computed Tomography uses X-rays to generate a three-dimensional image of the internals of an object. MRI uses strong magnetic fields and non-ionising radiations to accurately detect pathological and physiological changes in the living tissue.
- Antibodies against cancer-specific antigens are also used for detection of certain cancers.
- Techniques of molecular biology can be applied to detect genes in individuals with inherited susceptibility to certain cancers.

➤ **Treatment of Cancer:** Most cancers are treated by combination of surgery, radiotherapy and chemotherapy.

(a) **Radiation therapy:** Tumour cells are irradiated lethally without damaging surrounding normal tissues.

(b) **Chemotherapy:** Use of chemotherapeutic drugs. Many drugs have side effects like hair loss, anaemia, etc.

(c) **Immunotherapy:** The patients are given biological response modifiers (e.g., α- interferon) which activates their immune system and helps in destroying the tumour.

MNEMONICS

Concept Name: Cancer: Detection and Diagnosis

Mnemonics: Book Reader Club Manager

Interpretation: Biopsy, Radiography, CT, MRI

Drugs

Scan to know more about this topic

Drugs - Opioids, Cannabinoids, Cocaine

➤ Drugs have the ability to alter the activity of nervous system.

➤ They are also called as psychotropic drugs or mood altering drugs or neurological drugs.

➤ These drugs change the mood, feeling behaviour and power of perception.

➤ The sources of most of the drugs are mainly flowering plants and some fungi.

➤ The drugs, which are commonly abused, are opioids, cannabinoids and coca alkaloids.

➤ These drugs are of following main types :

1. Opioids:
- **Opioids are drugs which bind to specific opioid receptors present in our central nervous system and gastrointestinal tract.**

  Examples:

■ **Morphine:** It is strong analgesic and sedative extracted from the latex of poppy plant (*Papaver somniferum*). They are useful during surgery.

■ **Heroin (Diacetyl morphine):**
- Commonly called as smack.
- It is chemically diacetyl morphine, obtained by acetylation of morphine.
- It is a depressant and slows down body functions. It is taken by snorting and injection.

2. Cannabinoids
- They are group of chemicals which interact with cannabinoid receptors present in brain.
- Natural cannabinoids are obtained from *Cannabis sativa* (Hemp plant).
- Its flower tops, leaves and resin are used to produce bhang, ganja, charas (hashish), marijuana, etc.
- Affects cardiovascular system of body.
- These days cannabinoids are being abused by some sportspersons.

3. Coca alkaloid (Cocaine or coke / crack)
- Obtained from coca plant (*Erythroxylum coca*).
- Interferes with transport of neurotransmitter dopamine.
- It is a stimulant and activates central nervous system, producing a sense of euphoria and increased energy.
- Its excessive dosage causes hallucinations.

4. Hallucinogens
- It is obtained from *Atropa belladonna* and *Datura* species.
- LSD (Lysergic Acid diethylamide) is obtained from fungus.
- Cause hallucinations, changing thoughts, feelings and perceptions

5. Tobacco

Scan to know more about this topic

Tobacco, smoking, drugs- Effect

- Tobacco contains nicotine (an alkaloid) which stimulates adrenal gland to release adrenaline and nor-adrenaline causing high blood pressure and heart rate.
- Smoking causes cancers of lung, urinary bladder and throat, bronchitis, emphysema, coronary heart disease, gastric ulcer etc. Tobacco chewing causes oral cancer.
- Smoking increases CO (Carbon monoxide) content in blood and reduces oxyhaemoglobin. This causes O_2 deficiency in the body.

➤ When drugs are taken for a purpose other than medicinal use or in amounts/frequency that impairs one's physical, physiological or psychological functions, it constitutes drug abuse.

Adolescence and Drug/Alcohol Abuse.

➤ Adolescence is 'a period' and 'a process' during which a child becomes mature in terms of his / her attitudes and beliefs for effective participation in society.

➤ It is a bridge linking childhood and adulthood (period between 12-18 years of age). It is very vulnerable phase of mental and psychological development.

➤ **Causes of Drug or Alcohol use in Adolescence Period:**
- Curiosity and Experimentation.
- Need for adventure and excitement.
- To escape facing problems.
- Stress from pressure to excel in academics or examination.
- Television, movies, newspapers, internet etc.
- Unstable or unsupportive family structures and peer pressure.

Addiction

➤ It is a psychological attachment (euphoria and a temporary feeling of well being) with drugs and alcohol.

➤ With repeated use of drugs, the tolerance level of the receptors increases. Thus, the receptors respond only to higher doses leading to greater intake and addiction.

Dependence

- It is the tendency of the body to manifest a characteristic and unpleasant withdrawal syndrome if regular dose of drugs / alcohol is abruptly discontinued.
- This results in anxiety, shakiness, nausea and sweating.
- Dependence leads to social adjustment problems.

Effects of Drug or Alcohol Abuse

- Reckless behaviour, vandalism and violence.
- Coma and death due to respiratory failure, heart failure or cerebral hemorrhage.
- Drugs together with alcohol may cause death.
- Drop in academic performance and absence from school.
- Lack of interest in personal hygiene.
- Withdrawal and isolation.
- Depression, fatigue, aggressive and rebellious behaviour, deteriorating relationship between family and friends.
- Loss of interest in hobbies.
- Fluctuations in sleeping, eating habits, weight, appetite, etc.
- Social problems like stealing and spread of infectious diseases (e.g., AIDS, hepatitis B).
- Damage of nervous system and cirrhosis.
- Use of drugs and alcohol by pregnant woman adversely affects the foetus.
- Misuse of drugs by athletes (e.g., narcotic analgesics, anabolic steroids, diuretics and certain hormones to increase muscle strength and bulk and to promote aggressiveness).

Prevention and Control

- Avoid undue peer pressure.
- Education and counselling.
- Seeking help from parents and peers.
- Looking for danger signs.
- Seeking professional and medical help.
- Psychologists and psychiatrists.
- De-addiction and rehabilitation programmes.

Scan to know more about this topic

Drug and alcohol abuse-Effect and Prevention

NCERT CORNER

Exercise Questions

Q. 1. What are the various public health measures, which you would suggest as safeguard against infectious diseases? [NCERT Ex. Q.1, Page 148]

Ans. (i) Public health measures are preventive measures which are taken to check the spread of various infectious diseases. These measures should be taken to reduce the contact with infectious agents.

(ii) Some of these methods are given below:

(a) Maintenance of personal and public hygiene:

1. It is one of the most important methods of preventing infectious diseases. It includes maintaining a clean body, consumption of healthy and nutritious food, drinking clean water, etc.

2. Public hygiene includes proper disposal of waste material, excreta, periodic cleaning, and disinfection of water reservoirs.

(b) Isolation: It is essential to keep the infected person in isolation to reduce the chances of spreading air-borne diseases such as pneumonia, chicken pox, tuberculosis, etc.

(c) Vaccination:

1. It is the protection of the body against communicable diseases. It is a process of injecting killed microbe in order to stimulate the immune system against the microbe, thereby preventing disease. It provides passive immunisation to the body.

2. Several vaccines are available against many diseases, for e.g., tetanus, polio, measles, mumps, etc.

(d) Vector eradication:

1. Vector is a carrier of diseases. Various diseases such as malaria, filariasis, dengue, and chikungunya spread through vectors. Thus, these diseases can be prevented by providing a clean environment and by preventing the breeding of mosquitoes.

2. This can be achieved by not allowing water to stagnate around residential areas.

3. Also, measures like regular cleaning of coolers, use of mosquito nets and insecticides such as malathion in drains, ponds, etc. can be undertaken to ensure a healthy environment.

4. Introducing larvivorous fish, such as *Gambusia* in ponds also controls the breeding of mosquito larvae in stagnant water.

Q. 2. In which way has the study of biology helped us to control infectious diseases? [NCERT Ex. Q.2, Page 148]

Ans. (i) Advancements achieved in biological science have helped us gain a better understanding to fight against various infectious diseases. Biology has helped us to study the life cycle of various parasites, pathogens, and vectors along with the modes of transmission of various diseases and the measures for controlling them.

(ii) Discovery of vaccines and their timely use in immunisation programmes have helped in controlling and even eradicating certain infectious diseases. These programmes against several infectious diseases such as small pox, chicken pox, tuberculosis, etc. have helped to eradicate these diseases.

(iii) Biotechnology has helped in the preparation of newer and safer drugs and vaccines. Discovery of antibiotics and other drugs have also played an important role in treating infectious diseases.

Q. 3. How does the transmission of each of the following diseases take place?

(a) Amoebiasis **(b) Malaria**

(c) Ascariasis **(d) Pneumonia**

[NCERT Ex. Q.3, Page 148]

Ans.

S. No.	Disease	Causative organism	Mode of transmission
(a)	Amoebiasis	*Entamoeba histolytica*	It is spread by means of contaminated food and water. The vector involved in the transmission of this disease is the housefly.
(b)	Malaria	*Plasmodium sp.*	It is a vector-borne disease that spreads by the biting of the female *Anopheles* mosquito.
(c)	Ascariasis	*Ascaris lumbricoides*	It spreads via contaminated food and water.
(d)	Pneumonia	*Streptococcus pneumoniae*	It spreads by the sputum of an infected person.

Q. 4. What measure would you take to prevent water-borne diseases? [NCERT Ex. Q.4, Page 148]

Ans. (i) Water-borne diseases such as cholera, typhoid, hepatitis B, etc. spread by drinking contaminated water.

(ii) These water-borne diseases can be prevented by ensuring proper disposal of sewage, excreta, periodic cleaning. Also, measures such as disinfecting community water reservoirs, boiling drinking water, etc. should be observed.

Q. 5. Discuss with your teacher what does 'a suitable gene' means, in the context of DNA vaccines. [NCERT Ex. Q.5, Page 148]

Ans. (i) A 'suitable gene' refers to a specific DNA segment which can be injected into the cells of the host body to produce specific proteins.

(ii) This protein kills the specific disease-causing organism in the host body and provides immunity.

Q. 6. Name the primary and secondary lymphoid organs. [NCERT Ex. Q.6, Page 148]

Ans. (a) Primary lymphoid organs include the bone marrow and the thymus.

(b) Secondary lymphoid organs are the spleen, lymph nodes, tonsils, Peyer's patches of small intestine, and appendix.

Q. 7. The following are some well-known abbreviations, which have been used in this chapter. Expand each one to its full form.

(a) MALT , (b) CMI, (c) AIDS, (d) NACO, (e) HIV [NCERT Ex. Q.7, Page 148]

Ans.

S. No.	Abbreviations	Expanded form	Description
(a)	MALT	Mucosa-Associated Lymphoid Tissue	• It is located within the lining of the major tracts- respiratory, digestive and urogenital tracts and constitutes the most extensive component of human lymphoid tissue. • These surfaces protect the body from an enormous quantity and variety of antigens.
(b)	CMI	Cell-Mediated Immunity	• It refers to protective mechanisms that are not primarily characterised by antibody. • It is responsible for detecting and destroying intracellular pathogens. • It is important for graft rejection and destruction of tumour cells and for delayed-type hypersensitivity reactions.
(c)	AIDS	Acquired Immuno-deficiency Syndrome	• It is the final stage of infection with HIV (Human immuno deficiency Virus). • It alters the immune system, making people more vulnerable to infections and diseases.
			• It spreads through unprotected sex with an infected person. It may also spread by sharing drug needles or through contact with the blood of an infected person.
(d)	NACO	National AIDS Control Organisation	• It is a division of the Ministry of Health and Family Welfare, Government of India. • It was established in 1992 with the aim of providing leadership to the HIV/AIDS control Programme in India. • It is headquartered at New Delhi.
(e)	HIV	Human Immuno deficiency virus	• It is retrovirus which causes AIDS. • It infects and destroys certain white blood cells called CD4+ cells.

Q. 8. Differentiate the following and give examples of each.

(a) Innate and acquired immunity

(b) Active and passive immunity

[NCERT Ex. Q.8, Page 148]

Ans. (a) Differences between innate and acquired immunity.

S. No.	Innate immunity	Acquired immunity
1.	It is a non–pathogen specific type of defense mechanism.	It is a pathogen specific type of defense mechanism.
2.	It is inherited from parents and protects the individual since birth.	It is acquired after the birth of an individual.
3.	It operates by providing barriers against the entry of foreign infectious agents.	It operates by producing primary and secondary responses, which are mediated by B–lymphocytes and T-lymphocytes.
4	It does not have a specific memory.	It is characterised by an immunological memory.

(b) Differences between active and passive immunity

S.No.	Active immunity	Passive immunity
1.	It is a type of acquired immunity in which the body produces its own antibodies against disease-causing antigens.	It is a type of acquired immunity in which readymade antibodies are transferred from one individual to another.
2.	It has a long-lasting effect.	It does not have long lasting effect.
3.	It is slow and takes time in producing antibodies and giving responses.	It is fast and provides immediate relief.
4.	Injecting microbes through vaccination inside the body is an example of active immunity.	Transfer of antibodies present in the mother's milk to the infant is an example of passive immunity.

Q. 9. Draw a well-labelled diagram of an antibody molecule. **[NCERT Ex. Q.9, Page 148]**

Ans. Structure of an antibody molecule: The protein is composed of four polypeptide chains (two identical heavy chains and two identical and smaller light chains) held together by disulphide bonds. The antigen-binding site is formed where a heavy-chain variable domain (VH) and a light-chain variable domain (VL) come close together. These are the domains that differ most in their sequence and structure in different antibodies.

For Diagram: Refer Revision notes/ Fig 7.2.

Q. 10. What are the various routes by which transmission of human immunodeficiency virus takes place?

[NCERT Ex. Q.10, Page 148]

Ans. (i) AIDS (Acquired Immuno Deficiency Syndrome) is caused by the Human immunodeficiency virus (HIV).

(ii) Mode of transmission of HIV:

(a) Unprotected sexual contact with an infected person.

(b) Transfusion of blood from a healthy to an infected person.

(c) Sharing infected needles and syringes.

(d) From an infected mother to a child through the placenta.

Q. 11. What is the mechanism by which the AIDS virus causes deficiency of immune system of the infected person? **[NCERT Ex. Q.11, Page 148]**

Ans. (i) AIDS (Acquired Immunodeficiency Syndrome) is caused by the Human immunodeficiency virus (HIV) via sexual or blood to blood contact.

(ii) Mechanism by which the AIDS virus causes deficiency of immune system:

(a) After entering the human body, the HIV virus attacks and enters the macrophages. Inside the macrophages, the RNA of the virus replicates with the help of enzyme reverse transcriptase and gives rise to viral DNA.

(b) Then, this viral DNA incorporates into the host DNA and directs the synthesis of virus particles.

(c) At the same time, HIV enters helper T- lymphocytes. It replicates and produces viral progeny there.

(d) These newly formed viral progeny get released into the blood and attacks other healthy helper T-lymphocytes in the body. As a result, the number of T-lymphocytes in the body of an infected person decreases progressively, thereby decreasing the immunity of a person.

Q. 12. How is a cancerous cell different from a normal cell? **[NCERT Ex. Q.12, Page 148]**

Ans.

S. No.	Normal cell	Cancerous cell
(i)	Normal cells show the property of contact inhibition. Therefore, when these cells come into contact with other cells, they stop dividing.	Cancerous cells lack the property of contact inhibition. Therefore, they continue to divide, thereby forming a mass of cells or tumour.
(ii)	They undergo differentiation after attaining a specific growth.	They do not undergo differentiation.
(iii)	These cells remain confined at a particular location.	These cells do not remain confined at a particular location. They move into neighbouring tissues and disturb its function.
(iv)	It does not have a specific memory	It is characterised by an immunological memory.

Q. 13. Explain what is meant by metastasis.

[NCERT Ex. Q.13, Page 148]

Ans. (i) Metastasis is a pathological process of spreading cancerous cells to the different parts of the body. The property of metastasis is exhibited by malignant tumours.

(ii) These cells divide uncontrollably, forming a mass of cells called tumour. From the tumour, some cells get sloughed off and enter into the blood stream. From there these cells reach distant parts of the body and initiate the formation of new tumours by dividing actively.

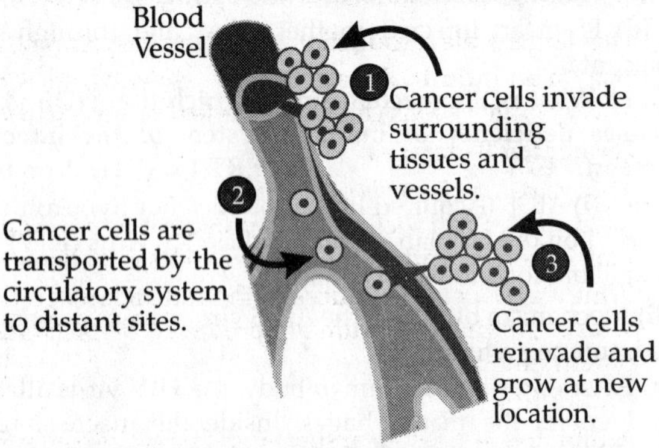

Process of metastasis

Q. 14. List the harmful effects caused by alcohol/drug abuse. **[NCERT Ex. Q.14, Page 148]**

Ans. Alcohol and drugs have several adverse effects on the individual, his family, and the society.

(i) Effects of alcohol:

(a) Effects on the individual: Alcohol has an adverse effect on the body of an individual. When an individual consumes excess alcohol, it causes damage to the liver and to the nervous system. As a result, other symptoms such as depression, fatigue, aggression, loss of weight, and appetite may also be observed in the individual. Sometimes, extreme levels of alcohol consumption may also lead to heart failure, resulting in coma and death. Also, it is advisable for pregnant women to avoid alcohol as it may inhibit normal growth of the baby.

(b) Effects on the family: Consumption of excess alcohol by any family member can have devastating effects on the family. It leads to several domestic problems such as quarrels, frustrations, insecurity, etc.

(c) Effects on the society:

1. Rash behaviour.
2. Malicious mischief and violence.
3. Deteriorating social network.
4. Loss of interest in social and other activities.

(ii) Effects of drugs: An individual who is addicted to drugs creates problems not only for himself but also for his family.

(a) Effects on the individual: Drugs have an adverse effect on the central nervous system of an individual. This leads to the malfunctioning of several other organs of the body such as the kidney, liver, etc. The spread of HIV is most common in these individuals as they share common needles while injecting drugs in their body. Drugs have long-term side effects on both males and females. These side effects include increased aggressiveness, mood swings, and depression.

(b) Effects on the family and society: A person addicted to drugs creates problems for his family and society. A person dependent on drugs becomes frustrated, irritated, and anti-social.

Q. 15. Do you think that friends can influence one to take alcohol/drugs? If yes, how may one protect himself/herself from such an influence?

[NCERT Ex. Q.15, Page 148]

Ans. (i) Yes, friends can influence one to take drugs and alcohol.

(ii) A person can take the following steps for protecting himself/herself against drug abuse:

(a) Increase your will power to stay away from alcohol and drugs. One should not experiment with alcohol for curiosity and fun.

(b) Avoid the company of friends who take drugs.

(c) Seek help from parents and peers.

(d) Take proper knowledge and counselling about drug abuse. Devote your energy in other extra-curricular activities.

(e) Seek immediate professional and medical help from psychologists and psychiatrists, if symptoms of depression and frustration become apparent.

Q. 16. Why is that once a person starts taking alcohol or drugs, it is difficult to get rid of this habit? Discuss it with your teacher. **[NCERT Ex. Q.16, Page 148]**

Ans. (i) Drug and alcohol consumption has an inherent addictive nature associated with euphoria and a temporary feeling of well-being.

(ii) Repeated intake of drugs increases the tolerance level of the body's receptors, leading to more consumption of drugs.

Q. 17. In your view what motivates youngsters to take to alcohol or drugs and how can this be avoided?

[NCERT Ex. Q.17, Page 148]

Ans. (i) Many factors are responsible for motivating youngsters towards alcohol or drugs, like curiosity, need for adventure and excitement, experimentation.

(ii) Some youngsters start consuming drugs and alcohol in order to overcome negative emotions (such as stress, pressure, depression, frustration) and to excel in various fields.

(iii) Several mediums like television, internet, newspaper, movies, etc. are also responsible for promoting the idea of alcohol to the younger generation. Amongst these factors, reasons such as unstable and unsupportive family structures and peer pressure can also lead an individual to be dependent on drugs and alcohol.

(iv) Preventive measures against addiction of alcohol and drugs:

(a) Parents should motivate and try to increase the will power of their child.

(b) Parents should educate their children about the ill-effects of alcohol. They should provide them with proper knowledge and counselling regarding the consequences of addiction to alcohol.

(c) It is the responsibility of the parent to discourage a child from experimenting with alcohol. Youngsters should be kept away from the company of friends who consume drugs.

(d) Children should be encouraged to devote their energy in other extra-curricular and recreational activities.

(e) Proper professional and medical help should be provided to a child if sudden symptoms of depression and frustration are observed.

CHAPTER 8

MICROBES IN HUMAN WELFARE

Microbes

- Microbes are very minute organisms which cannot be seen with the naked eyes but are viewed under the microscope.
- They are present everywhere such as in soil, water, air, inside our body and in and on the bodies of animals and plants.
- They are also present where no other life-form could possibly exist such as deep inside the geysers (thermal vents), where the temperature may be as high as 100°C, deep into the soil, under the layers of snow several metres thick and in highly acidic environments.
- Microbes are diverse group- **protozoa, bacteria, fungi and microscopic plants**.
- Microbes like bacteria and many fungi can be grown on nutritive media to form colonies that can be seen with the naked eyes. Such cultures are useful in studies of micro-organisms.
- Some microbes are harmful to the mankind, causing a number of infectious diseases but some are important in many ways for human welfare.
- **Viruses** are considered as intermediate between living and non-living organisms. **Viroids and also prions** are not considered as living entities, even though, they are considered as infectious agents.

Microbes in Household Products

- ***Lactobacillus* or Lactic Acid Bacteria (LAB)**
  - These bacteria grow in milk and convert it to the curd.
  - During its growth, it produces lactic acid that coagulates and partially digests the milk protein called **casein**.
  - It also improves the nutritional quality of curd by increasing vitamin B_{12}.
  - In our stomach too, it inhibits growth of pathogens.
- **Baker's Yeast (*Saccharomyces cerevisiae*):**
  - It is used to make bread by fermenting dough.
  - The puffed up appearance of dough is due to the production of CO_2 gas.
- **Toddy** is an alcoholic drink, made by fermenting flower sap of the palm tree by bacteria.
- Microbes are used to ferment fish, soyabean and bamboo-shoots to make foods.
- Microbes are used to produce cheese which are differing in flavour, taste and texture. e.g., Large holes in '**Swiss cheese**' are due to production of large amount of CO_2 by *Propionibacterium sharmanii* (a bacterium).
- '**Roquefort cheese**' is ripened by growing a specific fungus (*Penicillium roqueforti*) on them that gives them a particular flavour.

Microbes in Industrial Products

- The large scale production of beverages, antibiotics etc., on an industrial scale, requires growing microbes in very large vessels called **fermentors or bioreactors**.
- **Fermented Beverages**
  - The yeast *Saccharomyces cerevisiae* (Brewer's yeast) is used in the production of beverages by fermenting malted cereals and fruit juices to produce ethanol.
  - Wine and Beer are produced without distillation while, whisky , brandy and rum are produced by distillation of fermented broth.
- **Antibiotics**
  - Antibiotics are chemical substances produced by some microbes, that can kill or inhibit the growth of other disease-causing microorganisms.
  - They are used to treat plague, whooping cough, diphtheria, leprosy and many other infectious diseases.
  - **Penicillin was the first antibiotic discovered by Alexander Fleming in 1929**. It was a chance discovery.
  - **Discovery of Penicillin:** Alexander Fleming while working on *Staphylococci* bacteria, once observed a mould (*Penicillium notatum*) growing in one of his unwashed culture plates around which *Staphylococci* could not grow.
  - He found that it was due to chemical produced by the mould and he named it penicillin after the mould *Penicillium notatum.*
  - Later, Ernst Chain and Howard Florey established its full potential as an effective antibiotic.
  - Fleming, Chain and Florey were awarded Nobel Prize in 1945.

MNEMONICS

Concept Name: Organic Acid Microbes

Mnemonics: All Answers Clearly Labelled

Interpretation: Aspergillus niger, Acetobacter aceti, Clostridium butylicum, Lactobacillus

- **Chemicals, enzymes and other bioactive molecules**
  - **Organic Acids:** *e.g.*
    - *Aspergillus niger* (a fungus): Citric acid
    - *Acetobacter aceti* (a bacterium): Acetic acid
    - *Clostridium butylicum* (a bacterium): Butyric acid
    - *Lactobacillus* (a bacterium): Lactic acid

Scan to know more about this topic

Chemicals: Enzymes, Organic Acids

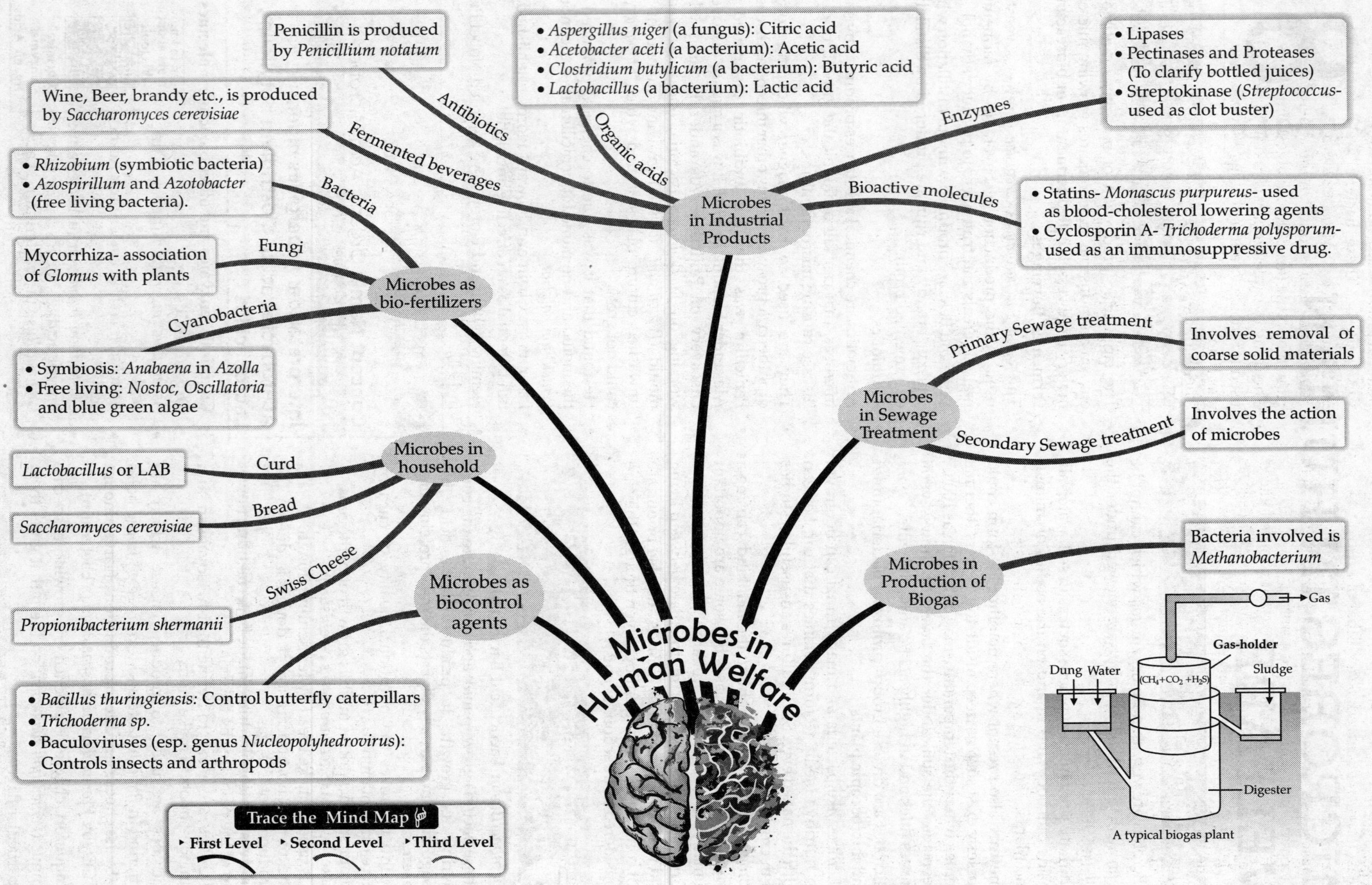
Microbes in Human Welfare
Microbes in Industrial Products
Antibiotics
Penicillin is produced by Penicillium notatum
Fermented beverages
Wine, Beer, brandy etc., is produced by Saccharomyces cerevisiae
Organic acids
• Aspergillus niger (a fungus): Citric acid
• Acetobacter aceti (a bacterium): Acetic acid
• Clostridium butylicum (a bacterium): Butyric acid
• Lactobacillus (a bacterium): Lactic acid
Enzymes
• Lipases
• Pectinases and Proteases (To clarify bottled juices)
• Streptokinase (Streptococcus- used as clot buster)
Bioactive molecules
• Statins- Monascus purpureus- used as blood-cholesterol lowering agents
• Cyclosporin A- Trichoderma polysporum- used as an immunosuppressive drug.
Microbes as bio-fertilizers
Bacteria
• Rhizobium (symbiotic bacteria)
• Azospirillum and Azotobacter (free living bacteria).
Fungi
Mycorrhiza- association of Glomus with plants
Cyanobacteria
• Symbiosis: Anabaena in Azolla
• Free living: Nostoc, Oscillatoria and blue green algae
Microbes in household
Curd
Lactobacillus or LAB
Bread
Saccharomyces cerevisiae
Swiss Cheese
Propionibacterium shermanii
Microbes as biocontrol agents
• Bacillus thuringiensis: Control butterfly caterpillars
• Trichoderma sp.
• Baculoviruses (esp. genus Nucleopolyhedrovirus): Controls insects and arthropods
Microbes in Sewage Treatment
Primary Sewage treatment
Involves removal of coarse solid materials
Secondary Sewage treatment
Involves the action of microbes
Microbes in Production of Biogas
Bacteria involved is Methanobacterium
Gas
Gas-holder
Dung Water
Sludge
(CH4+CO2 +H2S)
Digester
A typical biogas plant
Trace the Mind Map
First Level
Second Level
Third Level

- **Alcohol:**
- Yeast (*Saccharomyces cerevisiae*): Ethanol.
- **Enzymes:**
- **Lipases:** Used in the formation of detergents and help to remove oily stains from the laundry.
- **Pectinases and Proteases:** Used to clarify bottled juices.
- **Streptokinase:** Produced by *Streptococcus* and used as a '**clot buster**' to remove clots from the blood vessels of patients who have myocardial infections.
- **Bioactive molecules:**
- **Cyclosporine A:**
  * It is produced by *Trichoderma polysporum* (fungus).
  * It is used as an **immunosuppressive agent** in organ transplant patients.
- **Statins:**
  * It is produced by *Monascus purpureus* (a yeast).
  * It is used as lowering agent of blood cholesterol.
  * It inhibits the enzymes, responsible for synthesis of cholesterol.

Microbes in Sewage Treatment

➢ Sewage (municipal waste-water) contains large amount of human excreta, organic matter and microbes.

➢ Sewage is treated in Sewage Treatment Plants to make it less polluting.

➢ It includes stages namely primary treatment and secondary treatment.

(a) Primary Treatment

Scan to know more about this topic
Primary Sewage Treatment

- It is a physical treatment.
- It removes the large and small particles from sewage.
- It includes:
- Removal of floating debris by sequential filtration.
- Removal of the grit (soil and pebbles) by sedimentation.
- All solids that settle form the primary sludge and the supernatant forms the primary effluent.
- The effluent is taken for secondary treatment.

(b) Secondary treatment (Biological treatment)

- The primary effluent is passed into large aeration tanks and constantly agitated.
- This allows vigorous growth of useful aerobic microbes into flocs (masses of bacteria associated with fungal filaments to form mesh-like structures).
- These microbes consume the major part of the organic matter in the effluent.
- This reduces the **BOD (Biochemical Oxygen Demand)** of the effluent.
- The effluent is then passed into a settling tank, where the bacterial 'flocs' are allowed to sediment.
- This sediment is called '**activated sludge**'.
- A small part of the activated sludge is pumped back into the aeration tank to serve as the inoculum.
- The remaining major part of the sludge is pumped into large tanks called **anaerobic sludge digesters.**
- Here, some anaerobic bacteria digest the bacteria and fungi in the sludge by producing gases like CH_4, H_2S and CO_2. These gases form the biogas.
- The effluent from secondary treatment plant is released into natural water bodies like rivers and streams.

Microbes in Production of Biogas

➢ Biogas is a mixture of gases (mainly CH_4) produced by the microbial activity. It is used as fuel for cooking and lighting.

➢ Certain bacteria which grow anaerobically on cellulosic material produce large amount of methane along with CO_2 and H_2. These bacteria are collectively called **Methanogens**. e.g., *Methanobacterium.*

➢ *Methanobacterium* is found in the anaerobic sludge and rumen of cattle (for cellulose digestion).

➢ The dung of cattle (gobar) is rich in these bacteria and used for the generation of biogas (Gobar gas).

Biogas Plant

Scan to know more about this topic
Biogas Plant

➢ The technology of biogas production was developed in India mainly due to efforts of Indian **Agricultural Research Institute (IARI)**, and **Khadi and Village Industries Commission (KVIC)**.

➢ **A biogas plant consists of:**

(a) A concrete tank: It is 10-15 feet deep and collects bio-wastes and slurry of dung.

(b) A floating cover: A floating cover is placed over the slurry, which keeps on rising as the biogas is produced due to microbial activity.

(c) An outlet: It is connected to a pipe to supply biogas to nearby house. An outlet is used to remove spent slurry (used as fertilizer).

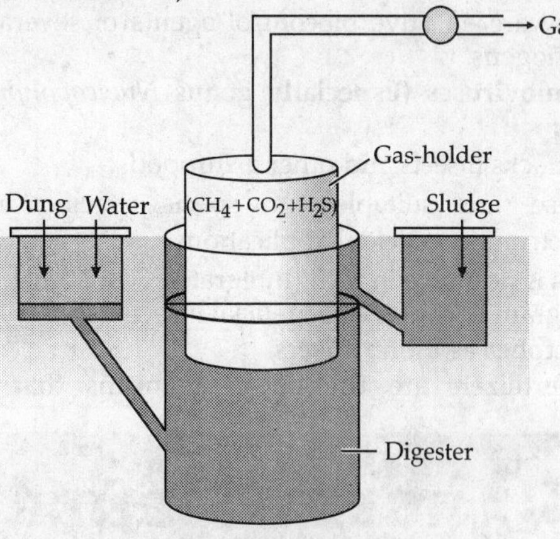

Fig. 8.1: A Biogas plant

Biocontrol agents

➢ It means the use of biochemical method for controlling plant diseases and pests.

➢ The chemicals which are used as pesticides and insecticides are toxic and harmful to all organisms including human beings and causes pollution.

➢ Biological control of pests and disease is a method of controlling pest on natural predation rather than chemicals. The organic farmer creates a system where the pests are not eradicated but kept at manageable level by complex system for check and balance within the living ecosystem.

MNEMONICS

Concept Name: Microbial Biocontrol Agents

Mnemonics: Back To Back

Interpretation: *Bacillus thuringiensis*, *Trichoderma* sp., Baculoviruses

Microbial biocontrol agents

➢ **Lady bird** is used to control aphids.

➢ **Dragon fly** is used to control mosquitoes.

➢ ***Bacillus thuringiensis* (Bt):**

- *Bacillus thuringiensis* is a common biological pesticide. This is to control butterfly caterpillar. These are available in sachets as dried spores which are mixed with water and sprayed on to vulnerable plants such as *Brassica* and fruit trees, where these are eaten by the insect larvae.
- In produces *insecticidal* proteins which kills certain insect such as *lepidopterans, coleoptera* and dipterans.
- In the gut of the larvae, the inactive toxin of Bt becomes active and thus, the larvae get killed.
- The scientists have introduced *B. thuringiensis* toxin genes into plants, e.g., Bt cotton.

Scan to know more about this topic

Biocontrol agents

➢ ***Trichoderma* sp (Fungus):**

- These are free livings species that are seen in the root ecosystems.
- They are effective biocontrol agents of several plant pathogens.

➢ **Baculoviruses (Especially genus *Nucleopolyhedrovirus*):**

- It attacks insects and other arthropods.
- These are suitable for species-specific, narrow spectrum insecticidal applications.
- This is desirable in IPM (Integrated Pest Management) program to conserve beneficial insects.

Microbes as Biofertilisers

➢ Biofertilizers are the micro-organisms that enrich nutrient quality of the soil.

➢ The main sources of biofertilizers are bacteria, fungi, cyanobacteria etc.

(i) Bacteria:

- **Symbiosis:** The root nodules formed by *Rhizobium* bacterium on root of leguminous plant increases the nitrogen level of soil. *Rhizobium* is a symbiotic bacterium that has the ability to fix atmospheric nitrogen.
- **Free-living bacteria:** *Azospirillum* and *Azotobacter* are free living bacteria that live in soil and enrich the nitrogen content of the soil.

(ii) Fungi:

- **Symbiosis:** Symbiotic association of fungi (e.g., the genus of *Glomus*) with the roots of angiospermic plants (mycorrhiza) also increases the fertility of the soil
- The fungal symbiont help to absorb phosphorous from soil and passes it to the plant, give resistance to root borne pathogens, tolerance to salinity and drought and also gives an overall increase in plant growth and development. The plant in return provides sugar and food to the fungus.

(iii) Cyanobacteria (Blue green algae):

- **Symbiosis:** *Anabaena* in *Azolla.*
- **Free living:** *Nostoc, Oscillatoria* and Blue green algae.

MNEMONICS

Concept Name: Cyanobacteria (Blue Green Algae Example)

Mnemonics: After Nasa's Operation

Interpretation: Anabaena, Nostoc, Oscillatoria

NCERT CORNER

Exercise Questions

Q. 1. Bacteria cannot be seen with the naked eyes, but these can be seen with the help of a microscope. If you have to carry a sample from your home to your biology laboratory to demonstrate the presence of microbes under a microscope, which sample would you carry and why? [NCERT Ex. Q.1, Page 159]

Ans. **(i)** Curd can be easy to carry from home to laboratory as a sample for the study of microbes. It contains numerous lactic acid bacteria (LAB) or *Lactobacillus,* which produce acids that coagulate and digest milk proteins called casein.

(ii) A small drop of curd contains millions of bacteria, which can be easily observed under a microscope.

Q. 2. Give examples to prove that microbes release gases during metabolism. [NCERT Ex. Q.2, Page 159]

Ans. Microbes that releases gases during metabolism are as follows:

(i) Bacteria and fungi carry out the process of fermentation and during this process, they release carbon dioxide.

(a) Fermentation is the process of converting a complex organic substance into a simpler substance with the action of bacteria or yeast.

(b) Fermentation of sugar produces alcohol with the release of carbon dioxide and very little energy.

$$\text{Glucose} \xrightarrow[\text{oxygen}]{\text{without}} \text{Alcohol+Energy+}CO_2$$

(c) The dough used for making *idli* and *dosa* gives a puffed appearance. This is because of the action of bacteria which releases carbon dioxide. This CO_2 released from the dough gets trapped in the dough, thereby giving it a puffed appearance.

(d) During secondary treatment of sewage in sewage treatment plants, a number of gases like methane are produced during microbial digestion of organic compounds.

Q. 3. In which food would you find lactic acid bacteria? Mention some of their useful applications. [NCERT Ex. Q.3, Page 159]

Ans. (i) Lactic acid bacteria (LAB) are commonly found in curd. It is also found in the human stomach where these prevent the growth of certain disease-causing microbes.

(ii) Application of lactic acid bacteria:

(a) It plays an important role in curdling of milk. Under suitable condition, these bacteria multiply and produce acids which coagulate and partially digest the milk proteins and change the milk into curd.

(b) It also increases the content of vitamin B_{12} in curd.

Q. 4. Name some traditional Indian foods made of wheat, rice and Bengal gram (or their products) which involve use of microbes.

[NCERT Ex. Q.4, Page 159]

Ans. Traditional Indian foods made of

(i) Wheat: Bread, Bhatura, Jalebi, cake, etc.

(ii) Rice: Idli, dosa, etc.

(iii) Bengal gram: Dhokla, Khandvi, etc.

Q. 5. In which way have microbes played a major role in controlling diseases caused by harmful bacteria?

[NCERT Ex. Q.5, Page 159]

Ans. (i) Microbes played a major role in controlling diseases caused by harmful bacteria by producing antibiotics.

(ii) Antibiotics are the chemical substances which are derived from certain useful microbes and are employed to kill or retard the growth of disease-causing microbes.

(iii) These medicines are commonly obtained from bacteria and fungi. They either kill or stop the growth of disease-causing micro-organisms.

(iv) Example of antibiotics are streptomycin, tetracycline and penicillin. So, antibiotics are being used in controlling a number of bacterial diseases like cholera, pneumonia, typhoid, syphilis, whooping cough, diphtheria, etc.

(v) Antibiotics destroy bacteria by weakening their cell walls as a result of which certain immune cells such as the white blood cells enter the bacterial cell and cause cell lysis.

Q. 6. Name any two species of fungus, which are used in the production of the antibiotics.

[NCERT Ex. Q.6, Page 159]

Ans. (i) Antibiotics are medicines that are produced by certain micro-organisms to kill other disease-causing micro-organisms. These medicines are commonly obtained from bacteria and fungi.

(ii) The species of fungus used in the production of antibiotics are:

S. No.	Fungus species	Antibiotics
(a)	*Penicillium notatum*	Penicillin
(b)	*Penicillium griseofulvin*	Griseofulvin
(c)	*Cephalosporium acremonium*	Cephalosporin

Q. 7. What is sewage? In which way can sewage be harmful to us? [NCERT Ex. Q.7, Page 159]

Ans. (i) Sewage is the municipal waste water containing human excreta. It contains large amount of biodegradable organic matter which when decomposed by naturally occurring microbes in the presence of oxygen, leads to sharp decline in dissolved oxygen (DO). This causes suffocation of large number of aquatic animals like prawns, fishes, etc. Such water become unfit for human consumption.

(ii) Sewage also contains many types of pathogenic micro-organisms which are responsible for causing diseases like cholera, typhoid, dysentery, hepatitis, etc.

(iii) Sewage water is a major cause of polluting drinking water. Hence, it is essential that sewage water is properly collected, treated and disposed.

Q. 8. What is the key difference between primary and secondary sewage treatment?

[NCERT Ex. Q.8, Page 159]

Ans. Differences between primary and secondary sewage treatment are as follows:

S. No.	Primary sewage treatment	Secondary sewage treatment
(i)	It is a mechanical process involving the removal of coarse particles.	It is a biological process involving the action of microbes.
(ii)	It is inexpensive and relatively less complicated.	It is a very expensive and complicated process.

Q. 9. Do you think microbes can also be used as source of energy? If yes, how? [NCERT Ex. Q.9, Page 159]

Ans. (i) Yes, microbes can be used as a source of energy. Bacteria such as *Methanobacterium* is used for the generation of gobar gas or biogas.

(ii) Biogas is produced from the degradable organic matter by the activity of various anaerobic micro-organisms present in cow dung. The micro-organisms involved in biogas production are mainly facultative or strictly anaerobic bacteria.

(iii) The major component of biogas is methane (~50–68%) which is highly inflammable. Other gases are carbon dioxide (25–35%), hydrogen (1–5%), nitrogen (2–7%), oxygen (0–0.1%) and (traces).

(iv) The generation of biogas is an anaerobic process in a biogas plant, which consists of a concrete tank (10–15 feet deep) with sufficient outlets and inlets.

(v) The dung is mixed with water to form the slurry and fed into the tank. The digester of the tank is filled with numerous anaerobic methane-producing bacteria, which produce biogas from the slurry. Biogas can be removed through the pipe which is then used as a source of energy, while the consumed slurry is removed from the outlet and is used as a fertilizer.

(vi) Biogas is used as fuel for heating and cooking, lighting, power for irrigation and other purposes as an alternative of fire wood, kerosene, dung cakes or even electricity and liquefied petroleum gas (LPG). It is considered as eco-friendly and pollution free source of energy.

Q. 10. Microbes can be used to decrease the use of chemical fertilisers and pesticides. Explain how this can be accomplished.

[NCERT Ex. Q.10, Page 159]

Ans. (i) Microbes plays an important role in organic farming, which is done without the use of chemical fertilisers and pesticides. Organic farming can be done by using biofertilizers.

(ii) Biofertilizers are the organisms that enrich the nutrient quality of the soil. The main sources of biofertilisers are bacteria, fungi and *Cyanobacteria.*

(iii) They increase the fertility of soil. It involves the selection of useful micro-organisms, that help in improving plant growth through the supply of plant nutrients.

(iv) Many species of bacteria and cyanobacteria have the ability to fix free atmospheric nitrogen.

(v) They can also act as biopesticides to control insect pests in plants (*e.g., Bacillus thuringiensis*) which produces a toxin that kills the insect pests. Similarly, *Trichoderma,* free living fungi, live in the roots of higher plants and protect them from various pathogens.

(vi) *Baculovirus* is another biopesticide that is used as a biological control agent against insects and other arthropods.

Q. 11. Three water samples namely river water, untreated sewage water and secondary effluent discharged from a sewage treatment plant were subjected to BOD test. The samples were labelled A, B and C; but the laboratory attendant did not note which was which. The BOD values of the three samples A, B and C were recorded as 20 mg/L, 8 mg/L and 400 mg/L, respectively.
Which sample of the water is most polluted? Can you assign the correct label to each assuming the river water is relatively clean? [NCERT Ex. Q.11, Page 159]

Ans. (i) BOD refers to the amount of the oxygen that would be consumed if all the organic matter in one litre of water were oxidised by bacteria. The BOD test measures the rate of uptake of oxygen by micro-organisms in a sample of water and thus, indirectly indicate the amount of organic wastes present in the water. The greater the BOD of waste water, more is its polluting potential.

(ii) On the basis of this criterion, it can be concluded in the given table.

Label	BOD value (mg/L)	Sample	Reason
A	20	Secondary effluent discharge from a sewage treatment plant	Because it comes after the primary treatment and is with less organic matter than untreated sewage water so has less BOD (i.e., 20 mg/L).
B	8	River water	It has minimum BOD (i.e., 8 mg/L) and it has been assumed that river water is relatively clean so BOD sample is of river water.
C	400	Untreated sewage water	Because such sewage water has highest quantities of organic matter and so has highest BOD value (i.e., 400 mg/L).

Q. 12. Find out the name of the microbes from which Cyclosporine A (an immunosuppressive drug) and Statins (blood cholesterol lowering agents) are obtained. [NCERT Ex. Q.12, Page 160]

Ans. (i) Cyclosporin A : It is an immunosuppressive drug which is produced by fungus *Trichoderma polysporum*.

(ii) Statin : It is a blood cholesterol lowering agents which is produced by the yeast *Monascus purpureus.*

Q. 13. Find out the role of microbes in the following and discuss it with your teacher.
(a) Single cell protein (SCP)
(b) Soil [NCERT Ex. Q.13, Page 160]

Ans. (a) Single cell protein (SCP).

1. A single cell protein is that protein, obtained from certain microbes, which forms an alternate source of proteins in animal feeds.

2. It contains about 45–55% proteins. So, it is a protein-rich powder and is an ideal supplement to conventional food supply.

3. It can be used to solve the problem of protein deficiency in the children of developing countries.

4. Most commonly employed bacterial strains to produce SCP are *Methylophilus, Paecilomyces, Chlorella, Spirulina,* etc.

(b) Soil

1. Soil contains a number of useful as well as harmful microbes. Many species of bacteria and cyanobacteria have the ability to fix atmospheric nitrogen into usable form.

2. Microbes play an important role in maintaining soil fertility. They help in the formation of nutrient-rich humus by decomposition.

3. The economically useful bacteria include the following :

- **Ammonifying bacteria:** These bacteria decompose the proteins of dead organisms and nitrogenous wastes of animals to ammonia (*e.g., Bacillus ramosus* and *B. vulgari*).
- **Nitrifying bacteria:** They oxidise ammonia to nitrites (*e.g., Nitrosomonas* and *Nitrobacter*).
- **Nitrates fixing bacteria:** These fix the atmospheric nitrogen as ammonia by the reduction process (*e.g., Rhizobium, Azotobacter* and *Clostridium*).

Q. 14. Arrange the following in the decreasing order (most important first) of their importance, for the welfare of human society. Give reasons for your answer.
Biogas, Citric acid, Penicillin and Curd
[NCERT Ex. Q.14, Page 160]

Ans. (i) The order of arrangement of products according to their decreasing importance is : Penicillin > Biogas > Curd > Citric acid.

(ii) It is so because :

(a) Penicillin, commonly called wonder drug, is a wide-spectrum antibiotic and is used to control a number of human diseases like syphilis, gonorrhoea, diphtheria, lung infections, etc.

(b) Biogas, produced from dung of cattle by the methanogens, is an alternative source of energy, especially in the rural areas. It is an ecofriendly source of energy. Its production also provides slurry which can be used as a manure to increase the soil fertility and crop yield.

(c) Curd: It is a milk product very commonly used in almost all the houses. It is obtained by the action of *Lactobacillus* bacteria on milk.

(d) Citric acid: It is least important but can be used as a food preservative.

Q. 15. How do biofertilizers enrich the fertility of the soil?
[NCERT Ex. Q.15, Page 160]

Ans. (i) Biofertilizers are cost effective and eco-friendly. They are living organisms which help in increasing the fertility of soil.

(ii) It includes the selection of useful micro-organisms that help in improving the plant growth through the supply of plant nutrients. These are introduced to seeds, roots, or soil to mobilise the availability of nutrients by their biological activity. Thus, they are extremely beneficial in enriching the soil with organic nutrients.

(iii) Many species of bacteria and cyanobacteria have the ability to fix free atmospheric nitrogen. For examples,

(a) *Rhizobium* is a symbiotic bacterium found in the root nodules of leguminous plants.

(b) *Azospirillium* and *Azotobocter* are free living nitrogen-fixing bacteria, whereas *Anabaena*, *Nostoc*, and *Oscillatoria* are examples of nitrogen-fixing cyanobacteria.

□□

CHAPTER 9

BIOTECHNOLOGY: PRINCIPLES AND PROCESSES

Biotechnology

- Biotechnology is the manipulation of living organisms and their genome for the welfare of human beings.
- It deals with different techniques of using live organisms or their enzymes for products and different processes.
- **The European Federation of Biotechnology** (EFB) defines Biotechnology as **'the integration of natural science and organisms, cells, parts thereof, and molecular analogues for products and services'.**
- **Biotechnology deals with:**
  - Microbe-mediated processes (making curd, bread, wine, etc).
  - *In vitro* fertilization ('test-tube' baby programme).
  - Synthesising a gene and using it.
  - Preparation of a DNA vaccine.
  - Correcting a defective gene.

Principles of Biotechnology

- **The two core techniques of modern biotechnology are:**

Scan to know more about this topic

Basic Concepts of Biotechnology

(a) Genetic engineering: It is the technique in which the genetic material (DNA and RNA) is chemically altered and introduced into host organisms to change its phenotype.

(b) Maintenance of sterile ambience: It is necessary in chemical engineering processes for growing only the desired microbe / eukaryotic cell in large quantities for the manufacture of antibiotics, vaccines, enzymes, etc.

- Genetic engineering offers a solution to the limitations of traditional techniques, where both desired and undesired genes often propagate together. It enables us to selectively isolate and introduce only the desired genes or a specific set of genes into the target organism, without the risk of introducing unwanted genes.
- In a chromosome, there is a specific DNA sequence called the origin of replication, which helps in initiating replication. Therefore, for the multiplication of any alien piece of DNA in an organism, it needs to be a part of chromosome which has specific sequence known as 'origin of replication'. Thus, an alien DNA is linked with the origin of replication, so that this alien piece of DNA can replicate and multiply itself in the host organisms. This process is known as cloning.
- The construction of the first recombinant DNA emerged from the possibility of linking a gene of antibiotic resistance with a native plasmid of *Salmonella typhimurium*.
- The cutting of DNA at specific locations became possible with the discovery of the restriction enzymes (also called Molecular scissors).
- The cut piece of DNA was linked with the plasmid DNA, with the help of another enzyme called **DNA ligase**. These plasmid DNA act as vectors to transfer the piece of DNA attached to it.
- A plasmid is a small , circular and double stranded DNA. It can be used as vector to deliver an alien piece of DNA into the host organisms.
- Vector is a DNA molecule which acts as a vehicle to carry a particular DNA segment into a host cell.
- Recombinant DNA technology also called **Genetic engineering**, deals with the production of new combinations of genetic material in the laboratory. These recombinant DNA (rDNA) molecules are introduced into host cells, where they can be propagated and multiplied.
- **Stanley Cohen and Herbert Boyer** (1972) constructed first recombinant DNA. They isolated the antibiotic resistance gene by cutting out a piece of DNA from a plasmid.

Steps involved in Genetically Modifying an Organism

- There are three basic steps in genetically modifying an organism:

(a) Identification and isolation of DNA with desirable genes.

(b) Introduction of the identified DNA into the host.

(c) Maintenance of introduced DNA into the host and transfer of the DNA to its progeny.

MNEMONICS

Concept Name: Enzymes Used in Biotechnology

Mnemonics: LiLY Rose Scent: Rose Daisy Carnation Sunflower

Interpretation:

Enzymes	**: Uses**
Ligase	**: DNA Repair enzyme**
Lyases	**: Dissolve cell wall**
Restriction enzymes	**: Cleaves DNA**
Synthetase	**: In-vitro DNA Synthesis**

- **Tools of Recombinant DNA technology**

1. Restriction Enzymes ('Molecular scissors')

- The restriction enzymes are called molecular scissors and are responsible for cutting of DNA.
- In 1963, two enzymes responsible for restricting the growth of bacteriophage in *E. coli* were isolated. One of these added methyl groups to DNA and the other (restriction endonuclease) cut DNA.

Scan to know more about this topic

Restriction Enzymes

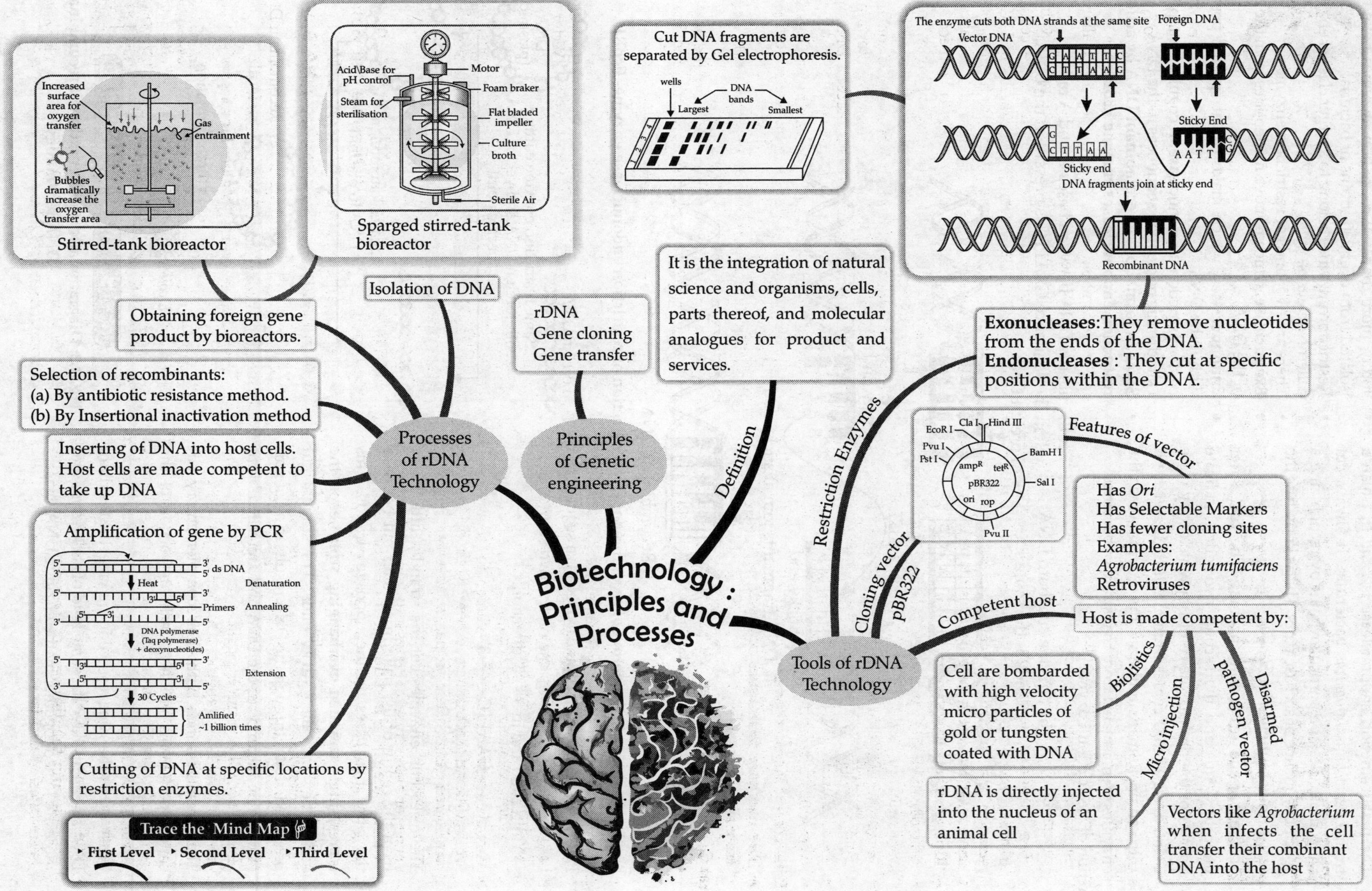
Biotechnology : Principles and Processes
Definition
It is the integration of natural science and organisms, cells, parts thereof, and molecular analogues for product and services.
Principles of Genetic engineering
rDNA
Gene cloning
Gene transfer
Processes of rDNA Technology
Isolation of DNA
Obtaining foreign gene product by bioreactors.
Stirred-tank bioreactor
Increased surface area for oxygen transfer
Gas entrainment
Bubbles dramatically increase the oxygen transfer area
Sparged stirred-tank bioreactor
Acid\Base for pH control
Steam for sterilisation
Motor
Foam braker
Flat bladed impeller
Culture broth
Sterile Air
Selection of recombinants:
(a) By antibiotic resistance method.
(b) By Insertional inactivation method
Inserting of DNA into host cells. Host cells are made competent to take up DNA
Amplification of gene by PCR
ds DNA
Heat
Denaturation
Primers
Annealing
DNA polymerase (Taq polymerase) + deoxynucleotides)
Extension
30 Cycles
Amlified ~1 billion times
Cutting of DNA at specific locations by restriction enzymes.
Cut DNA fragments are separated by Gel electrophoresis.
wells
DNA bands
Largest
Smallest
The enzyme cuts both DNA strands at the same site
Vector DNA
Foreign DNA
Sticky end
Sticky End
DNA fragments join at sticky end
Recombinant DNA
Tools of rDNA Technology
Restriction Enzymes
Exonucleases: They remove nucleotides from the ends of the DNA.
Endonucleases : They cut at specific positions within the DNA.
Cloning vector
pBR322
EcoR I
Cla I
Hind III
BamH I
Sal I
Pvu I
Pst I
Pvu II
ampR
tetR
ori
rop
Features of vector
Has Ori
Has Selectable Markers
Has fewer cloning sites
Examples:
Agrobacterium tumifaciens
Retroviruses
Competent host
Host is made competent by:
Biolistics
Cell are bombarded with high velocity micro particles of gold or tungsten coated with DNA
Micro injection
rDNA is directly injected into the nucleus of an animal cell
Disarmed pathogen vector
Vectors like Agrobacterium when infects the cell transfer their combinant DNA into the host
Trace the Mind Map
First Level
Second Level
Third Level

- The first restriction endonuclease is *Hind II*, isolated from *Haemophilus influenzae* bacterium. It always cut DNA molecules at a particular point by recognizing a specific sequence of six base pairs. This is known as the **recognition sequence** for *Hind II*.
- Naming of the restriction enzymes: The first letter indicate Genus and the second two letters indicate Species of the prokaryotic cell from which they were isolated, e.g., EcoRI comes from *E. coli* RY13, where R = the strain, Roman numbers = the order in which the enzymes were isolated from that strain of bacteria.
- Today, more than 900 restriction enzymes have been isolated from over 230 strains of bacteria.
- Restriction enzymes belong to a larger class of enzymes called **Nucleases**.
- There are two kinds of restriction enzymes:
  - **Exonuclease**, which remove nucleotides from the ends of the DNA.
  - **Endonucleases**, which make cut at specific position within the DNA.
- Each restriction endonuclease recognizes a specific Palindromic nucleotide sequences in the DNA.
- **Steps in formation of recombinant DNA by action of restriction endonucleases enzyme EcoRI:**

Action of Restriction Enzyme

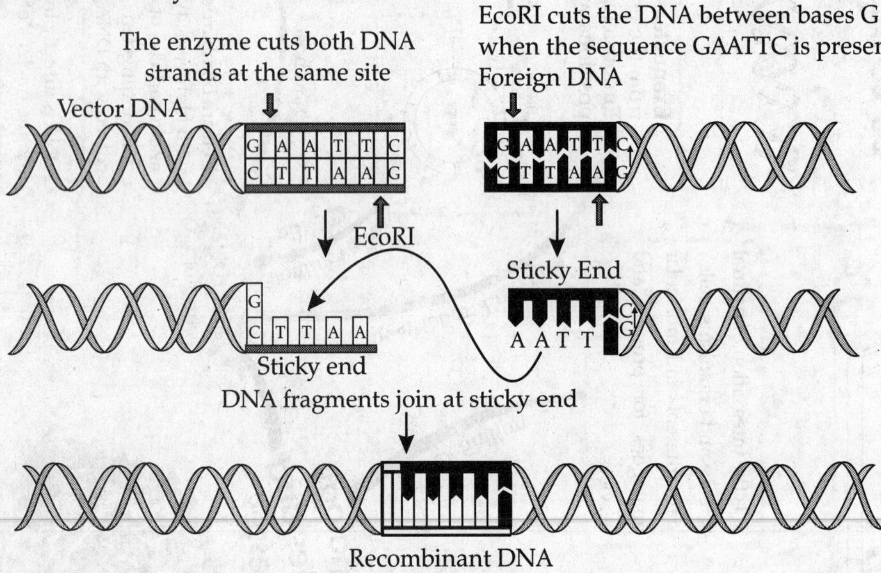

Fig. 9.1: Steps in formation of recombinant DNA by action of restriction endonuclease enzyme- EcoRI.

- **Palindromes:** The palindrome in DNA is a sequence of base pairs that read the same on the two strands in 5′ →3′ direction and in 3′ →5′ direction.

  5′ —— GAATTC —— 3′

  3′ —— CTTAAG —— 5′

- The restriction enzymes cut the strand a little away from the centre of the palindrome sites but between the same two bases on the opposite strands. This leaves **single stranded overhanging** stretches at the ends. They are called **sticky ends**. The straight cut produced, down through the DNA results in a flat pair of bases on the ends of the DNA and are called blunt ends.
- They form H-bonds with their complementary cut counterparts. This stickiness facilitates action of the enzyme, **DNA ligase**.
- When cut by the same restriction enzyme, the resultant DNA fragments have the same kind of sticky-ends and these are joined together by the enzyme DNA ligase.

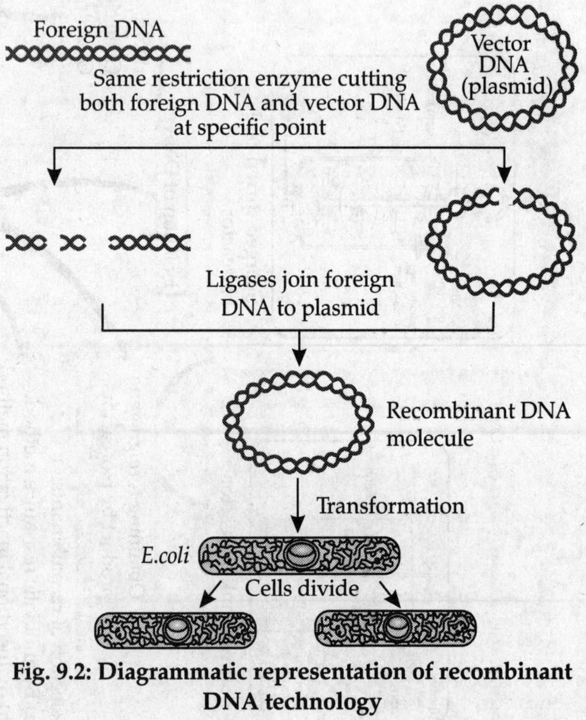

Fig. 9.2: Diagrammatic representation of recombinant DNA technology

Separation and isolation of DNA fragments (DNA of interest):

➢ DNA fragments formed by restriction endonucleases can be separated by a technique called **Gel electrophoresis**.

Scan to know more about this topic

Gel Electrophoresis

➢ DNA fragments are negatively charged. So, they can be separated by moving them towards the anode under an electric field through a medium / matrix such as **agarose.**

➢ The DNA fragments separate (resolve) according to their size through sieving effect provided by the agarose gel. The smaller sized fragments move farther.

➢ The separated DNA fragments can be visualized after staining the DNA with **ethidium bromide (EtBr)** followed by exposure to UV radiation. Bright orange coloured DNA bands can be seen.

➢ The separated DNA bands are cut out from agarose gel and extracted from gel piece. This step is called **elution**.

➢ These purified DNA fragments are used in constructing recombinant DNA by joining them with cloning vectors.

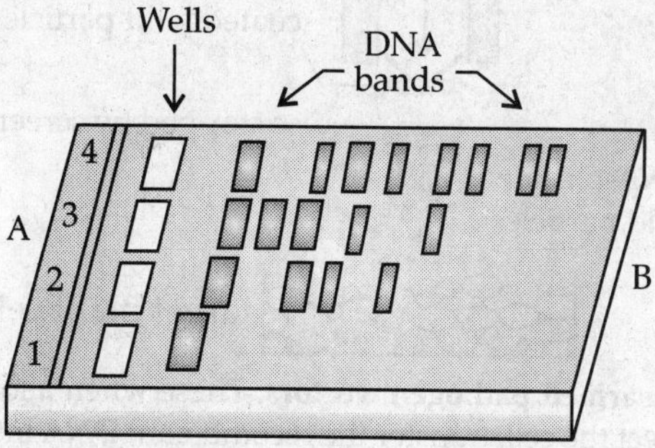

Fig. 9.3: Agarose gel electrophoresis (showing migration of undigested and digested set of DNA fragments)

2. Cloning Vectors

- Cloning vectors are vehicles to carry a foreign DNA sequence into a given host cell.
- They are the DNA molecules that carry a foreign DNA segment and replicate inside the host cells.

Scan to know more about this topic

Vectors

➢ **Salient Features of cloning vector:**

(a) Small size:

- Vector should be relatively small in size.

(b) Origin of replication (*ori*):

- Vector should contain an origin of replication so that it can replicate within the host cells.
- This is a DNA sequence from where the replication starts.
- This also controls the copy number of the linked DNA.
- So, for getting many copies of the target DNA, it should be cloned in a vector whose origin support high copy number.

(c) Selectable marker (marker gene)

- Vector should incorporate a selectable marker, which helps to select the transformants and eliminate the non-transformants.
- **Transformation** is a procedure in which a piece of DNA is introduced in a host bacterium.
- Selectable markers of *E. coli* include the genes encoding resistance to antibiotics like **ampicillin, chloramphenicol, tetracycline or kanamycin**, etc.
- The normal *E. coli* cells do not carry resistance against any of these antibiotics.

(d) Recognition site:

- The vector should have one unique restriction endonucleases recognition site to enable foreign DNA to be inserted into the vector during the generation of recombinant DNA molecule.
- In order to link the alien DNA, the vector needs one recognition site for restriction enzymes.
- Presence of more than one recognition sites generates several fragments, which complicates the gene cloning.
- The most commonly used vectors are **plasmids** (extra-chromosomal circular DNA of bacteria) and **bacteriophages.**
- Bacteriophages (high number per cell) have very high copy numbers of their genome within the bacterial cells.
- Some plasmids have only 1-2 copies per cell. Others may have 15-100 copies per cell.
- When the cloning vectors are multiplied in the host, the linked piece of DNA is also multiplied to the numbers equal to the copy number of the vectors.
- The ligation of alien DNA is carried out at a restriction site present in one of the two **antibiotic resistance genes**.
- **Identification of recombinants:**

■ The most efficient method of screening for the presence of recombinant plasmids is based on the principle that the cloned DNA fragments disrupt the coding sequence of a gene. This method is known as **insertional inactivation.**

e.g., ligation of a foreign DNA at the BamHI site of tetracycline resistance gene in the vector pBR322.

■ The recombinant plasmids lose tetracycline resistance due to insertion of foreign DNA but, they can be selected out from non-recombinant ones by plating the transformants on ampicillin containing medium. These transformants are then transferred on tetracycline medium.

■ The recombinants grow in ampicillin medium, not in tetracycline medium. But, non-recombinants will grow on the medium containing both the antibiotics.

■ In this case, one antibiotic resistance gene helps to select the transformants, whereas the other antibiotic resistance gene gets inactivated due to insertion of alien DNA and helps in the selection of recombinants.

■ Selection of recombinants due to inactivation of antibiotics requires simultaneous plating on two plates having different antibiotics.

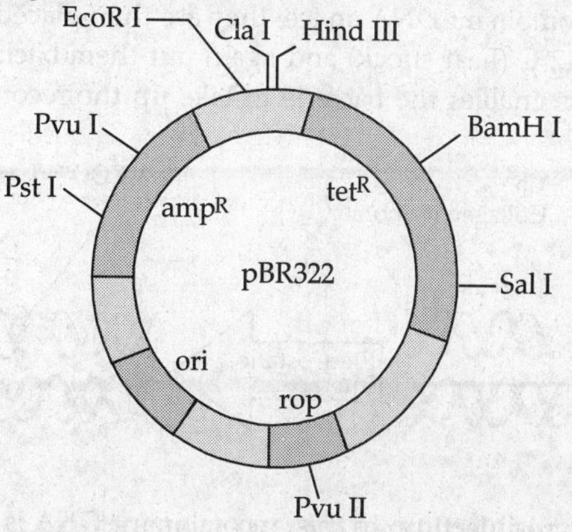

Fig. 9.4: Cloning vector pBR322

- Therefore, alternative selectable markers have developed to differentiate recombinants from non-recombinants on the basis of their ability to produce colour in the presence of a chromogenic substrate.
- A recombinant DNA is inserted within the coding sequence of an enzyme, **alpha-galactosidase**. So, the enzyme is inactivated. It is called insertional inactivation. Such colonies do not produce any colour. These are identified as **recombinant colonies.**
- If the plasmid in bacteria does not have any insert, then it gives blue colored colonies in presence of chromogenic substrate.

➢ **Vectors for cloning genes in plants and animals**

- Genetic tools of some pathogens can be transformed into useful vectors for delivering genes to plants and animals. Example: *Agrobacterium tumefaciens* (a pathogen of many dicot plants) can deliver a piece of DNA (T-DNA) to transform normal plant cells into a tumor.
- These tumor cells produce the chemicals required by the pathogen.
- The tumor inducing **(Ti) plasmid** of *A. tumefaciens* is modified into a cloning vector which is not pathogenic to the plants but is able to use the mechanisms to deliver genes of interest into plants.
- Retroviruses in animals can transform normal cells into cancerous cells. So, they are used to deliver desirable genes into animal cells.

3. **Competent Host (For Transformation with Recombinant DNA)**

- Competent cells are capable of taking DNA from the surrounding. For the process of transformation, bacterial cells are made competent, so that DNA can enter the cells.

➢ **Methods to introduce alien DNA into host cells are:**

(a) Chemical treatment with divalent calcium ions: DNA is a hydrophilic molecule. So, it cannot pass through cell membranes. To avoid this problem, bacterial cells are treated with a specific concentration of a divalent cations (*e.g.*, calcium), so as to increase the pore size in the cell wall. So, DNA enters the bacterium through pores in cell wall. Such cells are incubated with recombinant DNA on ice, they are then placed briefly at 42°C (heat shock) and again put them back on ice. This enables the bacteria to take up the recombinant DNA.

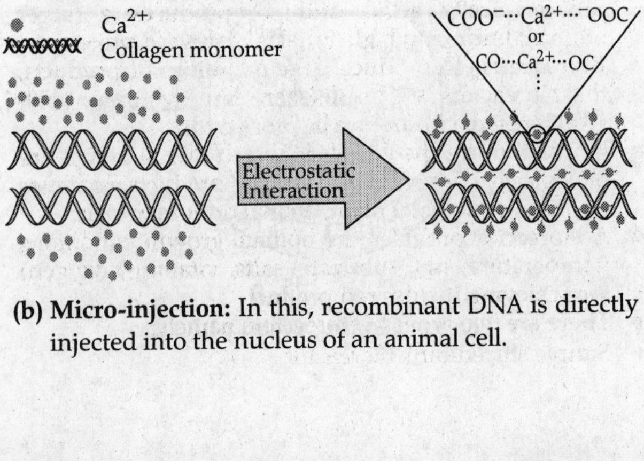

(b) Micro-injection: In this, recombinant DNA is directly injected into the nucleus of an animal cell.

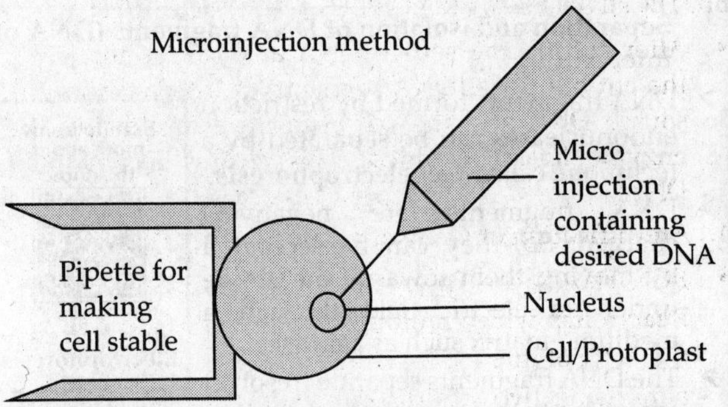

(c) Biolistics (gene gun) method: In this, cells are bombarded with high velocity micro-particles of gold or tungsten coated with DNA. This method is suitable for plants.

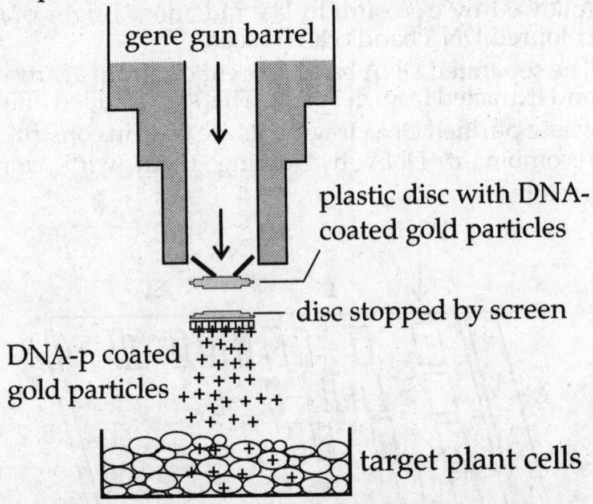

(d) 'Disarmed pathogen' vectors: These when allowed to infect the cell, transfer the recombinant DNA into host.

Steps involved in rDNA Tecnology

1. **Isolation of the Genetic Material (DNA)**

- To get pure DNA (free from other macro-molecules), the bacterial cells / plant or animal tissue are treated with enzymes such as **lysozyme** (bacteria), **Cellulase** (plant cells), **Chitinase** (fungus), etc.
- RNA is removed by treating with **ribonuclease.**
- Proteins are removed by treatment with **Protease.**
- Finally, the purified DNA precipitates out as a collection of fine threads in the suspension after the addition of chilled Ethanol.

Scan to know more about this topic

Polymerase Chain Reaction

2. **Cutting of DNA at specific locations**

- Restriction enzyme digestions are performed by incubating purified DNA with the restriction enzyme, at the optimal conditions.

3. **Isolation of derived DNA fragments.**

- Agarose gel electrophoresis is employed to check the progression of a restriction enzyme digestion. As DNA is negatively charged, it moves towards the anode. The process also repeats with vector DNA.

- After cutting the source DNA and the vector DNA, the cut out gene (DNA segment) of interest from the source DNA and the cut vector are mixed and the enzyme ligase is added. This creates recombinant DNA.

4. Amplification of Gene of Interest Using PCR

- PCR stands for **Polymerase Chain Reaction** in which multiple copies of the gene of interest is synthesized *in vitro* using two sets of primers and the enzyme **DNA polymerase.**
- Primers are small chemically synthesized oligonucleotides that are complementary to the regions of DNA.

Scan to know more about this topic

Screening of transformants

- The enzyme extends the primers using the nucleotides and the genomic DNA (template).
- For amplification, a thermostable DNA polymerase (isolated from a Thermophilic bacterium, *Thermus aquaticus*) is used.
- It remains active at high temperature during the high temperature induced denaturation of double stranded DNA.
- Source DNA and vector DNA are cut with the same endonuclease so as to obtain the sticky ends, these are then ligated by mixing the gene of interest vector DNA in presence of the enzyme DNA ligase to form recombinant DNA.
- The amplified fragment can be used to ligate with a vector for further cloning.

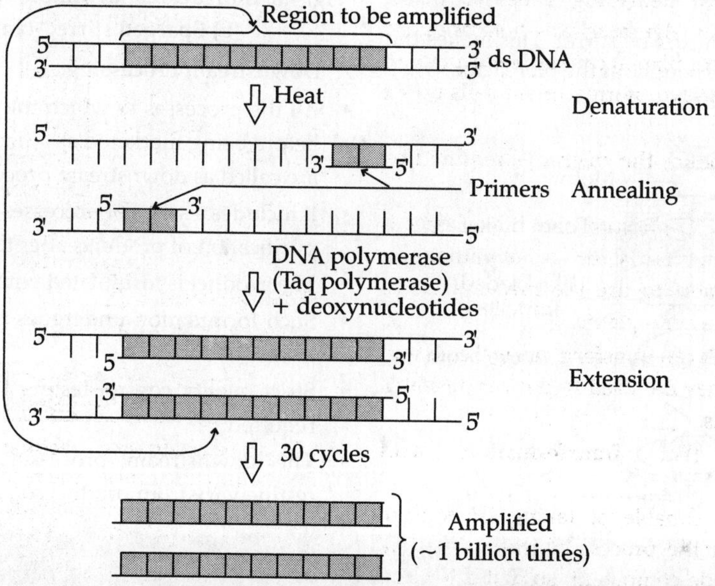

Fig. 9.5: Polymerase Chain reaction

Example: Write the functions of the following in biotechnology.

(i) Polymerase chain reaction technique

(ii) Restriction endonucleases

(iii) Bacterium Thermus aquaticus.

Ans. (i) Multiple copies of gene of interest can be obtained vithin short duration of time.

(ii) They can cut DNA molecule at a particular site by ecognizing a specific sequence of base pairs. Thus, they re useful in forming recombinant DNA.

(iii) Thermus aquaticus is the source of Taq-polymerase vhich remains active even at high temperature during he denaturation of DNA in PCR technique and therefore llows chain reaction to proceed.

. Insertion of Recombinant DNA into the Host Cell / organism

There are several methods of introducing the ligated DNA into recipient cells.

Recipient cells take up DNA present in its surrounding. If a recombinant DNA bearing ampicillin resistant gene (a selectable marker gene) is transferred into *E. coli* cells, the host cells become ampicillin-resistant cells.

If the transformed cells are spread on agar plates containing ampicillin, only transformants will grow, non- transformed recipient cells will die.

6. Obtaining the Foreign Gene Product

- The ultimate aim of the recombinant DNA technology is to produce a desirable protein.
- If a protein encoding gene is expressed in a heterologous host, it is called a **recombinant protein.**
- The cells with foreign genes may be grown on a small scale in the laboratory and the cultures may be used to extract the desired protein and purified using different separation techniques.
- The cells can also be multiplied on large scale in a continuous culture system. Here, the used medium is drained out from one side while fresh medium is added from the other. It maintains the cells more physiologically active and so, produces a larger biomass leading to higher yields of desired protein.
- **Bioreactors:** To produce large quantities of products, the bioreactors are used where large volumes (100-1000 litres) of culture can be processed.

■ Bioreactors are the vessels in which raw materials are biologically converted into specific products, enzymes etc., using microbial plant, animal or human cells.

■ A bioreactor provides the optimal growth conditions (temperature, pH, substrate, salts, vitamins, oxygen) for achieving the desired product.

■ There are two types of bioreactors namely,

- Simple stirred-tank bioreactor

- Sparged stirred-tank bioreactor

Stirred-tank Reactor

- It is the most commonly used bioreactors. It is usually cylindrical or with a curved base to facilitate the proper mixing of the reacting contents.
- The stirrer facilitates even mixing and oxygen availability throughout the bioreactor.
- Alternatively, air can be bubbled through the reactor.
- The bioreactor has:
  - **(a)** An agitator system.
  - **(b)** An oxygen delivery system.
  - **(c)** A foam control system.
  - **(d)** A temperature control system.
  - **(e)** pH control system.
  - **(f)** Sampling ports (for periodic withdrawal of the culture).
  - **(g)** The contents are mixed by stirrer. This makes the oxygen available throughout the bioreactor.

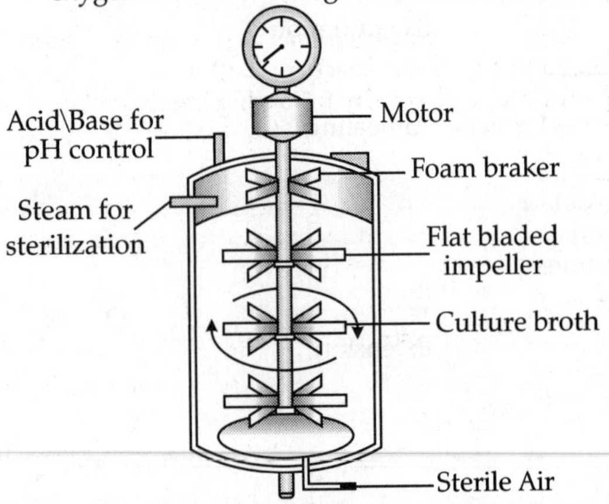

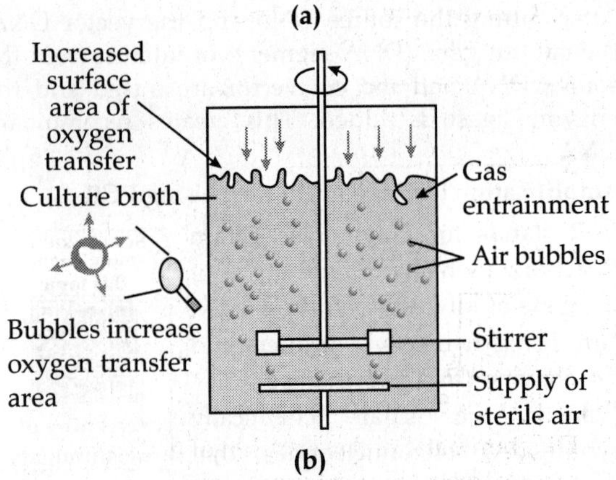

Fig. 9.6: Bioreactors- (a) Simple stirred-tank bioreactor, (b) Sparged stirred-tank bioreactor

7. Downstream Processing:

- All the processes to which the product is subjected to before being marketed as a final and finished product are called as downstream processing.
- It includes a series of processes such as, separation and purification of products after the biosynthetic stage.
- The product is formulated with suitable preservatives.
- Such formulation undergoes through clinical trials as in case of drugs.
- Strict quality control testing for each product is also required.
- The downstream processing and quality control testing vary from product to product.

NCERT CORNER

Exercise Questions

Q. 1. Can you list 10 recombinant proteins which are used in medical practice? Find out where they are used as therapeutics (use the internet).

[NCERT Ex. Q.1, Page 175]

Ans. 10 recombinant proteins, which are used in medical practice, are given in table below:

S. No.	Recombinant proteins	Therapeutic uses
(i)	Insulin	For the treatment of diabetes mellitus.
(ii)	Factor VIII	For treating haemophilia A.
(iii)	Factor IX	For treatment of haemophilia B.
(iv)	Interferons	For treatment of viral diseases, cancer and acquired immunodeficiency syndrome (AIDS).
(v)	OKT-3	For acute reversal of kidney transplantation rejection.
(vi)	DNAse-I	For treatment of cystic fibrosis.
(vii)	Bovine growth hormone	For increasing milk yield.
(viii)	Hepatitis-B surface antigen	Vaccine against hepatitis-B.
(ix)	Interleukins	For treatment of various types of cancers.
(x)	Antithrombin-III	To check the clot formation in heart patients.

Q. 2. Make a chart (with diagrammatic representation) showing a restriction enzyme, the substrate DNA on which it acts, the site at which it cuts DNA and the product it produces. [NCERT Ex. Q.2, Page 175]

Ans. Diagrammatic representation of action of restriction enzyme EcoRI:

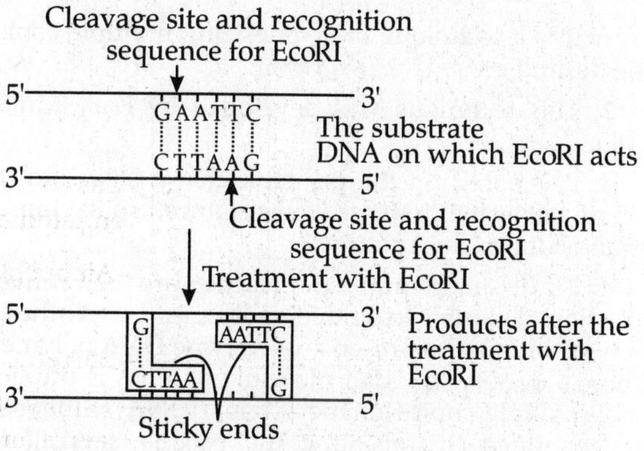

Diagrammatic representation of action of restriction enzyme EcoRI

Q. 3. From what you have learnt, can you tell whether enzymes are bigger or DNA is bigger in molecular size? How did you know? [NCERT Ex. Q.3, Page 175]

Ans. (i) Enzymes are smaller in size as compared to DNA molecules. This is because DNA contains genetic information for the development and functioning of all living organisms. It contains instructions for the synthesis of proteins and DNA molecules.

(ii) On the other hand, enzymes are proteins which are synthesized from a small stretch of DNA known as 'genes', which are involved in the production of the polypeptide chain.

(iii) The molecular weight of DNA in prokaryotes and eukaryotes are respectively 2.6×10^9 daltons (*E. coli*) and 1.8×10^{12} daltons (humans). Molecular weight of enzymes varies from 10,000 to 1 million. Thus, DNA is bigger in molecular size.

Q. 4. What would be the molar concentration of human DNA in a human cell? Consult your teacher. [NCERT Ex. Q.4, Page 175]

Ans. The molar concentration of human DNA in a human cell is as follows:

⇒ Human genome in total has 3.3×10^9 pairs.

⇒ The molecular weight of DNA = no. of pairs × 650 Daltons.

⇒ This totals as $(3.3 \times 10^9) \times 650 = 2.15 \times 10^{12}$ daltons which is equal to 3.5 picograms.

⇒ DNA with respect to moles—One mole is the Avogadro number.

⇒ Moles = 3.3×10^9 / Avogadro number $3.3 \times 10^9 \times 6 \times 10^{23}$ = 5.5 femtomoles of DNA

Q. 5. Do eukaryotic cells have restriction endonucleases? Justify your answer. [NCERT Ex. Q.5, Page 175]

Ans. (i) No, eukaryotic cells do not have restriction endonucleases.

(ii) Because,

(a) All the restriction endonucleases have been isolated from various strains of bacteria. Therefore, these enzymes are present in prokaryotes/bacteria as a defense mechanism to destroy the foreign DNA or to restrict the growth of bacteriophages.

(b) DNA of eukaryotes is highly methylated by a modification enzyme, called methylase. Methylation protects the DNA from the activity of restriction enzymes.

Q. 6. Besides better aeration and mixing properties, what other advantages do stirred tank bioreactors have over shake flasks? [NCERT Ex. Q.6, Page 175]

Ans. (i) The shake flask method is used for a small-scale production of biotechnological products in a laboratory, whereas stirred tank bioreactors are used for a large-scale production of biotechnology products.

(ii) There are several advantages of stirred tank bioreactors over shake flasks. These are as follows:

(a) They are cost effective.

(b) Capacity of fermenter is more.

(c) It has a foam breaker for regulating the foam.

(d) Due to presence of baffles, oxygen transfer rate is very high.

(e) It has a control system that regulates the temperature and pH.

(f) Small volumes of culture can be taken out from the reactor for sampling or testing.

Q. 7. Collect 5 examples of palindromic DNA sequences by consulting your teacher. Better try to create a palindromic sequence by following base-pair rules. [NCERT Ex. Q.7, Page 175]

Ans. (i) Palindromic nucleotide sequences in the DNA molecule are groups of bases that form the same sequence when read both forward and backward, that is, from 5′ → 3′ direction or from 3′→ 5′direction.

(ii) They are the sites for the action of restriction enzymes. Most restriction enzymes are palindromic sequences.

(iii) Examples:

(1)
5′—— G A A T T C ——3′
3′—— C T T A A G ——5′

(2)
5′—— G G A T C C ——3′
3′—— C C T A G G ——5′

(3)
5′—— T C G A ——3′
3′—— A G C T ——5′

(4)
5′—— A G C T ——3′
3′—— T C G A ——5′

(5)
5′—— A G G C C T ——3′
3′—— T C C G G A ——5′

Q. 8. Can you recall meiosis and indicate at what stage a recombinant DNA is made? [NCERT Ex. Q.8, Page 175]

Ans. Recombinant DNA is formed due to crossing over in prophase-I. During the pachytene stage of prophase I, crossing over of chromosomes takes place where the exchange of segments between non-sister chromatids of homologous chromosomes takes place. This results in the formation of recombinant DNA.

Q. 9. Can you think and answer how a reporter enzyme can be used to monitor transformation of host cells by foreign DNA in addition to a selectable marker? [NCERT Ex. Q.9, Page 175]

Ans. (i) Reporter gene can be used to monitor the transformation of host cells by foreign DNA. They act as a selectable marker to determine whether the host cell has taken up the foreign DNA or the foreign gene gets expressed in the cell.

(ii) Alternative selectable markers can differentiate recombinants from non-recombinants due to their capacity to form colour in the presence of a chromogenic substrate.

(iii) In coding sequence of enzyme galactosidase, recombinant DNA is inserted. Due to this, enzyme gets inactivated and step is called as insertional inactivation. If in plasmid of bacteria, insert is not present, blue coloured colonies appear due to presence of chromogenic substrate. In galactosidase, due to the presence of insert, process of insertional inactivation takes place and no colour is produced. Such colonies are identified as recombinant colonies.

Q. 10. Describe briefly the following:
(a) Origin of replication
(b) Bioreactors
(c) Downstream processing

[NCERT Ex. Q.10, Page 176]

Ans. (a) Origin of replication (*ori*):

1. It is one of the major component of a plasmid and is a sequence of bases where replication starts. This is a specific portion of plasmid genome that serves as start signal for self-replication (to make another copy of itself).

2. Any piece of DNA when linked to this sequence can be made to replicate within the host cells. This property is used to make a number of copies of linked DNA (or DNA insert).

(b) Bioreactors:

1. Bioreactors are vessels in which raw materials are biologically converted into specific products by microbes, plant and animal cells and their enzymes. They are allowed to synthesize the desired proteins which are finally extracted and purified from cultures. Small volume cultures are usually employed in laboratories for research and production of less quantity of products. However, large scale production of the products is carried out in ' bioreactors'.

2. The most commonly used bioreactors are of stirring type, that have a provision for batch culture or continuous culture. In continuous culture, the culture medium is added and the product is taken out continuously.

(c) Downstream processing:

1. After the formation of the desired product in the bioreactors, it undergoes through some processes before a finished product is ready for marketing. The processes include separation and purification of products which are collectively called the downstream processing.

2. The product is then subjected to quality control testing and kept in suitable preservatives.

3. A proper quality control testing for each product is also needed. The downstream process and quality control test are different from product to product.

Q. 11. Explain briefly:
(a) PCR
(b) Restriction enzymes and DNA
(c) Chitinase **[NCERT Ex. Q.11, Page 176]**

Ans. (a) Polymerase chain reaction (PCR):

1. It is a technique of synthesizing multiple copies of the desired gene (DNA) *in vitro*.

2. This technique was developed by Kary Mullis in 1985.

3. It is based on the principle that a DNA molecule, when subjected to high temperature, splits into two strands due to denaturation.

4. These single stranded molecules are then converted to original double stranded molecules by synthesizing new strands in the presence of enzyme DNA polymerase. Thus, a double stranded molecule of DNA is duplicated and multiple copies of the original DNA sequence can be generated by repeating the process several times. The basic requirements of PCR are, DNA template, two nucleotide primers usually 20 nucleotides long and DNA polymerase which is stable at high temperature (usually Taq polymerase)

5. Applications of PCR :
- Diagnosis of diseases.
- Diagnosis of specific mutations
- DNA fingerprinting
- In prenatal diagnosis
- In gene therapy.

(b) Restriction enzymes and DNA:

1. These enzymes are used to break DNA molecules. These are of two types : endonuclease and exonuclease.

2. Exonucleases remove nucleotides from the terminal ends (either 5′ or 3′) of DNA in one strand of duplex whereas endonucleases make cuts at specific position within the DNA.

3. These enzymes do not cleave the ends and involve only one strand of the DNA duplex. Restriction endonucleases were found by Arber in 1963 in bacteria.

4. They act as 'molecular scissors' or chemical scalpels. They recognise the base sequence at palindrome sites in DNA duplex and cut its strands.

5. Three main types of restriction endonucleases are type I, type II and type III. Out of the three types, only type II restriction enzymes are used in recombinant DNA technology because they can be used *in vitro* to recognise and cut within specific DNA sequence typically consisting of 4–8 nucleotides.

(c) Chitinase:

1. Chitinase is an enzyme which dissolves the fungal cell wall.

2. It results in the release of DNA along with several other macro-molecules from the cell.

Q. 12. Discuss with your teacher and find out how to distinguish between:
(a) Plasmid DNA and Chromosomal DNA.
(b) RNA and DNA.
(c) Exonuclease and Endonuclease.

[NCERT Ex. Q.12, Page 176]

Ans. (a) Plasmid DNA and chromosomal DNA

1. Plasmid DNA:
- It is a naked double-stranded DNA that forms a circle with no free ends.
- It is associated with few proteins but contains RNA polymerase enzymes.

- It is naked without histone protein and does not carry any vital gene necessary for cell.

2. Chromosomal DNA:

- It is a double-stranded linear DNA molecule associated with large proteins.
- This DNA exists in relaxed and supercoiled forms and provides a template for replication and transcription.
- The DNA is wrapped around the histone protein octamer and carries vital genes necessary for cell.

(b) Differences between DNA and RNA:

S. No.	DNA	RNA
1.	It is double-stranded nucleic acid.	It is single-stranded nucleic acid.
2.	It contains deoxyribose sugar.	It contains ribose sugar.
3.	It contains Thymine (T) as a nitrogenous base.	It contains Uracil (U) instead of Thymine.
4.	It is the genetic and hereditary material of the cells.	It is involved in synthesis of proteins.
5.	It is present in the nucleus of the cells.	It is present in both nucleus and cytoplasm.

(c) Differences between exonuclease and endonuclease:

S. No.	Exonuclease	Endonuclease
1.	These nucleases cleave base pairs of DNA at their terminal ends.	They cleave DNA at any specific point except the terminal ends.
2.	They act on single strand of DNA or gaps in double-stranded DNA.	They cleave one strand or both strands of double-stranded DNA.
3.	Exonulceases cleave DNA sequences, resulting in individual nucleotides or nucleosides.	Endonucleases cleave DNA sequences, resulting in oligonucleotides.

□□

CHAPTER 10

BIOTECHNOLOGY AND ITS APPLICATIONS

Biotechnology

- Biotechnology essentially deals with industrial scale production of bio-pharmaceuticals using genetically modified microbes, fungi, plants and animals.
- The applications of biotechnology include therapeutics, diagnostics, and genetically modified crops for agriculture, processed food, bioremediation, waste treatment and energy production.
- **Three critical research areas of biotechnology are:**
  - Providing the best catalyst in the form of improved organism usually a microbe or pure enzyme.
  - Creating optimal conditions through engineering for a catalyst to act.
  - Downstream processing technologies to purify the protein / organic compound.

Biotechnological Applications in Agriculture

- The three options for increasing food production are:
  - **(a)** Agro-chemical based agriculture.
  - **(b)** Organic agriculture.
  - **(c)** Genetically engineered crop-based agriculture.
- The Green Revolution succeeded in tripling the food supply but yet it was not enough to feed the growing human population. Scientists have decided that the use of genetically modified crops is a possible solution.
- Plants, bacteria, fungi and animals whose genes have been altered by manipulation are called **Genetically Modified Organisms (GMO).**

> **MNEMONICS**
>
> **Concept Name:** Achievement through transgenic crops or GM crops.
>
> **Mnemonics:** **P**roper **P**ackage of **M**uscular **B**ody: **H**ardwork **C**an **T**ransform
>
> **Interpretation:**
> **Achievements of: Example**
> **Protein of interest: Hirudin**
> **Production of desired genotype: Cry protein (Crystal protein)**
> **Modification of existing: Transgenic rice (higher content of vitamin A)**
> **Biosynthetic pathway**

- **Advantages of Genetic Modification in Plants:**
  - Made crops more tolerant to abiotic stresses (cold, drought, salt, heat, etc).
  - Helped to reduce post-harvest losses.
  - Increased efficiency of mineral usage by plants (this prevents early exhaustion of fertility of soil).
  - Enhanced nutritional value of food for e.g., Vitamin 'A' enriched rice.
  - Reduced reliance on chemical pesticides.

- **Bt Cotton**
  - Some strains of *Bacillus thuringiensis* produces a toxic insecticidal protein, that kill insects like coleopterans (beetles), lepidopterans (tobacco budworm, armyworm) and dipterans (flies, mosquitoes).
  - The Bt toxin protein does not kill the *Bacillus* as it exists as inactive protoxins.
  - When an insect ingests the inactive toxin, it is converted into active toxin due to the alkaline pH of the gut which solubilize the crystals.
  - The toxin binds to the surface of midgut epithelial cells and create pores.
  - It causes cells to swell and undergo lysis and ultimately leads to the death of the insect.
  - Bt toxin genes were isolated from *B. thuringiensis* and incorporated into crop plants such as cotton. Most Bt toxins are insect-group specific.
  - The toxin is coded by a gene named **cry**, e.g., the proteins encoded by the genes ***cryIAc*** and ***cryIIAb*** control the cotton bollworms and that of **cryI Ab** controls corn borer.

Biotechnological Applications in Medicine

- The recombinant DNA technology have made immense impact in the area of healthcare by enabling mass production of safe and more effective therapeutic drugs.
- At present, about 30 recombinant therapeutics have been approved for human-use in the world including India. In India, 12 of these are presently being marketed.
- **Genetically Engineered Insulin**
  - The management of adult-onset diabetes is possible by taking insulin at regular time intervals. Now, it is possible to produce human insulin using bacteria.
  - Insulin from the pancreas of animals (cattle and pigs) causes allergy or other types of reactions to the foreign protein.
  - Insulin consists of two short polypeptide chains (chain A and chain B) that are linked together by **disulphide bridges**.

Scan to know more about this topic
Genetically Engineered Insulin

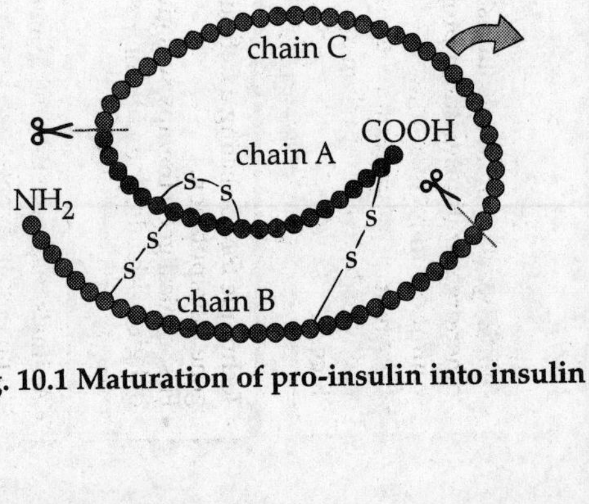

Fig. 10.1 Maturation of pro-insulin into insulin

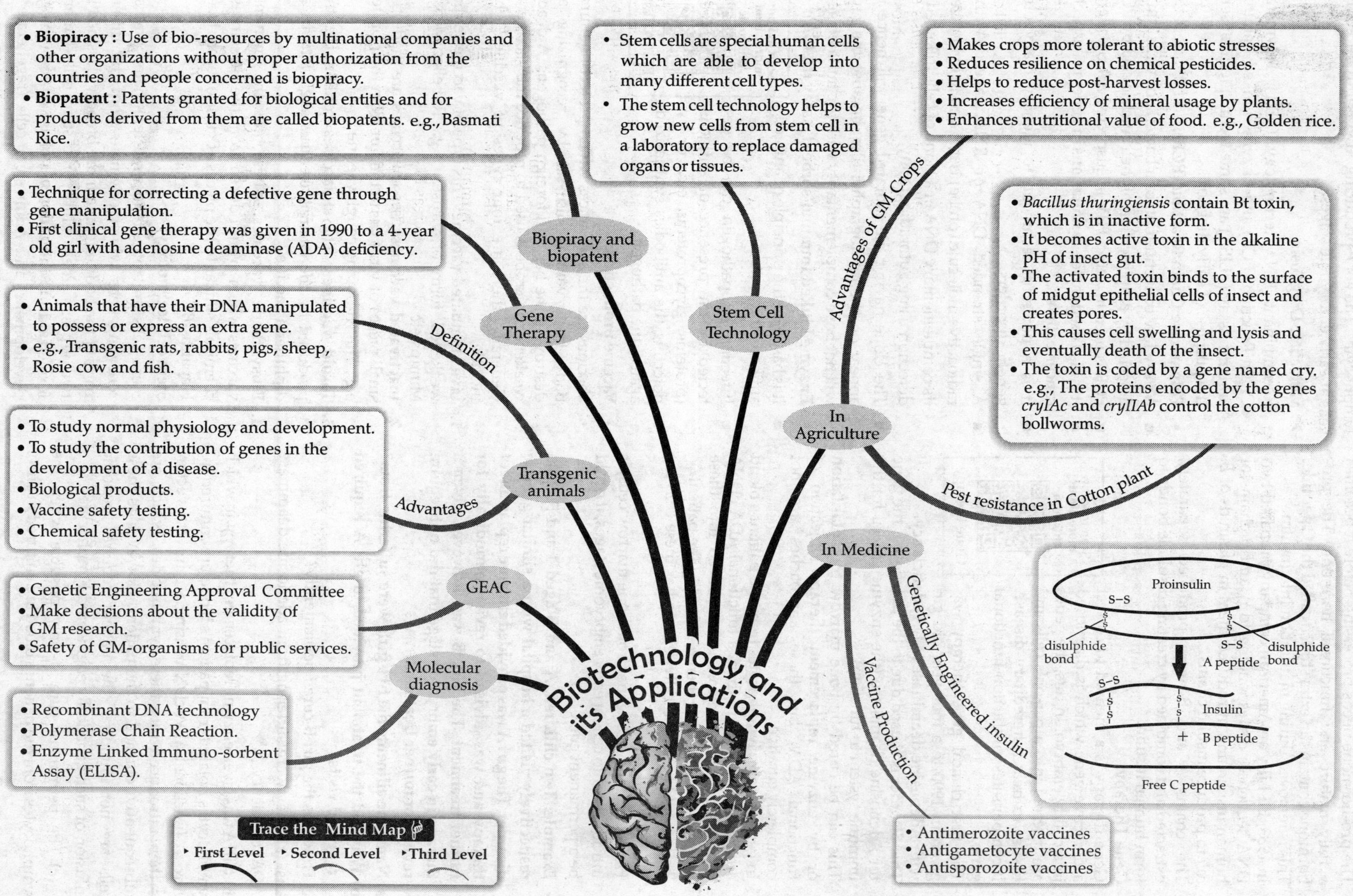
Biotechnology and its Applications
Biopiracy and biopatent
• Biopiracy : Use of bio-resources by multinational companies and other organizations without proper authorization from the countries and people concerned is biopiracy.
• Biopatent : Patents granted for biological entities and for products derived from them are called biopatents. e.g., Basmati Rice.
Gene Therapy
Definition
• Technique for correcting a defective gene through gene manipulation.
• First clinical gene therapy was given in 1990 to a 4-year old girl with adenosine deaminase (ADA) deficiency.
Transgenic animals
• Animals that have their DNA manipulated to possess or express an extra gene.
• e.g., Transgenic rats, rabbits, pigs, sheep, Rosie cow and fish.
Advantages
• To study normal physiology and development.
• To study the contribution of genes in the development of a disease.
• Biological products.
• Vaccine safety testing.
• Chemical safety testing.
GEAC
• Genetic Engineering Approval Committee
• Make decisions about the validity of GM research.
• Safety of GM-organisms for public services.
Molecular diagnosis
• Recombinant DNA technology
• Polymerase Chain Reaction.
• Enzyme Linked Immuno-sorbent Assay (ELISA).
Stem Cell Technology
• Stem cells are special human cells which are able to develop into many different cell types.
• The stem cell technology helps to grow new cells from stem cell in a laboratory to replace damaged organs or tissues.
In Agriculture
Advantages of GM Crops
• Makes crops more tolerant to abiotic stresses
• Reduces resilience on chemical pesticides.
• Helps to reduce post-harvest losses.
• Increases efficiency of mineral usage by plants.
• Enhances nutritional value of food. e.g., Golden rice.
Pest resistance in Cotton plant
• Bacillus thuringiensis contain Bt toxin, which is in inactive form.
• It becomes active toxin in the alkaline pH of insect gut.
• The activated toxin binds to the surface of midgut epithelial cells of insect and creates pores.
• This causes cell swelling and lysis and eventually death of the insect.
• The toxin is coded by a gene named cry. e.g., The proteins encoded by the genes cryIAc and cryIIAb control the cotton bollworms.
In Medicine
Genetically Engineered insulin
Proinsulin
S–S
S–S
disulphide bond
disulphide bond
A peptide
Insulin
+ B peptide
Free C peptide
Vaccine Production
• Antimerozoite vaccines
• Antigametocyte vaccines
• Antisporozoite vaccines
Trace the Mind Map
First Level
Second Level
Third Level

- In mammals, insulin is synthesized as a **pro-hormone**. The pro-hormone needs processing before it becomes a fully mature and functional hormone. The pro-hormone contains an extra stretch called the **C peptide**. This is removed during maturation into insulin.
- In 1983, **Eli Lilly** an American company prepared two DNA sequences corresponding to A and B chains of human insulin and introduced them in plasmids of *E. coli* to produce insulin chains.
- The chains A and B were produced separately, extracted and combined by creating disulfide bonds to form human insulin.

➢ **Gene Therapy:**

- Gene therapy is a method to correct a defective gene which is diagnosed in a child / embryo. In this, the genes are inserted into a person's cells and tissues to treat a **hereditary disease**. It compensates for the non-functional gene.

Scan to know more about this topic

Gene therapy

- The first clinical gene therapy was given in 1990 to a four year old girl with **Adenosine deaminase (ADA) deficiency**.
- This disorder is caused due to the deletion of the gene for Adenosine deaminase (the enzyme crucial for the immune system to function).
- This can be cured by **bone marrow transplantation** or **by enzyme replacement therapy** (injection of functional ADA) but these approaches are not completely curative.
- In gene therapy, lymphocytes from the patient's blood are grown in a culture then, a functional ADA cDNA (using a retroviral vector) is introduced into these lymphocytes. They are then returned to the patient.
- This should be periodically repeated as these cells are not immortal.
- However, if the ADA gene (from bone marrow cells) is introduced into cells at early embryonic stages, it could be a permanent cure.

➢ **Example: Two children, A and B aged 4 and 5 years respectively visited a hospital with a similar genetic disorder. The girl A was provided enzyme replacement therapy and was advised to revisit periodically for further treatment. The girl, B was, however, given a therapy in early embryonic stage that did not require revisit for further treatment.**

(a) Name the ailments the two girls were suffering from?

(b) Why did the treatment provided to girl A required repeated visits?

(c) How was the girl B cured permanently?

Ans. (a) They were suffering from adenosine deaminase (ADA) deficiency.

(b) Girl A was given enzyme replacement therapy, in which lymphocytes isolated from patient's blood are cultured in-vitro. A functional ADA cDNA (using a retroviral vector) is then introduced into these lymphocytes, which are subsequently returned to the patient. However, as these cells are not immortal, the patient requires periodic infusion of such genetically engineered lymphocytes.

(c) The permanent cure is only possible when the lymphocytes from the patient's blood are cultured in vitro. A functional ADA cDNA is then introduces into these lymphocytes. The gene producing ADA is introduced into cells at early embryonic stages.

➢ **Molecular Diagnosis**

- Recombinant DNA technology (RDT), Polymerase Chain Reaction (PCR) and Enzyme Linked Immuno-Sorbent Assay (ELISA) are some techniques that serve the purpose of early diagnosis.
- **Polymerase Chain Reaction (PCR):**

■ A very low concentration of a bacteria or virus can be detected by amplification of their nucleic acid by PCR.

■ PCR is used to detect **HIV** in suspected AIDS patients.

■ It is also used to detect **mutations** in genes in suspected cancer patients.

■ It is a powerful technique to identify many other genetic disorders.

■ A single stranded DNA or RNA, tagged with a radioactive molecule (probe) is allowed to hybridize to its complementary DNA in a clone of cells followed by detection using autoradiography.

■ The clone having the mutated gene will hence not appear on the photographic film, because the probe will not have complementarity with the mutated gene.

- **Enzyme Linked Immuno-sorbent Assay (ELISA):**

■ It is based on the principle of antigen-antibody interaction.

■ Infection by pathogen can be detected by the presence of antigens (proteins, glycoproteins, etc.) or by detecting the antibodies synthesized against the pathogen.

Scan to know more about this topic

ELISA Test

➢ **Vaccine production:**

- Vaccines are the substances which protect the human body from various diseases by recognizing and destroying the harmful foreign pathogens. A dead or weakened microbe is used to produce the vaccine.
- Generally, there are four types of vaccines which include:

1. **Live attenuated vaccine:** This type of vaccine contains weakened form of viruses. e.g., Rubella, Measles, Mumps etc.
2. **Inactivated vaccines:** These vaccines are made from small pieces of virus or bacteria or from their proteins e.g., The whooping cough vaccine.
3. **Toxoid vaccines:** These vaccines contain the toxin produced by the bacteria or virus. e.g., Tetanus and diphtheria vaccine.
4. **Biosynthetic vaccines:** These are the man-made vaccines which are produced from the substances or chemicals similar to the pieces of virus or bacteria. e.g., Hepatitis-B.

➢ **Stem cell technology:**

- Stem cells are totipotent, undifferentiated and self-renewing cells which originate from the different parts of the body. Stem cells are broadly classified into two types, namely Embryonic stem cells (embryos formed during the blastocyst phase of embryological development) and Adult stem cells (regenerate the damaged tissues).

- Stem cells technology is a rapidly growing field wherein efforts are made by cell biologist and geneticists in order to develop effective treatment for various malignant and non-malignant diseases.
- In this technology, stem cells are grown in lab by researchers. These are' later manipulated to differentiate into specific types of cells such as nerve cells, muscle cells etc.
- The specialized cells, then can be implanted into a person's target organ to treat the disease.
- In many people, heart tissue is repaired by manipulation of these stem cells under in vitro conditions.
- Cancer and blood related diseases like leukemia, lymphoma, myeloma has been cured by using adult stem cells.

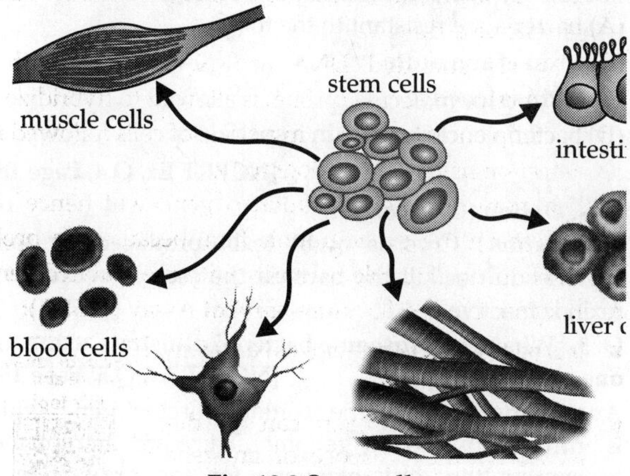

Fig. 10.2 Stem cells

Transgenic Animals

➢ Animals whose genome has been altered by introduction of an extra (foreign) gene by manipulation are known as transgenic animals.

➢ **Some example are:** Transgenic rats, rabbits, pigs, sheep, cows and fish. Over 95% of all existing transgenic animals are mice.

➢ Reasons for production of Transgenic Animals:

- **To study normal physiology and development**
  - Transgenic animals are used to study how genes are regulated and how they affect the normal body functions and its development.
  - For example study of complex factors such as insulin-like growth factor. Genes (from other species) that alter the formation of this factor are introduced and the biological effects are studied. This gives information about the biological role of the factor in the body.
- **To study the contribution of genes in the development of a disease**
  - Transgenic models help for investigation of new treatments for human diseases.
  - For e.g., transgenic models for many human diseases such as cancer, cystic fibrosis, rheumatoid arthritis and Alzheimer's.
- **To produce biological products**
  - Some medicines contain biological products, but they are often expensive.
  - Transgenic animals are used to produce useful biological products by introducing genes which codes for a particular product. For e.g., human protein (alpha-1-antitrypsin) used to treat **emphysema,** products for treatment of **phenylketonuria (PKU)** and **cystic fibrosis,** etc.
  - In 1997, the first transgenic cow, *Rosie* produced human protein-enriched milk (alpha lactalbumin - 2.4 gm per litre).
  - It contains the human **alpha-lactalbumin** and is nutritionally more balanced product for human babies than natural cow-milk.
- **For vaccine safety testing:** Transgenic mice are being developed for use in testing the safety of vaccines before they are used for humans. For example, Polio vaccine was tested in mice.
- **For toxicity testing:** Some transgenic animals carry genes which make them more sensitive to toxic substances than non-transgenic animals. They are then exposed to the toxic substances and the effects are studied. This is also known as toxicity / safety testing.

Ethical Issues

➢ Genetic modification may cause unpredictable results when such organisms are introduced into the ecosystem.

➢ Therefore, Indian Government has set up organizations like **GEAC (Genetic Engineering Approval Committee),** which makes decisions about the validity of GM research and the safety of GM-organisms for public services.

Biopatent

➢ A patent is the right granted by the government to an inventor to prevent others from making commercial use of his invention.

Scan to know more about this topic
Transgenic Animals

➢ Now patent is granted for biological entities and for products derived from biological resources.

➢ Certain companies have got patents for products and technologies that make use of the genetic materials, plants etc., that have been identified, developed and used by farmers and indigenous people of a specific country. For e.g., Basmati rice, herbal medicines like turmeric, neem, etc. India has 27 varieties of Basmati.

➢ In 1997, an American company got patent rights on Basmati rice through the US Patent and Trademark Office. This allowed the company to sell a 'new' variety of Basmati which had actually been derived from Indian farmer's varieties.

➢ Indian Basmati was crossed with semi-dwarf varieties and claimed as a novelty. Other people selling Basmati rice could be restricted by the patent.

Biopiracy

➢ It is the term used to refer to the use of bio-resources by multinational companies and other organizations without proper authorization from the countries and people concerned.

➢ Most of the industrialized nations are poor in biodiversity and traditional knowledge whereas the developing and the underdeveloped countries have rich biodiversity and traditional knowledge related to bio-resources. Therefore, some nations have developed laws to prevent unauthorized exploitation of bio-resources and traditional knowledge.

➢ Indian Parliament has cleared the second amendment of the Indian Patents Bill that takes such issues into consideration, including patent terms, emergency provisions and research and development initiative.

NCERT CORNER

Exercise Questions

Q. 1. Which part of the plant is best suited for making virus-free plants and why? [NCERT Ex. Q.1, Page 186]

Ans. The meristem of plants is the best part of the part to make virus-free plants. This is because even if the plant is infected with a virus, apical and axillary meristems are generally free from virus. Hence, the meristems can be removed and grown into in vitro to obtain virus-free plants.

Q. 2. What is the major advantage of producing plants by micropropagation? [NCERT Ex. Q.2, Page 186]

Ans. The major advantages of producing plants by micropropogation are:

(i) It is possible to achieve propogation of a large number of plants in very short durations.

(ii) The plants are genetically identical to the original plant from which they are grown.

Q. 3. Find out what the various components of the medium used for propagation of an explant *in vitro* are? [NCERT Ex. Q.3, Page 186]

Ans. The various components of the medium used for propagation of explants in vitro are carbon sources such as sucrose and also vitamins, amino acids, inorganic salts and certain growth regulators such as auxins, cytokinins etc.

Q. 4. Crystals of Bt toxin produced by some bacteria do not kill the bacteria themselves because,

(A) bacteria are resistant to the toxin

(B) toxin is immature

(C) toxin is inactive

(D) bacteria enclose toxin in a special sac

[NCERT Ex. Q.4, Page 186]

Ans. Option (C) is correct.

Explanation : Crystals of Bt toxin produced by some bacteria do not kill the bacteria themselves because the toxin is inactive.

Q. 5. What are transgenic bacteria? Illustrate using any one example. [NCERT Ex. Q.5, Page 187]

Ans. Transgenic bacteria contain foreign gene which is introduced into its genome. They are manipulated to express the desirable gene for the production of commercially important products.

Example of transgenic bacteria : *E.coli.* In the plasmid of *E.coli*, the two DNA sequences corresponding to A and B chain of human insulin are inserted, so as to produce the respective human insulin chains. Therefore, after the insertion of insulin gene into the bacterium, it becomes transgenic and starts producing chains of human insulin. Later on, these chains are extracted from *E.coli* and combined to form human insulin.

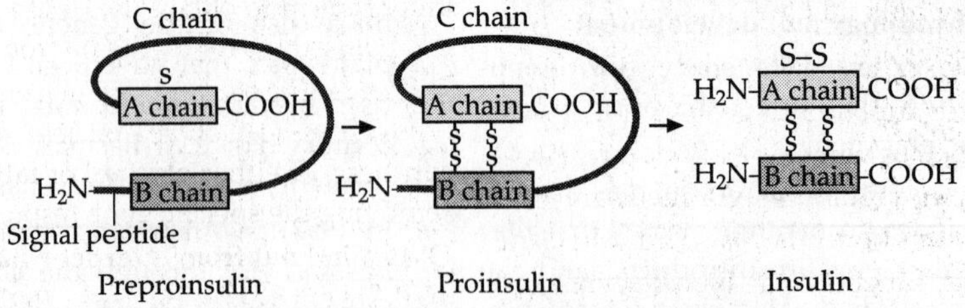

Q. 6. Compare and contrast the advantages and disadvantages of production of genetically modified crops. [NCERT Ex. Q.6, Page 187]

Ans. The production of genetically modified (GM) or transgenic plants has several advantages.

(i) Most of the GM crops are pest resistant, which increases the crop productivity and therefore, reduces the reliance on chemical pesticides.

(ii) GM food crops have enhanced nutritional quality. For example, golden rice is a transgenic variety in rice, which is rich in vitamin A.

(iii) These plants prevent the loss of fertility of soil by increasing the efficiency of mineral usage.

(iv) They are highly tolerant to unfavourable abiotic conditions.

(v) The use of GM crops decreases the post harvesting loss of crops.

However, there are certain controversies regarding the use of GM crops around the world. The use of these crops can affect the native biodiversity in an area. For example, the use of Bt toxin to decrease the amount of pesticide is posing a threat for beneficial insect pollinators such as honey bee.

If the gene expressed for Bt toxin gets expressed in the pollen, then the honey bee might be affected. As a result, the process of pollination by honey bees would be affected. Also, GM crops are affecting human health as they supply allergens and certain antibiotic resistance markers in the body. Also, they can cause genetic pollution in the wild relatives of the crop plants.

Hence, it is affecting our natural environment.

Q. 7. What are *Cry* proteins? Name an organism that produces it. How has man exploited this protein to his benefit? [NCERT Ex. Q.7, Page 187]

Ans. *Cry* proteins are encoded by cry genes.

These proteins are toxins, which are produced by *Bacillus thuringiensis* bacteria. This bacterium contains these proteins in their inactive form. When the inactive toxin protein is ingested by the insect, it gets activated by the alkaline pH of the gut. This results in the lysis of epithelial cell and eventually the death of the insect. Therefore, man has exploited this protein to develop certain transgenic crops with insect resistance such as Bt cotton, Bt corn, etc.

Q. 8. What is gene therapy? Illustrate using the example of adenosine deaminase (ADA) deficiency.

[NCERT Ex. Q.8, Page 187]

Ans. Gene therapy is an experimental approach aimed at treating or preventing diseases, including hereditary disorders, by addressing defective genes. It encompasses a range of methods designed to correct these faulty genes. The core principle involves introducing a healthy, functional gene into an individual to replace or supplement a defective one. For instance, a common application is the introduction of the adenosine deaminase (ADA) gene in individuals who lack ADA, effectively addressing their deficiency in this essential enzyme.

The adenosine deaminase enzyme is important for the normal functioning of the immune system. The individual suffering from this disorder can be cured by transplantation of bone marrow cells. The first step involves the extraction of lymphocyte from the patient's bone marrow. Then, a functional gene for ADA is introduced into lymphocytes with the help of retrovirus. These treated lymphocytes containing ADA gene are then introduced into the patient's bone marrow. Thus, the gene gets activated producing functional T- lymphocytes and activating the patient's immune system.

Q. 9. Diagrammatically represent the experimental steps in cloning and expressing a human gene (say the gene for growth hormone) into a bacterium like *E. coli*?

[NCERT Ex. Q.9, Page 187]

Ans. DNA cloning is a method of producing multiple identical copies of specific template DNA.

It involves the use of a vector to carry the specific foreign DNA fragment into the host cell. The mechanism of cloning and transfer of gene for growth hormone into *E. coli* is represented below.

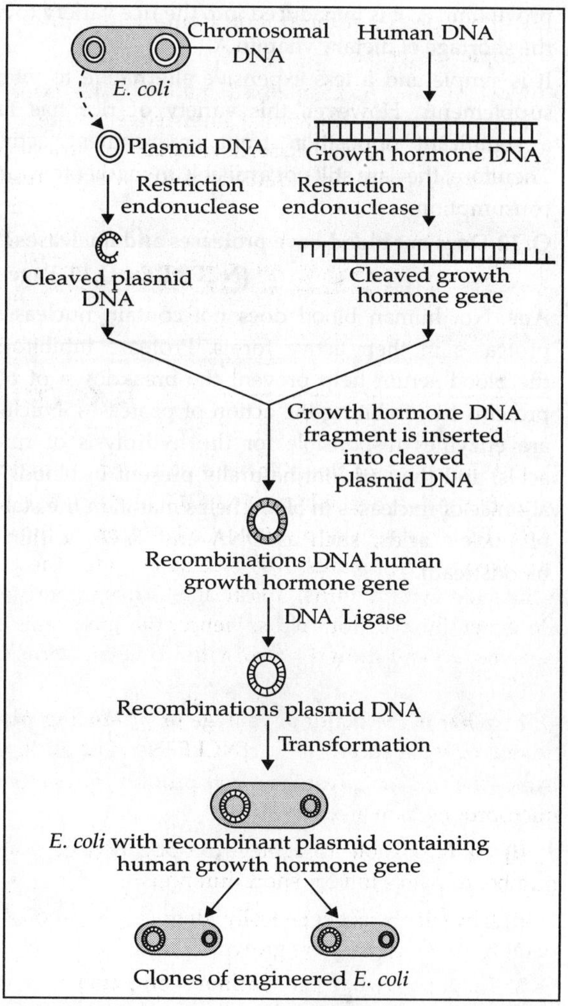

Q. 10. Can you suggest a method to remove oil (hydrocarbon) from seeds based on your understanding of rDNA technology and chemistry of oil?

[NCERT Ex. Q.10, Page 187]

Ans. Recombinant DNA technology (rDNA) is a technique used for manipulating the genetic material of an organism to obtain the desired result. This technology can be used for removing oil from seeds.

The constituents of oil are glycerol and fatty acids. Using *r*DNA, one can obtain oil less seeds by preventing the synthesis of either glycerol or fatty acids. This is done by removing the specific gene responsible for the synthesis.

Q. 11. Find out from internet what is golden rice.

[NCERT Ex. Q.11, Page 187]

Ans. *Golden rice* is a genetically modified variety of rice rich in the orange or red plant pigment beta-carotene, a substance important in the human diet as a precursor of vitamin A. It contains a precursor of pro-vitamin A, called beta-carotene, which has been introduced into the rice through genetic engineering. The rice plant, naturally, produces β-carotene pigment in its leaves.

However, it is absent in the endosperm of the seed. This is because beta-carotene pigment helps in the process of photosynthesis while photosynthesis does not occur in endosperm. Since, beta-carotene is a precursor of provitamin A, it is introduced into the rice variety to fulfil the shortage of dietary vitamin A.

It is simple and a less expensive alternative to vitamin supplements. However, this variety of rice has faced a significant opposition from environment activists. Therefore, they are still not available in market for human consumption.

Q. 12. Does our blood have proteases and nucleases?

[NCERT Ex. Q.12, Page 187]

Ans. No, human blood does not contain nucleases or proteases in their active forms. Protease inhibitors in the blood serum help prevent the breakdown of blood proteins by inhibiting the action of proteases. Nucleases are enzymes responsible for the hydrolysis of nucleic acids, and they are not naturally present in blood. This absence of nucleases in blood helps maintain the stability of nucleic acids, such as DNA and RNA, within the bloodstream.

Q. 13. Consult internet and find out how to make orally active protein pharmaceutical. What is the major problem to be encountered? [NCERT Ex. Q.13, Page 187]

Ans. Orally active protein contains pharmaceuticals biologically active materials such as peptides or proteins, antibodies, and polymeric beads. It is administered orally into the body through various formulations.

Process of manufacturing of orally active protein pharmaceutical involves the encapsulation of protein or peptide in liposomes or formulations using penetration enhancers.

These proteins or peptides are used for treatment of various diseases and are also used as vaccines.

However, the oral administration of these peptides or proteins has some problems related to it. Once these proteins are ingested, the proteases present in the stomach juices denature the protein. As a result, their effect will be nullified. Hence, it is necessary to protect the therapeutic protein from digestive enzymes, if taken orally. This is the reason for the proteins to be injected directly into the target site.

□□

ORGANISMS AND POPULATIONS

CHAPTER 11

- Ecology is the branch of biology that deals with the inter-relationship amongst the organisms and their environment.
- **Populations:** A population is defined as a group of individuals of the same species that live in a particular geographical area at a particular time and functioning as a unit.
- A population has certain attributes that an individual organism does not have. For example, individual may have births and deaths, but a population has birth rates and death rates.
- **The birth and death rates** are referred as per capita births or deaths respectively, which increases and decreases with respect to members of the population.
- **Sex ratio** is another attribute of population. An individual may be male or female but population has sex ratio.
- A population at given time is composed of different individuals of different ages. If the age distribution is plotted for the population, the resulting structure is called age pyramids. The shape of pyramids reflects the shape of growth status of population.

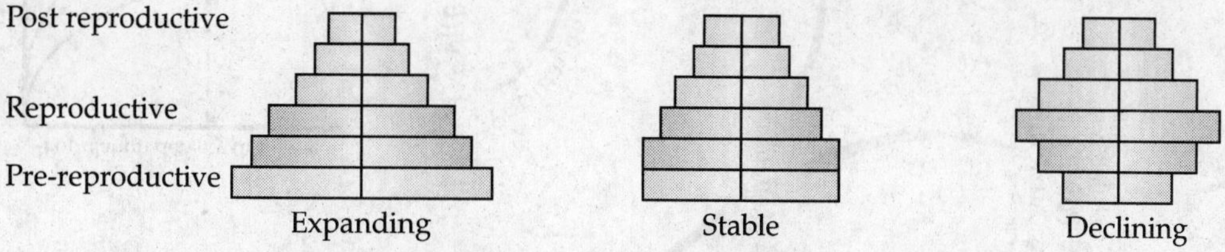

Fig. 11.1: Representation of age pyramids for human population

- **Population size or population density (N)** is measured in terms of number.
- **Population Growth:** The size of population is not static. It keeps changing with time, depending upon food availability, predation pressure and adverse weather. The main factors that determine the population growth are:

Scan to know more about this topic
Population density: Natality and Mortality

(i) Natality (number of births) [B]
(ii) Mortality (number of deaths) [D]
(iii) Immigration (individuals that come into habitat) [I]
(iv) Emigration (individual that leaves the habitat) [E]

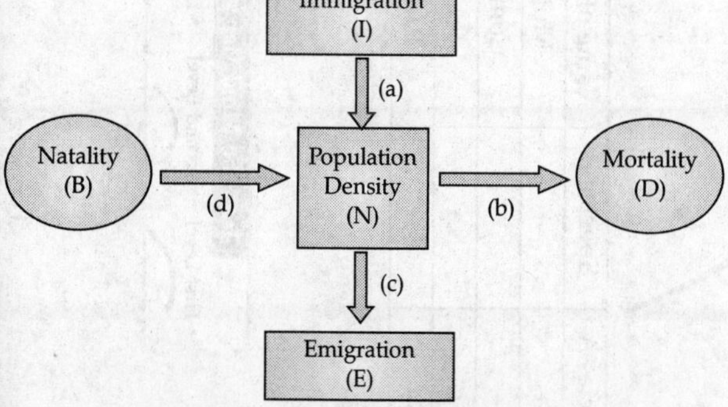

Fig. 11.2: Population Density

- **Differences between Natality Rate and Mortality Rate:**

S. No.	Natality Rate (B)	Mortality Rate (D)
1.	Addition of new individuals due to birth, hatching, germination or division.	Number of individuals in a population decreases with the death of the individuals.
2.	Natality shows the number of offsprings produced per unit time per unit population.	Population density and its size is decreased by death rate.

If 'N' is the population density at time 't', then its density at $t+1$ is

$$N_{(t+1)} = N_t + [(B + I) - (D + E)]$$

MNEMONICS

Concept Name: Population Density at time t+1

Mnemonics: Never tried Before I Dare to Exit

Interpretation: $N_t + [(B+I)-(D+E)]$

Growth model: Growth of population takes place according to availability of food, habitat condition and

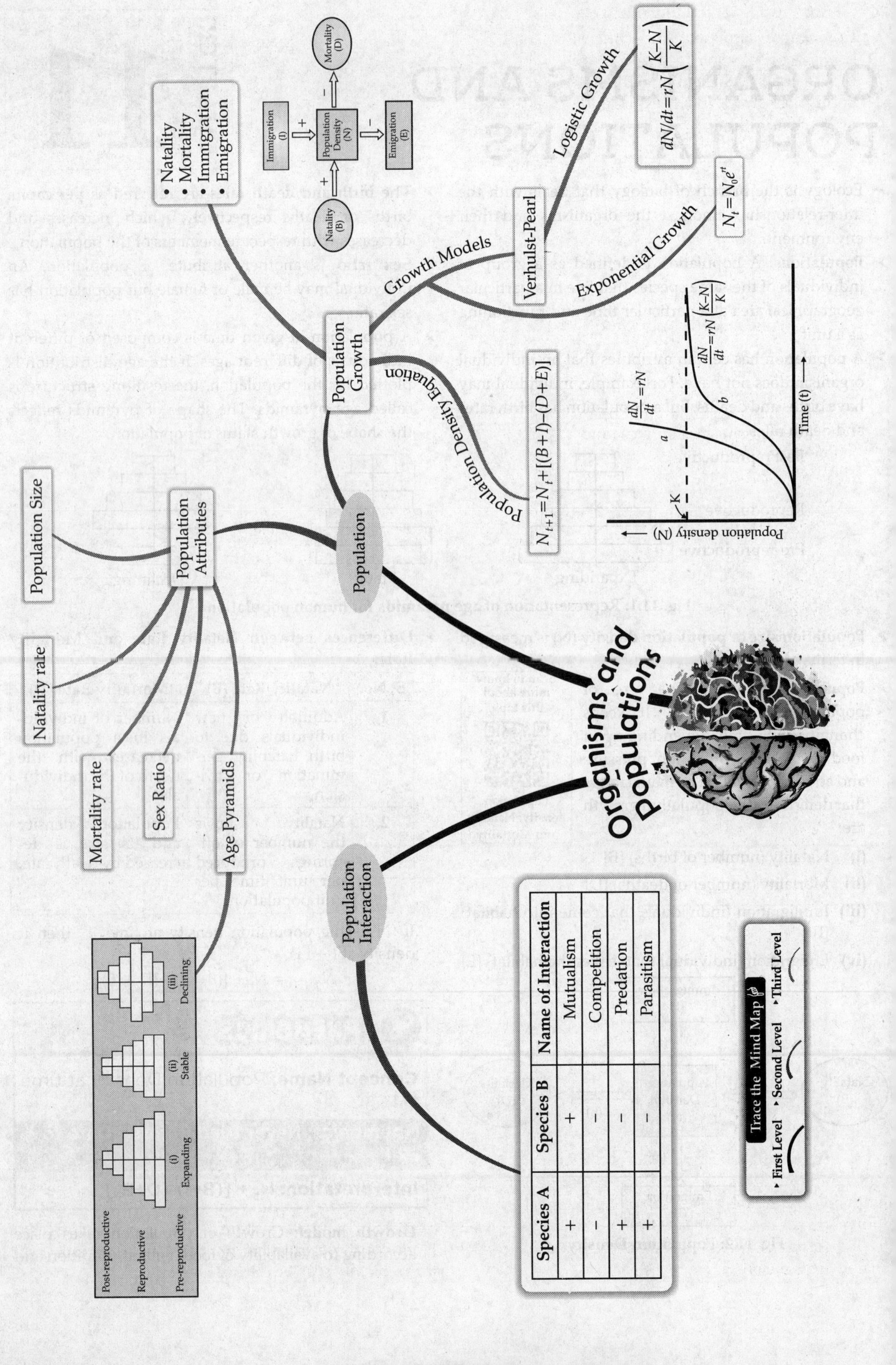
Organisms and Populations
Population
Population Attributes
Population Size
Natality rate
Mortality rate
Sex Ratio
Age Pyramids
Post-reproductive
Reproductive
Pre-reproductive
(i) Expanding
(ii) Stable
(iii) Declining
Population Growth
• Natality
• Mortality
• Immigration
• Emigration
Natality (B)
Immigration (I)
Population Density (N)
Emigration (E)
Mortality (D)
Growth Models
Verhulst-Pearl
Logistic Growth
$dN/dt = rN\left(\frac{K-N}{K}\right)$
Exponential Growth
$N_t = N_0 e^{rt}$
Population Density Equation
$N_{t+1} = N_t + [(B+I) - (D+E)]$
$\frac{dN}{dt} = rN$
$\frac{dN}{dt} = rN\left(\frac{K-N}{K}\right)$
Population density (N)
Time (t)
Population Interaction
Species A
Species B
Name of Interaction
Mutualism
Competition
Predation
Parasitism
Trace the Mind Map
First Level
Second Level
Third Level

presence of other biotic and abiotic factors. There are two main types of growth models:

(i) Exponential Growth: This kind of growth occurs when food and space is available in sufficient amount. The population grows in an exponential or geometric fashion. If the size of population is N, the birth rate is represented as '*b*' and death rate as '*d*', then increase and decrease in N during unit period time '*t*' will be

Scan to know more about this topic
Exponential Growth Model

$$dN/dt = (b-d) \times N$$

Let $(b-d) = r$.

Then $dN/dt = rN$

The *r* in this equation is called 'intrinsic rate of natural increase'.

(ii) Logistic Growth: There is a competition between the individuals of a population for food and space. The fittest organism survives and reproduces. This type of growth initially shows a lag phase followed by phases of acceleration and deceleration. K indicates the carrying capacity of the population.

Scan to know more about this topic
Logistic Growth

$$dN/dt = rN\left(\frac{K-N}{K}\right)$$

➢ **Population interaction:** All animals, plants and microbes in a biological community interact with each other. These interactions may be beneficial, detrimental or neutral to one species or both. Following types of interaction is seen:

Scan to know more about this topic
Population Interaction: Mutualism

(a) Predation: It is the interaction between two species members in which the members of one species capture, kill and eat up the members of other species.

(b) Parasitism: It is the relationship between two living organisms of different species in which one organism called parasite obtains its food directly from another living organism called host.

(c) Commonsalism: It is an interaction between two species in which one species gets benefited while the other remains unaffected

(d) Competition: It is the rivalry between two or more organisms for obtaining the same resources.

(e) Mutualism: It is the interaction between two organisms of different species where both the partners are benefitted but cannot live separately.

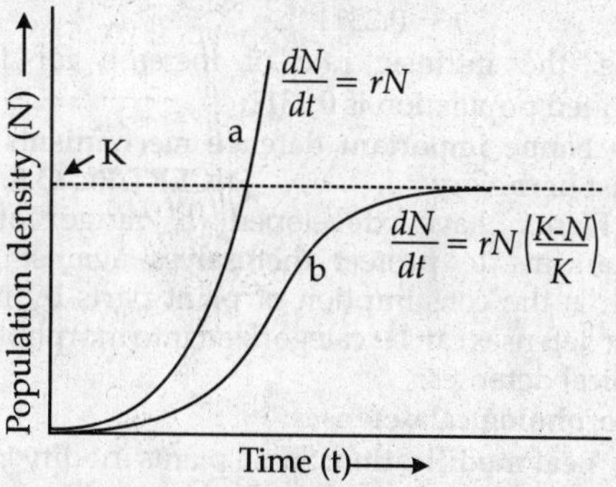

Fig. 11.3: Population Growth Curve

(a) When responses are not limiting the growth, plot is exponential.

(b) When responses are limiting the growth, plot is logistic. It produces (S-shaped) sigmoid curve, K is carrying capacity.

NCERT CORNER

Exercise Questions

Q. 1. List the attributes that populations possess but not individuals. **[NCERT Ex. Q.1, Page 204]**

Ans. (i) A population can be defined as a group of individuals of the same species residing in a particular geographical area at a particular time and functioning as a unit. It has some attributes which are not shown by its individual members. An individual may have births and deaths whereas the population has a birth rate and a death rate.

(ii) Each population has a certain pattern of distribution, variation in numbers, age structure, natality (birth rate), mortality (death rate), dispersal, biotic potential, growth forms, and sex ratio. All these attributes are not possessed by individuals. Further, a population has a gene pool shared by its members.

Q. 2. If a population growing exponentially double in size in 3 years, what is the intrinsic rate of increase (r) of the population? **[NCERT Ex. Q.2, Page 204]**

Ans. A population grows exponentially if sufficient amounts of food resources are available to the individual. Its exponential growth can be calculated by the following integral form of the exponential growth equation:

$$N_t = N_0 e^{rt}$$

Where,

N_t= Population density after time t

N_0= Population density at time zero

r = Intrinsic rate of natural increase

e = Base of natural logarithms (2.71828)

From the above equation, intrinsic rate of increase (r) of the population can be calculated as follows:

As per the given question,
Present population density = x
Then,
Population density after two years = 2x
t = 3 years
Substituting these values in the given formula, we get:

$\Rightarrow 2x = x\,e^{3r}$

$\Rightarrow 2 = e^{3r}$

Applying log on both sides:

$$\Rightarrow \log e^2 = 3r$$

$$\text{or, } r = \frac{1}{3}\log e^2$$

$$= \frac{1}{3} \times 2.303 \log 10^2$$

$$= \frac{1}{3} \times 2.303 \times 0.3010$$

$$r = 0.2311$$

Hence, the intrinsic rate of increase for the above illustrated population is 0.2311.

Q. 3. Name important defence mechanisms in plants against herbivory. [NCERT Ex. Q.3, Page 204]

Ans. Plants have developed a range of defense mechanisms to protect themselves against herbivory, which is the consumption of plant parts by herbivores. These defenses can be categorized into morphological and chemical defenses:

(i) Morphological defenses:

(a) **Leaf modification:** Some plants modify their leaves into spines or thorns to deter herbivores. These structures make it difficult for herbivores to feed on the plant's leaves. For example, cacti have spines that discourage herbivores from consuming their succulent tissues.

(b) **Thorns:** Sharp thorns on plant stems or branches act as physical barriers, making it challenging for herbivores to access plant tissues. Plants like roses and blackberries have thorns as a defense mechanism.

(c) **Spiny leaf margins:** Plants may have spiny leaf margins, which discourage herbivores from grazing on their leaves. This adaptation can be seen in plants like holly.

(ii) Chemical Defenses:

(a) Caffeine, nicotine, opium, and quinine are some chemical substances that are produced in some plants which is a response and defense mechanism against herbivory.

(b) All of the parts of Calotropis weeds consist of lethal cardiac glycosides (cause cardiac problems) that proved to be fatal if consumed by herbivores.

Q. 4. An orchid plant is growing on the branch of mango tree. How do you describe this interaction between the orchid and the mango tree? [NCERT Ex. Q.4, Page 204]

Ans. Orchids, as epiphytes, rely on other supporting plants like mango trees for physical support but do not derive their nutrition from them. This interaction is an example of commensalism, where one organism (the orchid) benefits by obtaining support, while the other organism (the mango tree) is not significantly affected by the presence of the orchid.

Q. 5. What is the ecological principle behind the biological control method of managing with pest insects? [NCERT Ex. Q.5, Page 204]

Ans. Biological control of pest management exploits predation. Predation is the ecological interaction between predators and preys where predators drives energy from preys. By this control method predator keeps the population size of pest and insects under control.

Q. 6. Define population and community. [NCERT Ex. Q.6, Page 204]

Ans. (i) Population may be defined as the total number of individuals of a species in a specific geographical area which can interbreed under natural conditions to produce fertile offsprings and share a common gene pool.

(ii) Community is the assemblage of all the populations of different species found in the same geographical area.

Q. 7. Define the following terms and give one example for each:
(a) Commensalism
(b) Parasitism
(c) Camouflage
(d) Mutualism
(e) Interspecific competition [NCERT Ex. Q.7, Page 204]

Ans.

S. No.	Term	Definition	Example
(a)	Commensalism	It is an interaction between two species in which one species gets benefited while the other remains unaffected.	An orchid growing on the branches of a mango tree.
(b)	Parasitism	It is an antagonistic interspecific interaction in which smaller partner, (called parasite) is benefitted and draws food and shelter from the body of larger partner (called host).	*Plasmodium* (malarial parasite) feeding upon liver cells and RBCs of man.
(c)	Camouflage	It is a phenomenon in which animal changes its body colour or body form and looks like another living organism or some inanimate object so as to defend itself or to capture the prey.	Praying mantis is green coloured so remains unnoticed in green grass.
(d)	Mutualism	It is an interspecific positive interaction in which both the partners are mutually benefitted and increase the chances of survival of each other.	Lichens and mycorrhizae.

(e)	Interspecific competition	It is an antagonistic interaction in which two or more members of different species compete for common resource like food, light, water, etc., which are in short supply.	Visiting flamingos and resident fishes competing for zooplanktons in S. American lake.

Q. 8. With the help of suitable diagram describe the logistic population growth curve.

[NCERT Ex. Q.8, Page 204]

Ans. (i) Logistic population growth curve or S-shaped or sigmoid growth curve is shown by the yeast cells grown under laboratory conditions. It is also shown by the populations of most organisms. S-shaped curve is also called Verhulst-Pearl logistic curve.

(ii) It includes five phases as shown below:

(a) Lag phase: There is little or no increase in population due to limited food resource in habitat.

(b) Positive acceleration phase: During this phase, the yeast cell adapts to the new environment and starts increasing its population. However, at the beginning of this phase, the growth of the cell is very limited.

(c) Exponential phase: Population of the yeast cell increases suddenly due to rapid growth. The population grows exponentially due to the availability of sufficient food resources, constant environment, and the absence of any interspecific competition. As a result, the curve rises steeply upwards.

(d) Negative acceleration phase: The growth rate finally slows down as environmental resistance increases. This occurs due to an increased competition among the yeast cells for food and shelter.

(e) Stationary phase: During this phase, the population becomes stable because number of cells produced in a population equals the number of cells that die. Also, the population of the species is said to have reached nature's carrying-capacity (designated as K) in its habitat.

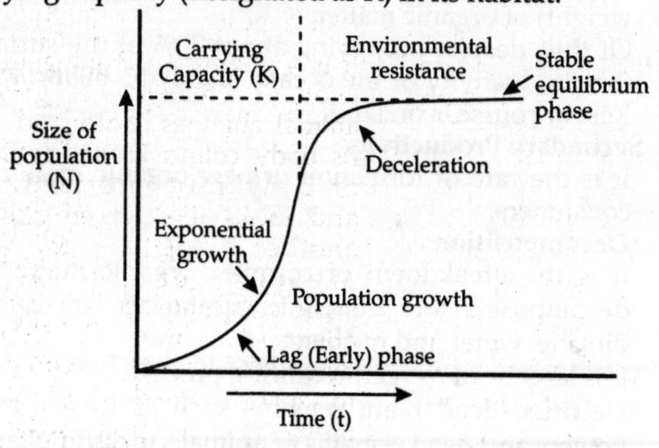

Figure: Logistic population growth curve

(iii) The sigmoid growth form is represented by the following equation:

$$\frac{dN}{dt} = rN\left(\frac{K-N}{K}\right)$$

Where,

$\frac{dN}{dt}$ = rate of change in population size

r = intrinsic rate of natural increase

N = population size

K = carrying capacity

(K – N/K) = environmental resistance

Q. 9. Select the statement which explains best parasitism.

(A) One organism is benefited.

(B) Both the organisms are benefited.

(C) One organism is benefited, other is not affected.

(D) One organism is benefited, other is affected.

[NCERT Ex. Q.9, Page 204]

Ans. Option (D) is correct.

Explanation: Parasitism is an interaction between two species in which one species (parasite) derives benefit while the other species (host) is harmed. For example, ticks and lice (parasites) present on the human body represent this interaction where in the parasites receive benefit (as they derive nourishment by feeding on the blood of humans). On the other hand, these parasites reduce host fitness and cause harm to the human body.

Q. 10. List any three important characteristics of a population and explain. [NCERT Ex. Q.10, Page 204]

Ans. The three important characteristics of a population are as follows:

(i) Birth rate (natality): It refers to the average number of young ones produced by birth, hatching or germination per unit time (usually per year). In the case of humans, it is commonly expressed as the number of births per 1,000 individuals in the population per year.

(ii) Death rate (mortality): It is the average number of individuals that die per unit time (usually per year). In humans, it is commonly expressed as the number of deaths per 1,000 persons in a population per year.

(iii) Age structure: It is the percentage of individuals of different ages such as young, adult and old in a given population. It is shown by organisms in which individuals of more than one generation coexist. The ratio of various age groups in a population determines the current reproductive status of the population.

□□

CHAPTER 12

ECOSYSTEM

Introduction

(a) An ecosystem is a functional unit of nature, where living organisms interact among themselves and also with the surrounding physical environment.

(b) The entire biosphere can be regarded as a global ecosystem.

➤ **Types of Ecosystems**

(a) Terrestrial ecosystem: Forest, grassland, desert, etc.

(b) Aquatic ecosystem: Pond, lake, wetland, river, estuary and ocean.

(c) Man-made ecosystem: Crop fields and aquarium.

Ecosystem: Structure and Function

(a) An ecosystem, consists of biotic and abiotic components. These components function as a unit. Unidirectional flow of energy takes place within these components of ecosystem.

(b) Vertical distribution of different species occupying different levels is called stratification. E.g., trees occupy top vertical strata (layer) of a forest, shrubs the second and herbs and grasses occupy the bottom layers.

➤ **Components of Ecosystem**

There are four main functions of ecosystem:

(i) Productivity (ii) Decomposition
(iii) Energy flow (iv) Nutrient cycling

Example: Pond - Aquatic Ecosystem

- A pond is a shallow, simple, self-sustainable water body that exhibits all basic components of an ecosystem.
- Abiotic components in pond: Water and the soil which is deposited at the bottom.
- Climatic conditions: The solar input, the cycle of temperature, day-length, etc.
- Autotrophic components: Phytoplankton, some algae and the floating, submerged and marginal plants.
- **Consumers (heterotrophs):** Zooplankton, free swimming and bottom dwelling forms.
- Decomposers: Fungi, bacteria and flagellates.
- **Pond performs all the functions of an ecosystem such as:**

(i) Conversion of inorganic into organic material with the help of the radiant energy of the sun by the autotrophs.

(ii) Consumption of the autotrophs by heterotrophs.

(iii) Decomposition and mineralization of the dead matter to release them back for reuse by the autotrophs.

- There is unidirectional movement of energy towards the higher trophic levels and its dissipation and loss as heat to the environment.

➤ **Productivity**

- A constant input of solar energy is the basic requirement for any ecosystem to function and sustain.
- The rate of biomass production is called productivity.
- The productivity is expressed in terms of $g^{-2}yr^{-1}$ or (kcal m^{-2}) yr^{-1}.
- It can be divided into gross primary productivity (GPP) and net primary productivity (NPP).

➤ **Primary Productivity**

- The amount of biomass or organic matter produced per unit area over a time period by plants during photosynthesis is called primary production.
- The primary production is expressed in terms of weight (g^{-2}) or energy (kcal m^{-2}).

➤ **Gross Primary Productivity**

- It is the rate of production of organic matter during photosynthesis.
- A considerable amount of GPP is utilized by plants in respiration.
- Gross primary productivity minus respiration losses (R) is the net primary productivity (NPP), i.e., NPP is the available biomass for the consumption of heterotrophs (herbivores and decomposers).

$$NPP = GPP - R$$

Scan to know more about this topic

Gross and Net primary productivity

- **Primary productivity depends on**

(i) The plant species inhabiting a particular area.

(ii) Environmental factors.

(iii) Availability of nutrients.

(iv) Photosynthetic capacity of plants.

Therefore, it varies in different types of ecosystems.

- The annual net primary productivity of the whole biosphere is approximately 170 billion tons (dry weight) of organic matter.
- Of this, despite occupying about 70% of the surface, the productivity of the oceans is only 55 billion tons. Rest of course is on land.

➤ **Secondary Productivity**

- It is the rate of formation of new organic matter by consumers.

➤ **Decomposition**

- It is the breakdown of complex organic matter by decomposers into inorganic substances like carbon dioxide, water and nutrients.
- It is largely an oxygen-requiring process.
- **Detritus** (dead plant remains such as leaves, bark, flowers and dead remains of animals, including faecal matter) is the raw material for decomposition.

MNEMONICS

Concept Name: Steps in decomposition

Mnemonics: Fly Like Crane with High Moral

Interpretation: Fragmentation, Leaching, Catabolism, Humification, Mineralisation

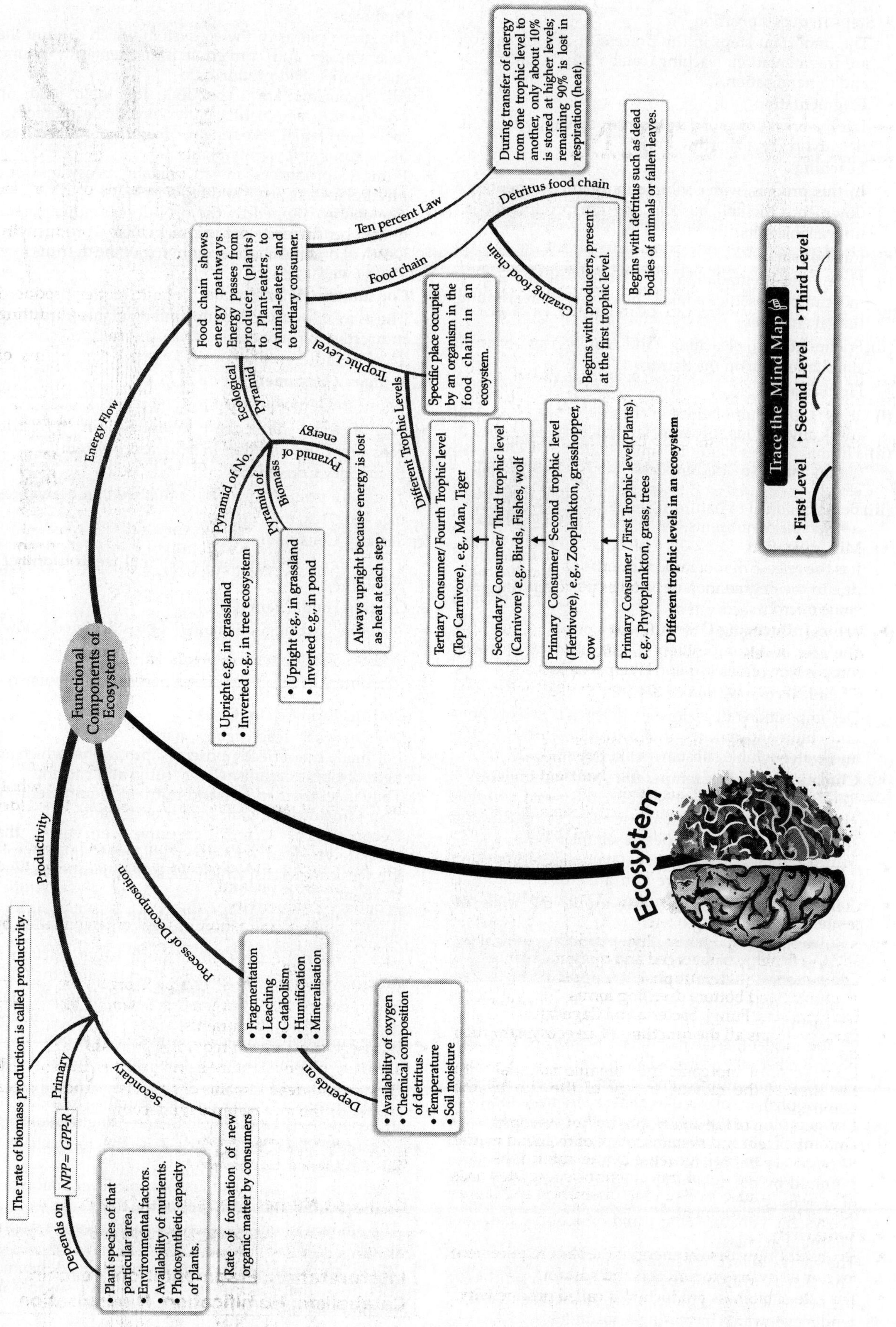
Ecosystem
Functional Components of Ecosystem
Productivity
The rate of biomass production is called productivity.
Primary
NPP= GPP-R
Depends on
• Plant species of that particular area.
• Environmental factors.
• Availability of nutrients.
• Photosynthetic capacity of plants.
Secondary
Rate of formation of new organic matter by consumers
Process of Decomposition
• Fragmentation
• Leaching
• Catabolism
• Humification
• Mineralisation
Depends on
• Availability of oxygen
• Chemical composition of detritus.
• Temperature
• Soil moisture
Energy Flow
Ecological Pyramid
Pyramid of No.
• Upright e.g., in grassland
• Inverted e.g., in tree ecosystem
Pyramid of Biomass
• Upright e.g., in grassland
• Inverted e.g., in pond
Pyramid of energy
Always upright because energy is lost as heat at each step
Trophic Level
Specific place occupied by an organism in the food chain in an ecosystem.
Different Trophic Levels
Tertiary Consumer/ Fourth Trophic level (Top Carnivore). e.g., Man, Tiger
Secondary Consumer/ Third trophic level (Carnivore) e.g., Birds, Fishes, wolf
Primary Consumer/ Second trophic level (Herbivore), e.g., Zooplankton, grasshopper, cow
Primary Consumer / First Trophic level(Plants). e.g., Phytoplankton, grass, trees
Different trophic levels in an ecosystem
Food chain shows energy pathways. Energy passes from producer (plants) to Plant-eaters, to Animal-eaters and to tertiary consumer.
Ten percent Law
During transfer of energy from one trophic level to another, only about 10% is stored at higher levels; remaining 90% is lost in respiration (heat).
Food chain
Grazing food chain
Begins with producers, present at the first trophic level.
Detritus food chain
Begins with detritus such as dead bodies of animals or fallen leaves.
Trace the Mind Map
First Level
Second Level
Third Level

➢ **Steps in decomposition**

The important steps in the process of decomposition are fragmentation, leaching, catabolism, humification and mineralization.

- **Fragmentation**

  It is the breakdown of detritus into smaller particles by detritivores (e.g., Earthworm).

- **Leaching**

  In this process, water soluble inorganic nutrients go down into the soil horizon and get precipitated as unavailable salts.

- **Catabolism**

(i) Here, the degradation of detritus into simpler inorganic substances takes place by bacterial and fungal enzymes.

(ii) Fragmentation, leaching and catabolism operate simultaneously on the detritus.

- **Humification**

(i) It is the accumulation of humus (dark amorphous substance) in soil.

(ii) Humus is resistant to microbial action and so decomposes very slowly.

(iii) Being colloidal in nature, it serves as a reservoir of nutrients.

- **Mineralization**

  It is the release of inorganic nutrients due to the degradation of humus by some microbes.

Scan to know more about this topic

Fragmentation leaching Humification Mineralization

➢ **Factors Influencing Decomposition**

The rate of decomposition is controlled by chemical composition of detritus and climatic factors.

- **Chemical composition of detritus:**

  Decomposition rate is slower if detritus is rich in lignin and chitin and quicker, if detritus is rich in nitrogen and water-soluble substances like sugars.

- **Climatic factors like temperature and soil moisture:**

– Temperature and soil moisture are the most important climatic factors that regulate decomposition through their effects on the activities of soil microbes.

– Warm and moist environment favours decomposition whereas low temperature and anaerobic conditions inhibits decomposition resulting in build up of organic materials.

Energy Flow

- Sun is the only source of energy for all ecosystems on the earth.
- Of the incident, solar radiation less than 50% of it is photosynthetically active radiation (PAR).
- Plants, photosynthetic and chemosynthetic bacteria (autotrophs) fix solar radiant energy to make food.
- Plants capture only 2-10% of the PAR and this small amount of energy sustains the entire living world. So, it is very important to know how the solar energy captured by plants flow through different organisms of an ecosystem.
- Ecosystem obeys First and Second Law of Thermodynamics.
- The energy of an ecosystem is constant.
- They need a constant supply of energy to synthesize the molecules they require, to counteract the universal tendency towards increasing disorderliness.

➢ **Producers**

- The green plants in the ecosystem which capture the solar energy and convert it into chemically bound energy are called producers.
- All organisms are dependent for their food on producers (green plants), either directly or indirectly.
- In a terrestrial ecosystem, major producers are herbaceous and woody plants.
- Primary producers in an aquatic ecosystem are phytoplankton, algae and higher plants.
- The energy trapped by the producer is either passed on to a consumer or the organism dies.
- Death of organism is the beginning of the detritus food chain / web.

➢ **Consumers (Heterotrophs)**

- These are all animals that depend on plants (directly or indirectly) for their food.
- They include:

(a) Primary Consumers

- These are herbivores that feed on plants.
- e.g., Insects, birds and mammals in terrestrial ecosystem and molluscs in aquatic ecosystem.

(b) Secondary Consumers

- These are primary carnivores that feed on herbivores, e.g., Frog, fox, man etc.

(c) Tertiary Consumers

- These are secondary carnivores that feed on primary carnivores.

➢ **Grazing Food Chain (GFC)**

- A simple grazing food chain (GFC) is depicted below:

Grass - - - - - - → Goat— - - - - - - - - - - → Man - — — — →

(Producer) (Primary Consumer) (Secondary Consumer)

➢ **Detritus Food Chain (DFC)**

- It begins with dead organic matter.
- It is made up of decomposers (saprotrophs) which are heterotrophic organisms, e.g., fungi and bacteria.
- They meet their energy and nutrient requirements by degrading dead organic matter or detritus.
- Decomposers secrete digestive enzymes that breakdown dead and waste materials into simple, inorganic materials, which are subsequently absorbed by them.

➢ In an aquatic ecosystem, GFC is the major conduit for energy flow.

➢ In a terrestrial ecosystem, a much larger fraction of energy flows through the DFC than through the GFC.

➢ DFC may be connected with GFC at some levels: some of the organisms of DFC are prey to the GFC animals.

➢ Some animals (cockroaches, crows etc.) are omnivores.

➢ These interconnections of food chains make a food web.

➢ Organisms occupy a place in the natural surroundings or in a community according to their feeding relationship.

➢ A specific place of organisms in the food chain is known as their trophic level.

➢ Producers belong to the first trophic level, herbivores to the second and carnivores to the third.

➢ The amount of energy decreases at successive trophic levels.

➢ When an organism dies, it becomes dead biomass (detritus) that serves as an energy source for decomposers.

- Organisms at each trophic level depend on those at the lower trophic level for their energy demands.
- Each trophic level has a certain mass of living material at a particular time called as the standing crop.
- The standing crop is measured as the mass of living organisms (biomass) or the number in a unit area. Biomass of a species is expressed in terms of fresh or dry weight.
- Measurement of biomass in terms of dry weight is more accurate.
- The number of trophic levels in the grazing food chain is restricted as the transfer of energy follows **Lindeman's 10 % law** –only 10% of the energy is transferred to each trophic level from the lower trophic level.
- In nature, it is possible to have so many levels – producer, herbivore, primary carnivore, secondary carnivore in the grazing food chain.
- **Ecological Pyramids**

- The representation of a food chain in the form of a pyramid is called ecological pyramid. It is the relationship between the producers and consumers of various order represented graphically.
- The base of each pyramid represents the producers (first trophic level) while the apex represents tertiary or top level consumer.
- **Ecological pyramids are of three types:**
  (a) Pyramid of number
  (b) Pyramid of biomass
  (c) Pyramid of energy

MNEMONICS

Concept Name: Types of Ecological Pyramids

Mnemonics: No **E**nergical **B**inding

Interpretation:

(i) Pyramid of Number

(ii) Pyramid of Energy

(iii) Pyramid of Biomass

- Any calculations of energy content, biomass or numbers, has to include all organisms at that trophic level.
- The trophic level represents a functional level, not a species as such.
- A given species may occupy more than one trophic level in the same ecosystem at the same time. For e.g., a sparrow is a primary consumer, when it eats seeds, fruits, peas, and a secondary consumer when it eats insects and worms.
- In most ecosystems, all the pyramids are upright i.e., producers are more in number and biomass than the herbivores and herbivores are more in number and biomass than the carnivores.

Also, energy at a lower trophic level is always more than at a higher level.

- Large number of insects feeding on a big tree is an example of an inverted pyramid of number.
- Pyramid of biomass in sea is generally inverted because the biomass of fish far exceeds that of phytoplankton.
- Pyramid of energy is always upright, because when energy flows from a trophic level to the next trophic level, some energy is always lost as heat at each step.
- **Limitations of Ecological Pyramids**
  (a) It does not take into account the same species belonging to two or more trophic levels.
  (b) It assumes a simple food chain that almost never exists in nature; it does not accommodate a food web.
  (c) Saprophytes are not included in ecological pyramids even though they play a vital role in the ecosystem.

Important Diagrams

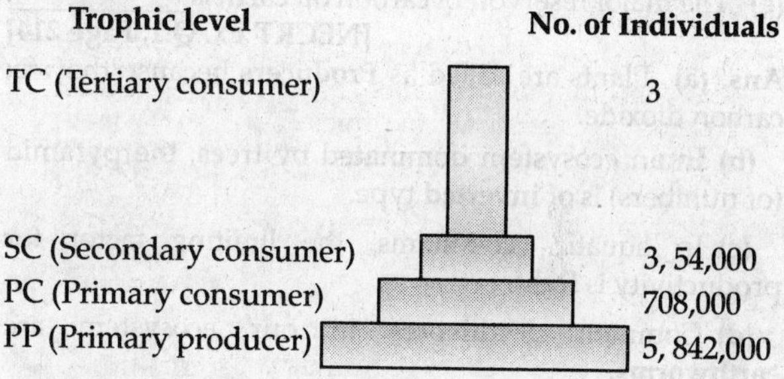

Fig 12.1: Pyramid of numbers in a grassland ecosystem

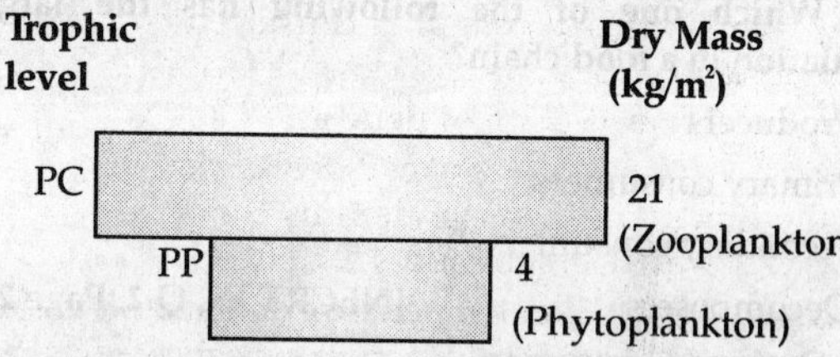

Fig 12.2: Inverted Pyramid of Biomass in Sea

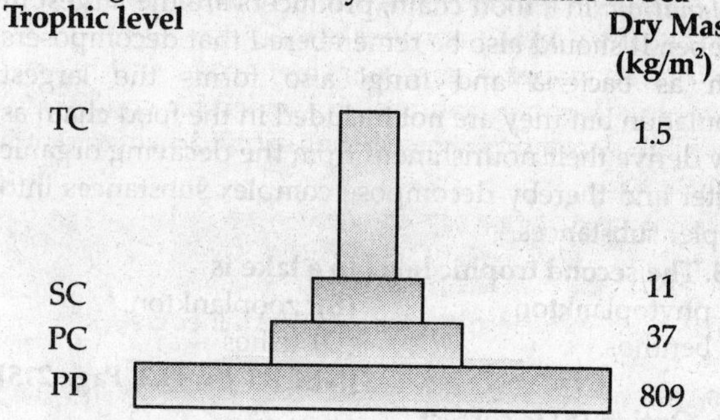

Fig 12.3: Pyramid of Biomass in most ecosystem

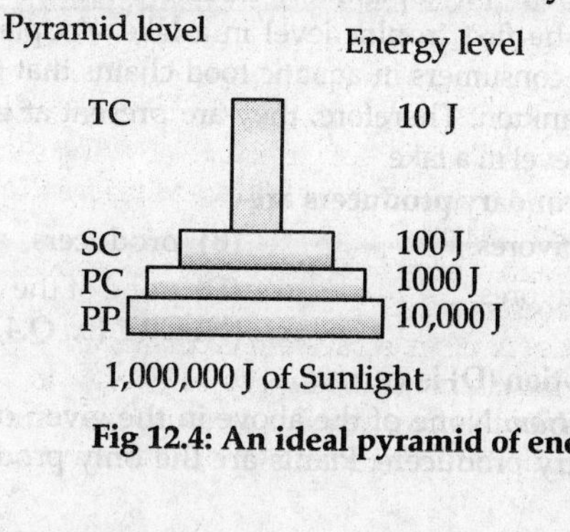

Fig 12.4: An ideal pyramid of energy

NCERT CORNER

Exercise Questions

Q. 1. Fill in the blanks.

(a) Plants are called as________ because they fix carbon dioxide.

(b) In an ecosystem dominated by trees, the pyramid (of numbers) is________ type.

(c) In aquatic ecosystems, the limiting factor for the productivity is________.

(d) Common detritivores in our ecosystem are________.

(e) The major reservoir of carbon on earth is________.

[NECRT Ex. Q.1, Page 214]

Ans. (a) Plants are called as **Producers** because they fix carbon dioxide.

(b) In an ecosystem dominated by trees, the pyramid (of numbers) is of **inverted** type.

(c) In aquatic ecosystems, the limiting factor for productivity is **light**.

(d) Common detritivores in our ecosystem are **earthworms.**

(e) The major reservoir of carbon on Earth is **oceans.**

Q. 2. Which one of the following has the largest population in a food chain?

(A) Producers

(B) Primary consumers

(C) Secondary consumers

(D) Decomposers **[NECRT Ex. Q.2, Page 215]**

Ans. Option (A) is correct.

Explanation: In a food chain, producers are the largest in number. It should also be remembered that decomposers such as bacteria and fungi also forms the largest population but they are not included in the food chain as they derive their nourishment from the decaying organic matter and thereby decompose complex substances into simpler substances.

Q. 3. The second trophic level in a lake is

(A) phytoplankton. (B) zooplankton.

(C) benthos. (D) fishes

[NECRT Ex. Q.3, Page 215]

Ans. Option (B) is correct.

Explanation: Phytoplankton exhibit photosynthesis and occupy the first trophic level in a lake. Zooplankton are primary consumers in aquatic food chains that feed upon phytoplankton. Therefore, they are present at the second trophic level in a lake.

Q. 4. Secondary producers are

(A) herbivores. (B) producers.

(C) carnivores. (D) none of the above.

[NECRT Ex. Q.4, Page 215]

Ans. Option (D) is correct.

Explanation: None of the above in the given options are secondary producers. Plants are the only producers and they are called primary producers. There are no other producers in a food chain.

Q. 5. What is the percentage of photosynthetically active radiation (PAR) in the incident solar radiation?

(A) 100% (B) 50 % (C) 1–5% (D) 2–10%

[NECRT Ex. Q.5, Page 215]

Ans. Option (B) is correct.

Explanation: About 50% of the total incident solar radiation constitutes photosynthetically active radiation.

Q. 6. Distinguish between

(a) Grazing food chain and detritus food chain

(b) Production and decomposition

(c) Upright and inverted pyramid

(d) Food chain and Food web

(e) Litter and detritus

(f) Primary and secondary productivity

[NECRT Ex. Q.6, Page 215]

Ans. (a) Difference between grazing food chain and detritus food chain

S. No.	Grazing food chain	Detritus food chain
(i)	Energy is provided by the sun.	Energy is provided by organic matter (or detritus) generated in trophic levels of the grazing food chain.
(ii)	It starts with producers, that is, first trophic level. The plant biomass is then eaten by herbivores, which in turn are consumed by variety of carnivores.	It starts with detritus such as dead bodies of animals or fallen leaves, which are then eaten by decomposers or detritivores. These detritivores in turn are consumed by their predators.
(iii)	Generally, this food chain is large.	Generally, this for chain is small.

(b) Difference between production and decomposition

S. No.	Production	Decomposition
(i)	It is the process of formation of organic matter by producers by means of photosynthesis.	It is the process of breaking down of complex organic matter or biomass from the body of dead plants and animals with the help of decomposers into simpler organic raw material such as CO_2, H_2O, and other nutrients.
(ii)	It relies on the photosynthetic capacity of the producers.	It relies on the decomposers.

(iii)	Sunlight is required by plants for primary production.	Instead of sunlight, dead and decaying organic material is required.

(c) Difference between upright and inverted pyramid

S. No.	Upright pyramid	Inverted pyramid
(i)	The pyramid of energy is always upright.	The pyramid of biomass and the pyramid of numbers can be inverted.
(ii)	In the upright pyramid, the number and biomass of organisms at the producer level of an ecosystem is the highest, which keeps on decreasing at each trophic level in a food chain.	In an inverted pyramid, the number and biomass of organisms at the producer level of an ecosystem is the lowest, which keeps on increasing at each trophic level.

(d) Difference between food chain and food web

S. No.	Food chain	Food web
(i)	It is a basic network that shows the linear flow of nutrients and energy from one trophic level to another.	It contains a number of interconnected food chains.
(ii)	Members present at higher trophic levels feed on single type of organisms.	One organism has alternate food sources of various interlinked food chains

(e) Difference between litter and detritus

S. No.	Litter	Detritus
(i)	Litter contains all kinds of wastes generated on the surface of earth.	Detritus is composed of the remains of dead plants and animals.
(ii)	Litter contains both biodegradable and non- biodegradable matter.	Detritus contains only biodegradable matter.

(f) Difference between primary and secondary productivity

S. No	Primary productivity	Secondary productivity
(i)	Organic matter produced by producers per unit area over a period of time is known as primary productivity.	It is the rate of production of organic matter by consumers over a period of time.

Q. 7. Describe the components of an ecosystem.

[NECRT Ex. Q.7, Page 215]

Ans. An ecosystem is an interacting unit composed of biological community (biotic) as well as the non-living components (abiotic) of an area.

The living and the non-living components of an ecosystem interact amongst themselves and function as a unit.

Living component of an ecosystem constitutes the biotic factors such as producers, consumers, decomposers, etc. Producers include plants and algae. They contain chlorophyll pigment, which helps them carry out the process of photosynthesis in the presence of light. Thus, they are also called converters or transducers. Consumers or heterotrophs are organisms that are directly (primary consumers) or indirectly (secondary and tertiary consumers) dependent on producers for their food. Decomposers include micro-organisms such as bacteria and fungi. They form the largest population in a food chain and obtain nutrients by breaking down the dead and decaying animal organic material.

Abiotic component of an ecosystem constitutes non-living factors such as light, temperature, water, soil, air, inorganic nutrients, etc.

Q. 8. Define ecological pyramids and describe with examples, pyramids of number and biomass.

[NECRT Ex. Q.8, Page 215]

Ans. An ecological pyramid is a graphical representation of various ecological parameters such as the number of individuals present at each trophic level, the amount of energy, or the biomass present at each trophic level. Ecological pyramids represent producers at the base, while the apex represents the top level consumers present in the ecosystem.

The three ecological pyramids that are usually studied are:

(a) Pyramid of number

(b) Pyramid of biomass and

(c) Pyramid of energy.

(a) Pyramid of number: It is a graphical representation of the number of individuals present at each trophic level in a food chain of an ecosystem. It can be upright or inverted depending on the number of producers. For example, in a grassland ecosystem, the pyramid of numbers is upright. In this type of a food chain, the number of producers (plants) is followed by the number of herbivores (mice), which in turn is followed by the number of secondary consumers (snakes) and tertiary carnivores (eagles). Hence, the number of individuals at the producer level will be the maximum, while the number of individuals present at top carnivores will be least.

(b) Pyramid of biomass: It is a graphical representation of the total amount of living matter present at each trophic level of an ecosystem. It can be upright or inverted. It is upright in grasslands and forest ecosystems as the amount of biomass present at the producer level is higher than at the top carnivore level. It is inverted in a pond ecosystem as the biomass of fishes far exceeds the biomass of zooplankton (upon which they feed).

Q. 9. What is primary productivity? Give brief description of factors that affect primary productivity.

[NECRT Ex. Q.9, Page 215]

Ans. Primary productivity refers to the rate of generation of biomass in an ecosystem by producers per unit area over a period of time. It depends on the variety of environmental factors such as light, temperature, water, precipitation, etc. It also depends on the availability of nutrients and the availability of plants to carry out photosynthesis.

Q. 10. Define decomposition and describe the processes and products of decomposition.

[NECRT Ex. Q.10, Page 215]

Ans. Decomposition is the process that involves the breakdown of complex organic matter or biomass from the body of dead plants and animals with the help of decomposers into inorganic raw materials such as carbon dioxide, water, and other nutrients. The various processes involved in decomposition are as follows:

Fragmentation: It is the first step in the process of decomposition. It involves the breakdown of detritus into smaller pieces by the action of detritivores, such as earthworms.

Leaching: It is a process where the water soluble nutrients go down into the soil layers and get locked as unavailable salts.

Catabolism: It is a process in which bacteria and fungi degrade detritus through various enzymes into simpler inorganic substances.

Humification: The next step is humification which leads to the formation of a dark coloured colloidal substance called humus, which acts as reservoir of nutrients for plants.

Mineralisation: The humus is further degraded by the action of microbes, which finally leads to the release of inorganic nutrients into the soil. This process of releasing inorganic nutrients from the humus is known as mineralization.

Decomposition produces a dark coloured, nutrient-rich substance called humus. Humus finally degrades and releases inorganic raw materials such as CO_2, water, and other nutrient in the soil.

Q. 11. Give an account of energy flow in an ecosystem.

[NECRT Ex. Q.11, Page 215]

Ans. Energy enters an ecosystem from the Sun. Solar radiations pass through the atmosphere and are absorbed by the Earth's surface. These radiations help plants in carrying out the process of photosynthesis. Also, they help maintain the Earth's temperature for the survival of living organisms.

Some solar radiations are reflected by the Earth's surface. Only 2–10% of solar energy is captured by green plants (producers) during photosynthesis to be converted into food.

The rate at which the biomass is produced by plants during photosynthesis is termed as 'gross primary productivity'. When these green plants are consumed by herbivores, only 10% of the stored energy from producers is transferred to herbivores. The remaining 90% of this energy is used by plants for various processes such as respiration, growth, and reproduction. Similarly, only 10% of the energy of herbivores is transferred to carnivores. This is known as 10% law of energy flow.

□□

BIODIVERSITY AND ITS CONSERVATION

CHAPTER 13

Biodiversity

- It is the diversity (or heterogeneity) of biological organisation ranging from cellular macromolecules to biomes.
- **Edward Wilson:** Popularized the term 'biodiversity' to describe the combined diversity at all levels of biological organization.

MNEMONICS

Concept Name: Components of Biodiversity

Mnemonics: Grand School Exhibition

Interpretation: Genetic diversity, Species diversity, Ecological diversity

- **Components of Biodiversity**

  Biodiversity has been divided into three hierarchial levels of biological organization.

1. Genetic diversity

(a) Diversity shown by a single species at genetic level. *e.g., Rauwolfia vomitoria* in Himalaya shows genetic variation in the potency and concentration of the chemical reserpine.

(b) India has more than 50,000 different strains of rice and 1,000 varieties of mango.

2. Species diversity

Diversity at species level. e.g., Western Ghats have greater amphibian species than Eastern Ghats.

3. Ecological diversity

Diversity at ecosystem level. e.g., In India, deserts, rain forests, mangroves, coral reefs, wetlands, estuaries & alpine meadows, all can be seen, whereas the Scandinavian countries (like, Norway, Sweden) have less ecological diversity.

- **Number of Species on Earth (Global Species Diversity)**

- According to IUCN or International Union for Conservation of Nature and Natural Resources (2004) more than 1.5 million species have been described so far.
- According to Robert May, global estimate is about 7 million (considering the species are to be discovered in the tropics, i.e., only 22% of the total species have been recorded so far).
- Animals are more diverse (above 70%) than plants including plantae and fungi (22%).
- Most species-rich taxonomic group among animals are: Insects (70%, i.e., out of every 10 animals, 7 are insects).
- Number of fungi species is more than the combined total of the species of fish, amphibians, reptiles and mammals.
- Biologists are not sure about total number of prokaryotic species because:

(a) Conventional taxonomic methods are not suitable for identifying microbial species.

(b) Many species are not culturable under laboratory conditions.

- India has only 2.4% of world's land area, but has 8.1% of the species diversity.
- India is one of the 12 mega diversity countries of the world.
- Nearly 45,000 species of plants and twice as many of animals have been recorded from India.
- Applying May's global estimate, India would have more than 1 lac plant species and 3 lac animal species.

Patterns of Biodiversity

- Biodiversity is not uniform throughout the world. It varies with the change in latitude and altitude, it is affected by latitudinal gradients and species-area relationship. Following are the main patterns of biodiversity.

(a) Latitudinal Gradients

- Species diversity decreases from the equator to the poles.
- Tropics (latitudinal range of 23.5° N to 23.5° S) have more species than temperate or polar areas.
  - **(i)** Colombia (near equator) has about 1400 species of birds.
  - **(ii)** New York (41° N): 105 species of birds
  - **(iii)** Greenland (71° N): 56 species of birds
  - **(iv)** India (tropical latitudes): > 1200 species
- Tropical forest region like Ecuador has up to 10 times species of vascular plants as compared to a forest of equal area in a temperate region like the Midwest of USA.
- Tropical Amazonian rain forest (South America) has the greatest biodiversity on earth. It contains:
  - **(i)** 40,000 species of plants
  - **(ii)** 3,000 species of fish
  - **(iii)** 1,300 species of birds
  - **(iv)** 427 species of mammals
  - **(v)** 427 species of amphibians
  - **(vi)** 378 species of reptiles
  - **(vii)** 1,25,000 species of invertebrates
- Biodiversity (species richness) is highest in tropics because
  - **(i)** Tropics had more evolutionary time.
  - **(ii)** Relatively constant environment (less seasonal).
  - **(iii)** They receive more solar energy which contributes to greater productivity.

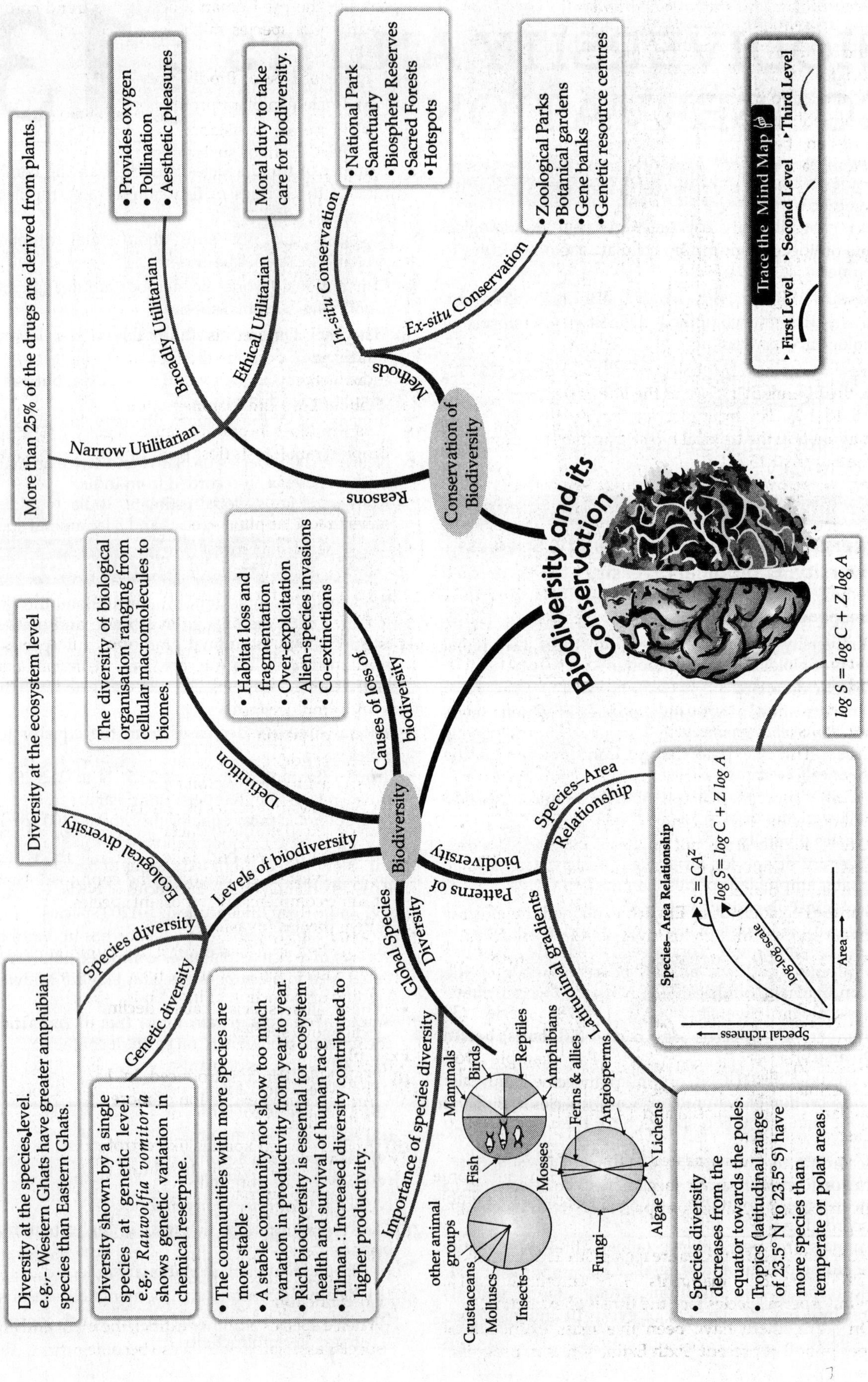
Biodiversity and its Conservation
Biodiversity
Definition
The diversity of biological organisation ranging from cellular macromolecules to biomes.
Levels of biodiversity
Ecological diversity
Diversity at the ecosystem level
Species diversity
Diversity at the species level. e.g., Western Ghats have greater amphibian species than Eastern Ghats.
Genetic diversity
Diversity shown by a single species at genetic level. e.g., Rauwolfia vomitoria shows genetic variation in chemical reserpine.
Importance of species diversity
• The communities with more species are more stable.
• A stable community not show too much variation in productivity from year to year.
• Rich biodiversity is essential for ecosystem health and survival of human race
• Tilman : Increased diversity contributed to higher productivity.
Global Species Diversity
Mammals
Birds
Reptiles
Amphibians
Fish
other animal groups
Crustaceans
Molluscs
Insects
Ferns & allies
Angiosperms
Mosses
Lichens
Algae
Fungi
Patterns of biodiversity
Latitudinal gradients
• Species diversity decreases from the equator towards the poles.
• Tropics (latitudinal range of 23.5° N to 23.5° S) have more species than temperate or polar areas.
Species–Area Relationship
Species– Area Relationship
S = CA^Z
log S = log C + Z log A
log-log scale
Special richness
Area
log S = log C + Z log A
Causes of loss of biodiversity
• Habitat loss and fragmentation
• Over-exploitation
• Alien-species invasions
• Co-extinctions
Conservation of Biodiversity
Reasons
Narrow Utilitarian
More than 25% of the drugs are derived from plants.
Broadly Utilitarian
• Provides oxygen
• Pollination
• Aesthetic pleasures
Ethical Utilitarian
Moral duty to take care for biodiversity.
Methods
In-situ Conservation
• National Park
• Sanctuary
• Biosphere Reserves
• Sacred Forests
• Hotspots
Ex-situ Conservation
• Zoological Parks
• Botanical gardens
• Gene banks
• Genetic resource centres
Trace the Mind Map
First Level
Second Level
Third Level

(b) Species - Area Relationship

Scan to know more about this topic
Species- Area Relationship

- According to the study of **Alexander von Humboldt** (German naturalist and geographer) in South American jungles, within a region, species richness increases with increase in explored area, but only up to a limit.
- Relation between species richness and area for a wide variety of taxa (like, angiosperm plants, birds, freshwater fishes) gives a rectangular hyperbola.
- On a logarithmic scale, the relationship is a straight line or linear, described by the equation:
  $\log S = \log C + Z \log A$
  where, S = Species richness, A = Area, C = Y-intercept, Z = slope of the line (regression co-efficient)
- The value of Z lies in the range of 0.1 to 0.2.
- In species-area relationship, among the large areas like entire continents, slope of the line is steeper (Z value: 0.6 to 1.2). For example, for frugivorous birds and mammals in the tropical forests of different continents, the slope is 1.15.

Importance of Species Diversity to the Ecosystem

- For many decades, ecologists believed that communities with more species, generally, tend to be more stable than those with less species.
- A stable community should not show too much variation in productivity from year to year; it must be either resistant or resilient to occasional disturbances (natural or man-made), and it must also be resistant to invasions by alien species.
- **David Tilman** found that plots with more species showed less year-to-year variation in total biomass.
- He also showed that in his experiments, increased diversity contributed to higher productivity.
- A rich biodiversity is not only essential for ecosystem health but imperative for the survival of the human race on this planet.
- Stanford ecologist **Paul Ehrlich** explained the effect of loss of species through his 'rivet popper hypothesis'.

Loss of Biodiversity

- IUCN Red List (2004) says that 784 species (338 vertebrates, 359 invertebrates and 87 plants) became extinct in the last 500 years. For example Dodo (Mauritius), Quagga (Africa), Thylacine (Australia), Stellar's sea cow (Russia) and 3 subspecies (Bali, Javan, Caspian) of tiger.
- 27 species have disappeared in the last 20 years.
- The extinctions across taxa are not random. Some groups (like amphibians) appear to be more vulnerable to extinction.
- More than 15,500 species are facing threat of extinction.
- 12% birds, 23% mammals, 32% amphibians, 31% gymnosperm species face the threat of extinction.
- On earth, there have been five mass extinction of species and at present 'Sixth Extinction' is in progress.
- The current extinction rate is 100 - 1000 times faster than in the pre-human times. If this trend continues, nearly 50% species might be extinct within the next 100 years.

➤ **Impacts of Loss of Biodiversity**

(a) Decline in plant production

(b) Lowered resistance to some environmental perturbations such as drought.

(c) Increased variability in ecosystem processes such as plant productivity, water use and pest and disease cycles.

Causes of Biodiversity Losses ('The Evil Quartet')

- "The Evil Quartet" is the phrase coined by **Jared Diamond** to describe the four human induced causes of extinction.

Scan to know more about this topic
Loss of Biodiversity and Causes

(a) Habitat Loss and Fragmentation

- It is the most important cause, e.g., Tropical rain forests (loss from 14% to 6%).
- Thousands of hectares of rain forests is being lost within hours.
- The Amazon rain forest ('lungs of the planet') is being cut for cultivating soya beans or for conversion of grasslands for cattle.
- When large habitats are broken up into small fragments due to various human activities, mammals and birds requiring large territories and certain animals with migratory habits are badly affected, leading to population declines.

(b) Over-exploitation

- The dependence of humans on nature for food and shelter led to over-exploitation of natural resources.
  Example: Many species like Stellar's sea cow, passenger pigeon, etc., became extinct due to over exploitation.
- Many marine fish populations around the world are over harvested, endangering the continued existence of some commercially important species.

(c) Alien Species Invasions

- When alien species are introduced unintentionally or deliberately, some of them turn invasive, and cause decline or extinction of indigenous species.
- These alien species cause decline or extinction of indigenous species.

Example:

(i) The Nile Perch introduced in Lake Victoria (East Africa) caused extinction of more than 200 species of cichlid fish.

(ii) Invasive weed species like carrot grass (*Parthenium*), *Lantana* and water hyacinth (*Eichhornia*) caused damage to our native species.

(iii) The illegal introduction of the African Catfish (*Clarias gariepinus*) for aquaculture is posing a threat to the indigenous catfishes (*Clarias batrachus*) in our rivers.

(iv) Co-extinction

When a species becomes extinct, the plant and animal species associated with it also become extinct.

Example:

(a) Extinction of the parasites takes place when the host is extinct.

(b) In co-evolved plant-pollinator mutualism extinction of one leads to the extinction of the other.

➢ There are three main reasons for conserving the biodiversity which are categorized as follows:

(a) Narrowly Utilitarian Arguments

- Humans derive economic benefits from nature such as food, firewood, fibre, construction material, industrial products (tannins, lubricants, dyes, resins, perfumes) and medicines.
- More than 25% of the drugs are derived from plants.
- 25,000 species of plants have medicinal value.
- Exploring molecular, genetic and species-level diversity, i.e., 'bioprospecting' for products of economic importance may enormously benefit nations with rich biodiversity.

(b) Broadly Utilitarian Arguments

- Biodiversity has many ecosystem services.
- Amazon forest produces 20% of total O_2 in the earth's atmosphere by the process of photosynthesis.
- Pollination service takes place through bees, bumblebees, birds and bats.
- Aesthetic pleasures such as walking through thick woods, watching spring flowers in full bloom or waking by hearing a bulbul's song in the morning.
- Other indirect benefits are pest control,climate moderation and flood control.

(c) Ethical Arguments

- Every species has an intrinsic value.
- We have a moral duty to take care for their well-being.

MNEMONICS

Concept Name: Conservation of Biodiversity– *In-Situ* Conservation

Mnemonics: **N**ational **S**ervice **B**est **S**ervice **H**ai

Interpretation: National Park, Sanctuary, Biosphere reserve, Sacred forest, Hotspots

➢ **Biodiversity Conservation**

Types of Conservation

(a) *In situ* conservation (on site)

- It is the conservation of genetic resources within natural or human-made ecosystems in which they occur.
- e.g., Protected areas such as National Parks, Sanctuaries, Biosphere reserves, cultural landscapes, national monuments.

Scan to know more about this topic

Ex situ and In situ conservation

(i) National Park

- Strictly reserved for the welfare of the wildlife where private ownership, cultivation, grazing etc, are prohibited.
- There are 90 national parks in India.

(ii) Sanctuary

- Here, protection is given only to the animals.
- Collection of timbers, minor forest products and private ownership are allowed so long as they do not harm the animals.
- There are 448 wildlife sanctuaries in India.

(iii) Biosphere Reserves

- Areas of land or coastal environments to conserve ecosystem and genetic resources contained therein.
- There are 14 biosphere reserves in India.

(iv) Sacred Forests (Sacred Groves)

- Sacred groves are highly protected forests because they are of religious and cultural values.
- Sacred groves in Khasi and Jaintia Hills in Meghalaya
- Aravalli Hills of Rajasthan
- Western Ghat regions of Karnataka & Maharashtra
- Sarguja, Chanda and Bastar areas of Madhya Pradesh.
- In Meghalaya, the sacred groves are the last refuges for a large number of rare and threatened plants.

(v) Hotspots

- These are the richest and the most threatened reservoirs of plant and animal life on earth.
- There are 34 hotspots in the world.
- In total, all the biodiversity hotspots cover less than 2% of the earth's land area but could reduce the ongoing extinctions by almost 30%.
- Three main hotspots (Western Ghats and Sri Lanka, Indo-Burma and Himalaya) cover India's high biodiversity regions.

(b) *Ex situ* conservation (off site)

- It is the conservation of organisms outside their habitats.
- In this approach, threatened animals and plants are taken out from their natural habitat and placed in special setting where they can be protected and given special care. e.g., genetic resource centres, zoological parks, botanical gardens, gene banks etc.
- In recent years, *ex-situ* conservation has advanced by preserving the gametes of threatened species in viable and fertile condition for long periods using cryopreservation techniques, eggs can be fertilised *in-vitro*, and plants can be propagated using tissue culture methods.
- Seeds of different genetic strains of commercially important plants can be kept for long periods in seed banks.

➢ **International Efforts for Conserving Biodiversity**

- **The Earth Summit (Rio de Janeiro, 1992) - Three objectives:**
  - **(a)** Conservation of biodiversity
  - **(b)** Sustainable use of biodiversity
  - **(c)** Sharing of benefits in the utilization of genetic resources.
- The World Summit on Sustainable Development (Johannesburg, South Africa, 2002): 190 countries pledged to reduce the current rate of biodiversity loss.

NCERT CORNER

Exercise Questions

Q. 1. Name the three important components of biodiversity. [NCERT Ex. Q.1, Page 226]

Ans. (i) Biodiversity refers to the varieties of life forms that can be found on the Earth (plants, animals, fungi and micro-organisms) as well as to the communities that they form and the habitats in which they live.

(ii) Genetic diversity, species diversity and ecological diversity are three important components of biodiversity.

(iii) Genetic diversity takes into account the genetic variations present in a species whereas species diversity refers to species richness. Ecological diversity refers to types of ecosystem present on earth.

Q. 2. How do ecologists estimate the total number of species present in the world? [NCERT Ex. Q.2, Page 226]

Ans. (i) The diversity of living organisms present on the Earth is very vast. According to the ecologists, the total number of species present in the world is about 7 millions.

(ii) The total number of species is calculated by statistical comparison between a species richness of a well-studied group of insects of temperate and tropical regions. Then, these ratios are extrapolated with other groups of plants and animals to calculate the total species richness present on the Earth.

Q. 3. Give three hypothesis for explaining why tropics show greatest levels of species richness. [NCERT Ex. Q.3, Page 227]

Ans. There are three different hypothesis proposed by scientists for explaining species richness in the tropics. These are as follows:

(i) Tropical latitudes receive more solar energy than temperate regions which leads to high productivity and high species diversity.

(ii) Tropical regions have less seasonal variations and a more or less constant environment. This promotes the niche specialisation and thus, high species richness.

(iii) Temperate regions were subjected to glaciations during the ice age, while tropical regions remained undisturbed which led to an increase in the species diversity in this region.

Q. 4. What is the significance of the slope of regression in a species-area relationship?[NCERT Ex. Q.4, Page 227]

Ans. (i) According to Alexander Von Humboldt, the diversity of species increases with increase in explored area up to a certain limit. It can be expressed in two main measures: species richness and species evenness.

(ii) The relationship can be given by

Log S = Log C + Z Log A.

where,

S = Species richness, A = Area, C = Y intercept, Z = Slope of the line (regression coefficient)

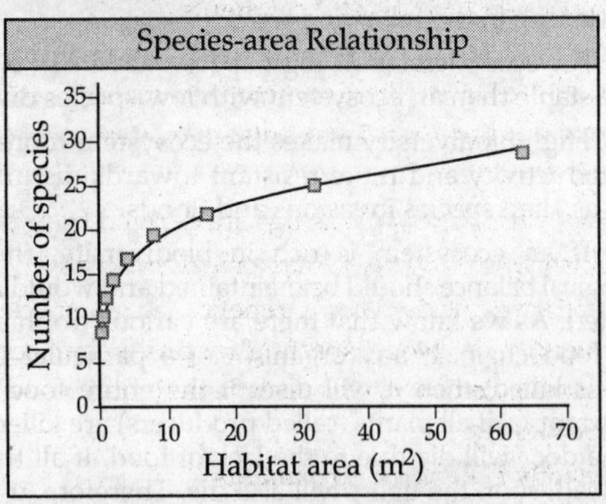

Figure: Species-area relationship

(iii) The relation between species richness and area for a wild variety of taxa is a rectangular hyperbola.

(iv) The slope of regression (Z) has a great significance in order to find a species-area relationship. It has been found that in smaller areas (where the species-area relationship is analysed), the value of slopes of regression is similar regardless of the taxonomic group or the region. However, when a similar analysis is done in larger areas, then the slope of regression is much steeper.

Q. 5. What are the major causes of species losses in a geographical region? [NCERT Ex. Q.5, Page 227]

Ans. (i) Loss of biodiversity means extinction of species.

(ii) Major causes for the loss of biodiversity around the world are as follows:

(a) Habitat loss and fragmentation:

1. Habitats of various organisms are altered or destroyed by uncontrolled and unsustainable human activities (e.g., deforestation, slash and burn agriculture, mining and urbanisation).

2. This leads to breaking up of the habitat into small pieces, which affect the movement of migratory animals and also, decrease the genetic exchange between populations leading to a decline in species.

(b) Over-exploitation:

1. Due to over-hunting and over-exploitation of various plants and animals by humans, many species have become endangered or extinct.

2. For example, Tiger, Steller's sea cow, and the passenger pigeon.

(c) Alien species invasions:

1. Deliberate or unintentional introduction of non-native species into a habitat has caused decline or extinction of indigenous species.

2. For example, the Nile perch introduced in Lake Victoria in Kenya led to the extinction of more than 200 species of native fish in the lake.

(d) Co–extinction:

1. In a native habitat, one species is connected to the other in an intricate network.

2. The extinction of one species causes the extinction of other species which is associated with it in an obligatory way.

3. For example, the extinction of the host will cause the extinction of its parasites.

Q. 6. How is biodiversity important for ecosystem functioning? [NCERT Ex. Q.6, Page 227]

Ans. (i) Biodiversity is important for ecosystem functioning in the following ways:

(a) An ecosystem with high species diversity is much more stable than an ecosystem with low species diversity.

(b) High biodiversity makes the ecosystem more stable in productivity and more resistant towards disturbances such as alien species invasions and floods.

(c) If an ecosystem is rich in biodiversity, then the ecological balance should be maintained and would not get affected. As we know that there are various trophic levels in a food chain. If any organism of a particular trophic level is killed, then it will disrupt the entire food chain. For example, if all plants (called producers) are killed, then all the deer will die due to the lack of food. If all the deer are dead, soon the tigers will also die. Therefore, it can be concluded that if an ecosystem is rich in species, then there will be other food alternatives at each trophic level which would not allow any organism to die due to the absence of their food resource. Hence, biodiversity plays an important role in maintaining the health and ecological balance of an ecosystem.

Q. 7. What are sacred groves ? What is their role in conservation? [NCERT Ex. Q.7, Page 227]

Ans. (i) Sacred groves are areas of forest or trees which are regenerated around places of worship. These areas are dedicated to local deities or ancestral spirits and are protected by local communities through social traditions and taboos that incorporate spiritual and ecological values.

(ii) These groves are found in Rajasthan, Western Ghats of Karnataka, Maharashtra, Meghalaya and Madhya Pradesh.

(iii) They help in the protection of many rare, threatened and endemic species of plants and animals found in that area. Deforestation is strictly prohibited in this region by local people.Hence, the sacred grove biodiversity is a rich area.

Q. 8. Amongst the ecosystem services are control of floods and soil erosion. How is this achieved by the biotic components of the ecosystem? [NCERT Ex. Q.8, Page 227]

Ans. (i) The biotic components of an ecosystem include the living organisms such as plants, animals, fungi and micro-organisms that make up ecological communities.

(ii) Plants play an important role in controlling floods and soil erosion. The roots of plants hold the soil particles together, thereby preventing the top layer of the soil to get eroded by wind or running water. The roots also make the soil porous, thereby allowing ground water infiltration and preventing floods.

(iii) Hence, plants are able to prevent soil erosion and natural disasters like floods and droughts. They also increase the soil fertility and biodiversity.

Q. 9. The species diversity of plants (22%) is much less than that of animals (72%). What could be the explanations to how animals achieved greater diversification? [NCERT Ex. Q.9, Page 227]

Ans. (i) More than 70% of species recorded on the Earth are animals and only 22% species are plants. There is quiet a large difference in their percentage. This is because animals have adapted themselves to ensure their survival in changing environments in comparison to plants.

(ii) For example,

(a) Insects and other animals have developed a complex nervous system which control and co-ordinate their body structure.

(b) Similarly, repeated body segments with paired appendages and external cuticles have made insects versatile and given them the ability to survive in various environments as compared to other life forms.

Q. 10. Can you think of a situation where we deliberately want to make a species extinct? How would you justify it? [NCERT Ex. Q.10, Page 227]

Ans. (i) Yes, there are different types of parasites and disease-causing microbes that we deliberately want to eradicate from the Earth. Since these micro-organisms are harmful to human beings, scientists are working hard to fight against them.

(ii) Scientists have been able to eliminate small pox virus from the world with the help of vaccinations. This shows that humans want to make these species extinct. Several other eradication programmes such as polio and hepatitis B vaccinations are aimed to eliminate these disease-causing microbes.